KV-143-448

DOGS
AND THEIR
HUMANS

DOGS
AND THEIR
HUMANS

*Stories of Healing and Hope from
the Supervet's Surgery*

NOEL FITZPATRICK

GALLERY BOOKS UK

First published in Great Britain by Gallery Books,
an imprint of Simon & Schuster UK Ltd, 2024

Copyright © Noel Fitzpatrick, 2024

1 3 5 7 9 10 8 6 4 2

Simon & Schuster UK Ltd
1st Floor
222 Gray's Inn Road
London WC1X 8HB

Simon & Schuster: Celebrating 100 Years of Publishing in 2024

www.simonandschuster.co.uk
www.simonandschuster.com.au
www.simonandschuster.co.in

Simon & Schuster Australia, Sydney
Simon & Schuster India, New Delhi

A CIP catalogue record for this book is available from the British Library

Hardback ISBN: 978-1-3985-3943-3
Trade Paperback ISBN: 978-1-3985-4149-8
eBook ISBN: 978-1-3985-3944-0

Typeset in Bembo by Palimpsest Book Production Ltd, Falkirk, Stirlingshire

Printed and Bound in the UK using 100% Renewable Electricity at CPI Group (UK) Ltd

To Keira and Pirate, for allowing me to trust them
and
To all of the dogs and their humans who
have placed their trust in me

Contents

Dogs and their humans   1

1. In the doghouse
   Franky the West Highland Terrier, Tanya (and George)   11

2. Taking the lead
   Larry the Labrador and Gavin   25

3. A perfect life
   Fairy the Berdoodle and Cheryl   43

4. More than everything
   Teddy the Doberman, Rosie and Ryan   61

5. But will he love me again?
   Bertie the Pomeranian and Cynthia   79

6. The Queen, the King and I
   Willow the Corgi and Elizabeth   93

7. The right thing to do
   Xīngxīng the Chow and Anton   113

8. He saved me from myself
   Bob the Staffordshire Bull Terrier and Dave   131

9. There was a hole in my soul, which he filled with
   his love
   Thor the Pyrenean Mountain Dog,
   Natalie and John   147

10. Everyone deserves a second chance
    Lucia the mongrel and Sheila   161

11. Unspeakable things
    Mabel the Cocker Spaniel and Mark   179

12. I don't trust anyone who doesn't like dogs
    Prince the Labrador and Craig   199

13. We are all the same
    Guy the Beagle and Meghan   213

14. He knows me better than I know me
    Bobby the Springer Spaniel and Finley   229

15. What is death?
    Sparkle the Bouvier des Flandres and Nicola   245

16. He smells like peace
    Captain the Labrador and Mary   267

17. Everything is impossible until it happens
    Irena the Airedale Terrier and Sarah   285

Snatched moments   301

Dogs and their humans

There is no love like that which our dog friends feel when we come home. No happiness. No joy. A bounding, over-leaping, urgent love that blots out everything else. And for that moment, as we share in it, we are pulled blinking into the absolute present. Into the eternal now of that love. The greatest 'present' that has ever been gifted and shared. We echo their love back, as we kneel on the floor, as we scratch behind their ears, as we rub their bellies. As we use that voice that we use for no one else in our life and tell them how good, so good, the best of all dogs they are. As the day's hardships melt away. Our joy begins as a reflection of theirs, but as a glorious tingling flame infuses our entire being, in that moment we are truly happy. Because what could be more joyful than to love and be loved without condition? To those who have never experienced it, it is like trying to describe music to someone who has never heard it.

Wherever this melody of unconditional love plays in our lives, our world is immeasurably better. It allows us to be the best humans we can be. Those of us who have known and felt this love will hold it inside us forever. So much so, that a dog isn't just 'at home', a dog '*is* home' – the place we feel most safe, where we are allowed to be truly ourselves in total peace and without judgement.

I know this for a fact because I know what I lost when, after fourteen years, my best friend, Keira, left my life. The slipper-chewing, room-flooding, bristly-eyed centre of my universe. It was as if the sun had gone behind a cloud and would never come out again. As if some essential sense, some limb, some part of me had died with her. Life was darker, quieter, colder and emptier. Since then, however, her light has gradually re-emerged, first in the smaller and then in the really big things. Her love and her light have transcended time and space. They live on both beside me and within me forever, guiding my way through fears and crises, and radiating through moments of joy. Her light shines in even my smallest triumphs and she is there during my difficult surgeries, day or night, my beacon of hope when all seems dark and lost and my safety net when I fall. She came and found me when I sat, slumped on the floor, unable to stop crying; she came and sat by me, then walked, nuzzled, muttered, stretched up onto her hind legs and licked my tears. And she still does.

It is estimated that all mammals, apart from humans, get a billion heartbeats. It is a fact inscribed by nature that at some point we will lose each other. And yet, in spite of this immutable law, there are studies suggesting that, in fact, our heartbeats can synchronise with those of our canine companions.

I have spent my life trying to maximise the number of synchronised heartbeats that dogs and their humans are allowed to share. That is the centre of it. I have never believed that humans own dogs and I don't routinely use the term owner in my veterinary practice. You cannot own love. It is an echo of one sound, a reflection of one light, a sharing of the same heartbeat. The dogs we share our lives with give us permission to be truly human. I have witnessed every sort of human come into my consulting room – monarchs, presidents, generals and global celebrities alongside the rest of us. Dogs arrive in expensive 4x4s and beaten-up old hatchbacks, in the baskets of mobility scooters, cradled in the arms of crying children and held on the laps of doting elderly people. Every shape of family, every sort of relation-ship, every type of person, every kind of life. All of them come with the same need, the same urgent prayer they offer to the universe. 'Please, not now. Not like this. Please, just a bit more time.' They all feel the same thing and come for the same thing – hope.

In my consulting room, every family is the only family at that moment in time, and their challenges, fears and hopes are the only focus of my attention. For this family, I am totally in the present and completely available to them and them alone.

Sometimes they have come to me because everyone else has said no, there's nothing that can be done. There are many reasons why no one else does some of the things I do. They may not have the technology or the experience or they may have other practical constraints that I don't, or different perspectives from mine. But I have never preserved a life where I truly felt that it was ethically more appropriate to hold a paw and a hand and let life pass. I have never performed a surgery just to please a guardian, no matter how much they beg. It has to be in the patient's best interest. It's not enough to be able to do something; it must be the right thing to do. But there have been, and continue to be, those who feel that some of the operations I perform are not actually 'right'. That the 'kindest' thing is to amputate the limb or put the animal to sleep. But what some may perceive as 'an unethical step too far' may be a procedure I have performed a dozen times successfully. I only ever offer procedures that I believe can provide a tangible, pain-free quality of life – and such procedures, to me, are no more or less difficult than those which others may recommend.

This is a paradigm I have fought for all my career – that the life of a dog or a cat deserves the same respect as my own, and that they deserve the same access to treatment options too. And it is through this prism that I have lived my life. I have committed my life to advancing medical care of dogs, cats and other animals, domestic and wild, because there is no value I could place on a thousand, on a hundred, on one more shared heartbeat with Keira. In 1985, I was offered a place at both human and veterinary medical schools on the same day. I chose to care for animals and to do my very best for them, as I would have done for humans if they were my patients. So, I find it very frustrating when rational, caring people do not feel as I do that treatment options for animals must continually be improved. Earlier in my career, I could only provide limited options by comparison with those we have now brought into existence. I want to leave medicine for animals better off when I'm finished than when I started, and to do that, someone must take the first step within a good ethical framework. I believe that animals have taught me more about humanity than I could ever have imagined, which is why I have called this book *Dogs and Their Humans*.

There is always a place for kindness and there is, of course, a time and a place for death, but I have seen again and again where that place or time is not here or now.

I have euthanised hundreds of patients where I believed it was the right thing to do, and I have advised euthanasia for patients where clients have declined to do so. Also, let me emphasise that I believe vets are good people who every single day seek to do the very best they can for their clients and for the animals of whom they are the guardians. I am the biggest and most ardent supporter of vets and vet nurses, all of whom have big hearts and minds and dedicate their lives to the care of some of the most vulnerable beings on earth.

My fifty-six years on this planet originated from a childhood growing up on a farm in Ballyfin, County Laois, where animals were functional. One of my earliest memories is crying my heart out over a dead lamb in a frozen winter field. My best and only true friend was Pirate, the sheepdog. I went to vet school in Dublin and moved as fast as I could to America to further my studies. I spent my first years as a vet in a large animal practice back in Ireland, performing cow Caesareans, delivering lambs and piglets and stomping about on misty Irish hillsides. Then I came to England where I worked all kinds of jobs and attended as many courses and training periods at universities and specialist practices as I could in pursuit of the dream of becoming the best surgeon I could be.

I performed most of my early orthopaedic surgeries in a wooden shed in a garden, then in a room next to a pub and a kebab shop, and then in my first referral practice, a converted army building in the middle of woods. I borrowed a few million pounds, lost a few million pounds and now reside in my world-class facilities near Godalming, in Surrey, where I do what I was put here to do. I studied for exam after exam, performed thousands of surgeries and wrote innumerable scientific papers, getting lots of letters after my name and becoming a professor as I helped to found a vet school. And of course, my patients care about none of these letters or ambitions; all they care about is being held and being healed. I can hold and comfort any animal in a shack, but the kind of healing I want to offer demands a massive infrastructure.

Over thousands of hours, my colleagues and I have developed techniques, mechanisms, procedures and protocols that have made the impossible possible. We have built an engineering hub and a factory where paradigms shift and where the future of medicine is born in every molecule of titanium, polyethylene and cobalt chromium that we sculpt into limbs and life. We built a regenerative medicine facility where fat cells grow into anti-inflammatory cells for treating arthritis and where bone and cartilage cells grow to patch up broken biology. All with a single aim – to provide good quality of life in the best way possible for our patients. It is because of this, and the work of countless vets, nurses and other members of the team I am blessed to call colleagues, that I have been lucky enough to witness time and again that look in the eyes of dogs and their humans, as they realise that they have indeed been given more time. As they bound, or limp or crawl towards each other, into that glorious 'now'. I have seen every scale of tragedy, every extreme of high and low that a family can face. I have shared their tears, but often I have been lucky enough to be part of their joy, their relief and their immense gratitude. Over the last three decades plus, I have been humbled and honoured to be present at that moment when dim hopes become brightest reality more times than I can remember.

I never forget the responsibility inherent in what I do. My job is much like that of a paediatric human surgeon, in that babies can't give informed consent and neither can dogs or cats. So, their guardian and I must weigh up all available information, all potential risks and benefits, all personal and medical circumstances and make a fully informed recommendation.

There are so many similarities between dogs and humans. The skeletal structure of a human and a dog are remarkably similar. Our bones have the same names and are moved by the same muscles, more or less. A human down on 'all fours' with toes and fingers outstretched even looks like a dog. Most of the basic principles of every surgery I have ever performed are the same for a dog or a human. Humans and dogs share a common ancestor that lived approximately 90–100 million years ago. Dogs share human patterns of voice-recognition in the anterior temporal lobes of the brain. Humans and dogs have about 84 per cent shared DNA. There are at least 500 diseases of genetic origin that dogs share with humans and our immune systems are near identical. The types of cancer that humans and dogs may be affected by are also often identical. In the USA, humans condemned to certain death because of genetic mutations of their cancer have been saved because their cancer ultimately proved susceptible to drugs that had been trialled only in dogs at that point, bringing a whole new meaning to the phrase 'my dog saved my life'.

So, it's little wonder that we are each other's best friend.

While it's fairly predictable that similar personality types in humans and dogs attract each other, and I often see dogs who are nervous, reclusive, ebullient or plain angry as a reflection of certain personality traits of their human guardians or in response to the particular environment their humans have created, it is also surprisingly common for animals and the humans they love to share physical ailments too.

And yet, though our skeletal, organ and immune systems are nigh-on identical, little effort is expended on studying naturally occurring cancer, arthritis, infections and other challenges in dogs that are identical challenges for humans. Human and animal doctors rarely communicate with each other. I deeply respect my human doctor and surgeon counterparts, but sadly my experience has been that they often feel 'it's only a dog'; most people don't know that dogs get the same diseases as us humans, and most of us don't like to think about our safe drugs and implants coming from experiments on dogs and other animals who are sacrificed for our benefit.

The central goal of my life is to promote the concept of One Medicine, whereby drugs and implants developed in animals and humans can be shared equally. At the moment that isn't the case because human life is understandably considered more valuable. Human and veterinary medicine are two separate, parallel worlds that have much to teach each other, but hardly any bridges have been built since their divergence a few hundred years ago. I founded a charity called Humanimal Trust to build these bridges of mutual respect and understanding for the benefit of all living beings. We still have a very long way to go.

The reason for this book's existence is to celebrate our most special of friends, to entertain and to educate and to advocate that we demand only the best-intentioned efforts for the treatment of their ailments in return for the immense love they share with us. Trust should be a two-way street, hence the name of the charity: human + animal + trust. I believe that it's the moral responsibility of the profession I love to make it so.

To that end, this book is a collection of just some of those tales (tails) of dogs and their humans. And because dogs free us to be more human, it runs the range of the human experience too, from laughter and joy to all the times I have sat in silence, holding the hands of those too sad to speak. The bit people think is hard – the surgery – is the easy bit. It's all the other stuff that's the hard stuff. I get to hear about everyone's lives. Families speak to me with a freedom they don't have with anyone else. Perhaps it's partly to impress on me how much this matters. Of course, I try my hardest every time. But I think it's also that when their most important of friends is hurt and in danger, everything else falls away. Everyone becomes a child in my consulting room. They want someone to make the hurt disappear.

I have changed most names and identifying details in this book to protect the privacy of dogs and their humans, and have sought permissions where necessary. I have also conflated some stories for your ease as a reader and because several journeys may have had a similar central message to share with all of us. Every story I tell is the absolute truth and it's the distillation of my thirty-plus years of meeting dogs and their humans. Their personalities, their foibles, their bravery, their fears and their love.

In the 30,000 years since human and dog first began to walk in step, they have been there for us and they have given us the gift of being there for them. They have been present at every moment, often the centre of our universe. They come in every shape and size, with every sort of personality: from mischievous to long-suffering, from boisterous to dignified, from slobbering to self-contained. I want to take you on a journey through the full range of what we can mean to each other. It will involve laughter, tears, paw prints, chew marks and lots of dog hair.

As I write this, I can see Keira's gravestone in the garden outside my practice. I can hear the gentle patter of her paws on the floor. I can feel the insistent brush of her rough wiry hair against my chin as she nudges me while I type. This book is a thank you to her. For all that she gave to me.

1

In the doghouse

Franky the West Highland Terrier, Tanya (and George)

'I'm telling you I need a vet right now!'

The deep male voice came booming through from the waiting room, impossible to ignore. I heard the quiet tones of our infinitely patient receptionist, Hannah, as she attempted to calm him down. But it clearly wasn't working.

'I don't care what he's bloody doing. Get him here now!'

I sighed and caught the eye of Benji the Shih Tzu, who I was attempting to carefully examine, and he seemed to raise an eyebrow at the kerfuffle. What you gonna do?

This particular afternoon had already seen a run of drama. There'd been Max the beautiful Border Collie with a broken hind leg after being hit by a car, Chairman Meow the cat who had his paw crushed under a bookcase, and an unending succession of poorly animals affected by varying magnitudes of crises alongside their concerned guardians. I had been hoping things were winding down for the day, but clearly not. At this time in my life I was new enough to this to feel I was still earning my stripes. Only a couple of years out of veterinary school, I had come straight from mixed practice in Ireland where I had been calving cows, lambing sheep and operating on dogs, all in an afternoon. Though I covered it up with a decent dose of the blarney, I didn't feel like I'd quite got my bearings in this new environment – in a village near Guildford in Surrey.

After a few minutes, I got Benji safely back into his cage and headed out to see what was going on. I was greeted by the sight of a very large man pacing up and down our tiny reception. He was wearing an expensive-looking suit and the sort of pink shirt I was to learn only a certain sort of English geezer wears. Sitting in a shiny Bentley immediately outside in our equally small yard was a distraught but extremely glamorous blonde woman, and on her lap was an extremely glum-looking West Highland Terrier. The car door was open. They both had panicked looks on their faces.

I looked at the man and held out my hand. 'I'm Noel,' I said. He didn't shake it, but rather ushered me in the direction of the car. The blonde woman in the Bentley was dressed like a queen, and as we approached, she made to get out of the car.

'It's Franky,' she said, standing up as I drew aside her. 'He's dying!'

As I reached to take Franky from her arms, pink-shirt guy fired up the loudhailer again. 'You've got to sort him out, guvnor!'

He strode over and took my hand before I could do anything else and I saw there was a fifty-pound note in it.

'I'm George. Give Franky the premium service, doc. He's like Tanya's actual basin. Most important member of the manor, if you get my drift? And you know what they say – happy wife, happy life.' I didn't get his drift at all and it was only several years later that I learned that 'basin of gravy' is rhyming slang for baby, and his manor was his big house.

I beckoned them all inside, carrying Franky myself. He was panting and whining gently. I could see he was spasming, gasping and retching, his little body heaving, his abdomen sucking in and out with each violent effort to vomit. Normally Westies are bouncing around, irrepressible balls of white spiky-haired fun and energy. Or they watch the world go by and grin. But Franky was not in a happy place. He lay his head on my arm and looked up at me with his almond-shaped blue eyes, asking for help. And lovingly drooled all over me. Tanya seemed very timid and had apparently acquiesced to George always taking the lead. They clearly had the lifestyle and the material possessions, but in that moment, I felt sorry for her as she clutched the love of her life in her hands on my consulting room table, her perfectly manicured and varnished nails at odds with the dribble trickling down Franky's soggy chin.

'Has he eaten anything he shouldn't have?' I asked.

'I don't know. I was out all day and came back to him like this,' said Tanya. We both looked at George. There was something shifty about him I couldn't quite place. He looked at the floor.

'No, I was playing golf all day. I told you,' he said. 'I only got back just before you.'

I knelt down and listened to Franky's heart. *Lub-dub, lub-dub.* The heartbeat sounded fine. But there was definitely something amiss. He had a temperature too.

'He keeps retching but there's nothing left to come out,' Tanya wailed.

'But what does that mean?' asked George. 'Will he be all right?'

I continued to examine Franky on my table. George seemed to look disapprovingly at how close I was to his wife but all I could think of was the mingling of the poshest perfume I'd ever smelled with the bilious tang of fresh vomit in the same whiff.

'Right,' I said, taking control of the situation as best I could. 'I've checked his heart. It's fine. I've felt his stomach and it feels to me like there could be something in there. I am going to give him a drug called an emetic to try to make him bring up whatever is in there. But you must understand that if that doesn't work, I'll need to knock him out and take some X-ray pictures and possibly operate. Do you understand?'

Realising the gravity of the situation, and also the increasing distress of his wife, who had by now started to cry, George simply said, 'Do what you have to, doc.'

I was very aware that the emetic might not work, but wanted to avoid anything more invasive if I could. We carried Franky out to the patch of grass in front of the surgery, where I popped him down and administered the emetic. After a couple of minutes, he shuffled over under a hedge, sniffing the ground and retching, smacking and licking his lips agitatedly. I felt very sorry for the poor fella. Tanya ambled nervously nearby, blowing her nose on some tissue and struggling to stay erect on her high heels. George held back near the Bentley, growing impatient.

And then it happened. All of it. Quicker than I could take in at the time. Franky squatted and, with what seemed like horrendous contractions of his abdomen, and the loudest honking *bleagh* sound – a mixture of a grunt, a gag and a heave all in one – out it came . . . whatever it was! It looked like a long piece of red string covered with the contents of his stomach.

Tanya stood by his side almost retching herself with dismay and holding the tissue to her mouth. George marched over. We all stared down at Franky and the foreign body lying on the grass. Franky licked his lips and looked up at all of us, immensely relieved and, it seemed to me, a little bit proud that he had finally eructated the alien object from within. Then he sniffed at it curiously, as dogs do, and I knelt down beside him.

I pulled a precautionarily pocketed glove out, popped it on and picked up the offending item. And it was only as I held it up, and the morning sun glistened off it, that all there present could immediately see that it wasn't a red string at all, but a delicate crimson-red suspender belt. It was like dominos falling as first I realised what I was holding, then George's realisation, and then him turning to see if Tanya had seen and rapidly clocking that she had indeed.

I have never witnessed a person's demeanour change more quickly from 'authoritative overbearing man in control' to 'little boy with tail firmly between legs' as the blood drained from George's face. My hand hovered as I stood up, not intentionally but rather unfortunately, holding the puke-covered scrap of fabric between George and his wife.

'Well, what are the chances—' started George.

'Shut up, George,' Tanya said.

'He must have been in your underwear drawer, babes.'

In quicker than the blink of an eye, this petite, reserved, submissive wife suddenly grew six feet tall in front of my very eyes, as she snatched Franky from the grass, clutched him to her chest and screamed, 'That. Is not mine, George!' almost as disgusted that he had not noticed that, as anything else.

She marched off across the car park, her high heels ringing with righteous fury before deciding they were slowing her down, taking them off with one hand, while clutching bewildered Franky with the other, turning and throwing them directly at George. One missed, and as I shuffled out of the way, the heel of the other hit him squarely on the chest. By then she was out the gate, barefoot on the road. Undoubtedly, whichever expensive designer had made these shoes hadn't had their use as missiles in mind, but the shoe was certainly effective, and I saw George wince as it hit. He called out, 'But, babes!' after her ever more forlornly.

There's nothing quite like witnessing the innocent honesty of a dog silencing the greatest bravado of a man, putting him firmly in the doghouse rather than his own house. His manner had indeed cost him his manor in the end. We let dogs into every area of our lives, including our embarrassment and heartbreak. They hear our argu-ments, our reconciliations, our tears and our joy. They are there at the beginning of a relationship, as we can hardly contain our excitement. They are there at the end, watching baffled as we bawl along to break-up songs or cope with our heartache in whichever way we see fit. And they are there by our side at every stage in between.

There was the time a client had locked his friend Bilbo the British Bulldog in his sports car, while he popped off for a cheeky dalliance with someone who was not his boyfriend. Bilbo somehow got the pin of a badge stuck into the pad of his foot, nicking a blood vessel, and spent the next half an hour jumping around inside the car, covering it in blood. When Bilbo arrived at the surgery, he had a tie wrapped around his foot as a kind of tourni-quet to stem the bleeding. I'd thought nothing of it, concentrating on getting Bilbo into my consulting room. But once Bilbo's other dad arrived, he certainly did think something of it.

'Whose tie is this?! Whose bloody tie is this?!' he screamed at my client. They went outside, where we all pretended not to listen to what was being shouted, as we attended to Bilbo's wound. It was easy enough to bandage and give a dose of antibiotics, in contrast with the 'blood-letting' outside, which would take more than a bandage to fix, it seemed. I kept Bilbo in overnight, sensing that this was probably best for both him and his humans. Thankfully, by the following day they seemed to have patched up their own wounds. Bilbo checked in on them both when they arrived, with a good long sniff of both faces to see how they were doing as they snuggled him. Bilbo the Bulldog may have landed one of his dads in the doghouse, but now he was a bridge over troubled water. He may in fact have saved that relationship as, a few months afterwards, I received a card to say thanks, with a picture of all three of them on holiday, smiling broadly.

I have seen many times how dogs have sent their humans to the doghouse in no uncertain terms. It would appear that dogs not only inherently bring out the best in people, but they also often expose the worst. They don't mean to. They don't understand the concept of adultery and our other transgressions. They just wander through life innocently wondering who or what this new person or situation in their life is. They can't speak, of course, but it's amazing how often they find a way to show what is really going on.

There was a time very early in my days of small animal practice when I couldn't work out why a client was so embarrassed. I could hear a buzzing sound coming from her canine friend's stomach that was even louder than his heartbeat. 'He's right out of sorts. Pacing, trembling . . . won't settle . . . and . . . well, I guess it must be his stomach rumbling then?' she said. Her friend was a droopy-eyed St Bernard. A slobber of drool spun like a strand of cooked spaghetti down from his even droopier lips. Then he suddenly and without warning shook his big shaggy head, splattering this sticky token of his affection across my cheek as I stooped to place my stethoscope on him. I heard a dull, repetitive monotone, something I had definitely never heard before. It wasn't the heart, and it wasn't the chest. I moved my stethoscope further backwards, following the sound as it seemed to get louder. And louder. Finally, with my stethoscope resting over the stomach, where normally I heard very little, or maybe a few gurgles, I could definitely hear an intense buzzing.

I sedated him to take a radiograph and, when I held up the X-ray picture, saying, 'It looks like some sort of blurry torpedo,' the client looked very sheepish indeed. I explained I'd have to operate to get it out. It was only when I quizzically held up the pink plastic torpedo I'd removed from his stomach that one of the nurses had to whisper to this poor innocent Irish farm boy what it actually was.

He made a full recovery and, when she came to pick him up, she immediately fell down on her knees, cuddling him and losing her face in the huge bed of fur on the top of his head. When she finally emerged from fur-hiding, she looked up and hesitantly reached forward as I gave her his lead and a carrier bag containing what we'd taken out of his stomach. She blushed as red as I've ever seen a human's cheeks go and said, 'Oh dear. It's amazing what they can swallow when rummaging around in the park, isn't it!'

It sure is amazing what happens in parks when dogs are around! Dogs are smile-making and conversation-making machines wherever they go. It's remarkable how many people have met their partner while out walking a dog, especially in parks, which is exactly what happened for Eric and Fi. Dogs like nothing better than to spread love and to introduce their humans to other humans. Norman the Norfolk

Terrier nearly pulled Eric's arm off to meet Fi's dog, a Cockapoo called Cricket, when they first bumped into each other. They touched noses and sniffed each other's bottoms as their two humans awkwardly said hello and, before long, did the human equivalent.

One thing led to another and, over the months, Eric and Fi started to see each other. They left leads and dog treats at each other's houses. Each dog would look for the other if one of their humans ever went for a walk without each other's company. And the two humans felt exactly the same way. Walks just didn't seem right without all four of them being present. So finally, several hundred walks later, the two dogs ended up with their humans on a hiking trip together. Eric had intended to propose to Fi in a delightful woodland cottage, perhaps on the balcony beneath the stars, undoubtedly with both Norman and Cricket curled up beside them supervising.

He had the engagement ring in the pocket of his trousers, from whence he had planned to pull it out nonchalantly at the perfect moment. But he had absent-mindedly also put doggie treats in the same pocket for calling the wayward doggies back when on the heath. Off he went to have a shower before dinner, leaving said trousers on the bed. He came out of the shower, put his trousers on, checked his left pocket, panicked, checked his right pocket, panicked. And then he looked over at both dogs, who had the contented look that only dogs who have recently stolen a treat can have.

Eric had the distinct impression that he was in the doghouse during the not-so-romantic balcony dinner that followed.

In their idyllic solitude, Fi had that look which was most certainly expecting a ring to be produced. But nothing was said at all. And for the next three days, Eric followed both dogs around every time they even looked like they might be going for a poo. Fi found it sweet at first, that he was always more than willing to pick up the poo. But she had to admit it was getting weird when he went sprinting into clumps of gorse to bag one up. She also began to secretly feel that it did slightly take the shine off some of the romance. As for Eric, this really had not been how he imagined the trip going. Though, as I pointed out to him later, searching through dog poos for diamonds is about as good a metaphor for life, married or otherwise, as there is. (I think it was still too soon for him to find it funny.)

Anyway, finally, on the very last day of the trip, there, glistening in the steam, a diamond ring!

Using boiled water and a huge amount of antiseptic handwash, he was satisfied the ring was as good as new. He proposed on the last night of the trip. Right on the balcony as planned. Eric couldn't help but notice that it was the starriest night imaginable, so he gave Norman and Cricket a knowing nod as they sat there contentedly, looking at each other and then up at their humans with smiles that made the moment even more special, as only happy dogs can. She said yes, admired the ring, and was secretly glad the poo bag obsession seemed to have gone away. The two dogs just sat there smiling. Apparently, Fi doesn't know to this day, and of course, dogs will never let your secret be known, unless you've been very naughty indeed . . . in which case, beware . . . because you just might end up in the doghouse like George.

I have often wondered if a dog might one day introduce me to their human in a romantic way. Keira was always suspicious of anyone she felt was getting too friendly with me. Not rude, but you could tell she was watching and judging. Something about the tilt of her head. A decisive sniff. She knew that I wanted, and still would like, to be a dad to a human baby, so she was super-fussy on my behalf in deciding which dogs she might deliberately tangle her lead with, rom-com style. The truth is that I've been married to the vocation. And it's hard for anyone to compete with that. There's always the next patient to be saved, and I have always wanted to build the best practice possible; mediocre was never good enough for me. But there's only so many times you can come home at 2 a.m., smelling of antiseptic solution, before it gets old. As a good friend said to me, if I had put a fraction of the effort into my relationships that I put into my job, I'd be married with six kids by now. He's probably right. I'm hoping there is still time for me to have children of my own.

I would be lying if I said that being a vet hasn't some-times led to admirers. Maybe it's one of those jobs that has a kind of competence that some people find attractive. Vet isn't quite firefighter, but you're often helping folks in a difficult situation. Even before I was on television, there were a fair few clients who got the flirt on. I remember one particular client who seemed to keep wandering by the practice in ever more elaborate formal wear. One time,

I was mid-procedure and heard a knock on the window, to find her peering in wearing a red sequinned dress. This was at a time when I was operating in a remote place in the middle of some woods. There was literally no way you could be passing through, unless you were a squirrel. I had to try and politely mime with my head for her to go away, as both my hands were busy trying to do my best for a poorly dog. I was in my own chosen 'doghouse' and that's where I firmly intended to stay.

A few months after Franky and the suspender belt saga, I was filling up my car at a local petrol station when I caught the eye of someone who looked familiar. It was George. I didn't know whether he'd be embarrassed, but he strode across to me. 'Maaaaaate. Hello, me old china.'

Without any shame or awkwardness, he told me everything. How he'd come home the next day to find his suits cut up on the lawn, strewn as sleeveless torsos, with particular attention spent on one particular part of his trousers. He'd had to sell the manor and the Bentley. These things happen. I couldn't help but notice that he'd 'downgraded' to a Mercedes. He said he wanted to thank me for what I'd done for Franky. He was a lovely dog. Funny thing was, he hadn't thought he would, but he missed him. 'You never think you're going to miss dog drool on your trousers but it turns out you do.' He stood for a moment, lost in thought, and I couldn't help thinking how remarkably well he had taken being sent to the doghouse. Then he sniffed.

'Still, onwards and upwards. A lump of ice for ya, guvnor . . . There's no point crying over spilt satin and silk,

23

is there? Anyway, there wasn't enough room for all of us in the bed. Probably makes sense this way around.'

Then he strode off shouting 'Be lucky!' over his shoulder. And not for the first time, I really felt like I was.

2

Taking the lead

Larry the Labrador and Gavin

Gavin found trusting people almost impossible. How could you when you'd seen them doing what he had over three tours of active military service? When you'd seen what war demanded of all those involved. How it burns away humanity with every minute you are exposed to it. You learned not to trust anything at all: every pile of rubble at the side of the road could have an improvised explosive device hidden in it. Every person in the street could have a suicide vest on. Every child running towards you could be carrying a hand grenade. How could you trust what that did to you? The decisions that were made, the commands that were issued and followed. The innocent people who died. He couldn't stop thinking about them. The men and the women and children who were 'collateral damage'.

I didn't know any of this when he came into my consulting room on a windy autumn morning. I saw someone who was pale and clearly shaken. I told him to sit down, to tell me what had happened. Obviously, Gavin's story didn't all come out in the first consultation, which was focused on the dog that this particular human carried in his arms, but a bit of background will help you understand what followed.

When he'd gone home to Newcastle, every loud or sudden noise made him flinch. At night, he was back there again, in Afghanistan, back in the heat and the dust and the terror. He could be walking down the street and suddenly he'd feel that he was in a sniper's sights and, overcome with fear, he'd need to duck into a shop and wait until his heart stopped pounding and he could talk again. He'd lost mates out there. Good mates. The ones who'd come back, he found he couldn't see. They seemed to want to pretend nothing had happened, talk even louder, as if they could drown out everything they'd seen with beer and laughter. They stopped inviting him after a while because he just sat there, his pint getting flatter and flatter as he stared into the middle distance, his knee jerking uncontrollably. So, Gavin just stayed indoors, with the curtains drawn. It was easier that way.

His small three-roomed cottage was sparse; he slept on a small bed, he had a small microwave, a small refrigerator, a small radio, a small television and a small allowance from the army. Everything in his life was small except for his fear and the demons in his head. Post-traumatic stress disorder or depression or anxiety didn't really capture what was going on for Gavin. His life was suspended in a pain from which he could not escape and didn't want to. Because outside the pain was guilt, and that was even worse.

One day, there was a knock on the window.

'Hello, Gavin? Are you there? My name's Hugo.'

It turned out Hugo was from the mental health service of the British Armed Forces. Gavin told him the same thing he'd told the last person they sent: 'Go away' (in slightly stronger terms). They'd tried to talk to him, but he'd just ignored them till they went away. His day was set up to see the fewest people possible. He got food deliveries on apps and shouted at them from inside to leave the bags on the doorstep. Usually he would get to the end of the day and realise the only thing he'd said to another human being was 'leave it there'. But this time, the person outside didn't go. This time Hugo said, 'Gavin. I've brought someone to meet you. He's called Larry.'

Gavin got up and went to the door, intending to tell Hugo and Larry that they could both go away (again in stronger terms). But when he opened the door just a tiny bit, he could see that Larry was a lot shorter and hairier than he was expecting. Looking up at him was a waggy-tailed, bouncy-eared, effusive coiled spring on a lead – a bundle of yellow Labrador happiness who was jumping up and down on the spot. He seemed genuinely pleased to see Gavin.

'We're just here to check in on you, Gavin.'

'Well, now you've checked,' said Gavin and closed the door.

Hugo opened the letterbox and called back, 'Well, maybe Larry and I can come and check on you tomorrow?'

'Free country,' said Gavin.

It took two weeks of daily visits before Gavin finally let Larry over the threshold. Hugo held back, but at least the door was open. He asked Gavin questions as Larry strained at his lead to come further into the cottage and properly say hello to his new friend. Eventually Gavin said, 'You're all right, you can let him come over.'

And suddenly Gavin was enveloped in an avalanche of licks and fur and panting. He waited for the panic to come but it didn't. Subconsciously, his brain somehow knew that this dog meant him no harm. Sensed it with every cell in his body. For the first time since he had been home, he didn't feel afraid. He felt like a kid again. Somehow, he felt like he was a person who deserved this small moment of pleasure. There was an odd sound he didn't recognise and he realised it was himself laughing. It all happened so quickly, though; he didn't realise all of this stuff until later.

Then Gavin let Hugo in. He was very hesitant at first, but Hugo explained that he could help Larry to be happy in Gavin's company. Hugo was a trained psychologist, specialising in mental trauma, as well as a damn-fine dog trainer. He knew that if Gavin wouldn't or couldn't talk to a therapist, then an intervention of another kind – the canine kind – might bring some small chink of light into the darkness of his mind – and he was right. They chatted for a few minutes while Larry went on a sniffing expedition around the room, and when Hugo asked him if he could bring Larry back another time, Gavin said, 'Yeah, yeah, I'd like that.'

It didn't all go smoothly of course; it never does with a boisterous Labrador. The next time Gavin held the door ajar for him to come in, Larry sniffed him all over and then went utterly mental, jumping off his sofa onto his bed, off his bed onto his chairs and off his chairs and actually head-first into the small microwave in the kitchen within which there was a half-eaten carton of something brown and liquidy. Down came the microwave on his head with an enormous bang. Gavin came running in, followed by Hugo.

That was day one of training.

Larry had been trained by Hugo to pick things up and bring them to people. These things included water bottles, phones and bottles of medication. His training involved smearing food on each of these items, and along the way, Larry had burst many plastic bottles, mangled several phones and exploded quite a few pill bottles, but eventually he got the hang of it. Larry's favourite thing in the whole world was a dirty old tennis ball, which was his reward for doing most things.

Hugo knew that Gavin would also benefit from medication and he managed to persuade him that if he could bring himself to have an examination and a chat with a proper medical doctor, he might be able to have Larry stay for longer, maybe overnight. He suggested that they could train Larry to bring Gavin his medication and water. That way Gavin would never 'forget' to take it. They set things up so that Larry's favourite tennis ball was suspended from a rope on the door of Gavin's fridge.

Larry would open the door by tugging on the tennis ball, pick up Gavin's medication and bring it to him followed by a bottle of water. Though Gavin did not trust humans, he did trust Larry, and if Larry brought the medication he felt obliged to take it. He would also answer the phone if it rang and Larry brought it to him. Hugo explained that he had to do that, so he could check if everything was OK with Larry. Gavin nodded along. If it was for Larry then it all made sense.

Larry seemed to know when Gavin's body started to move of its own accord, when his knee started tapping or his jaw started clenching, his body trying to take him physically back to where he did not want to go. Larry would sense it and come over to him, touch him. Lay his head on his lap, or get up onto his hind limbs, planting his paws against him as he leaned forward with his head in his hands. And that would sometimes be enough, just that touch, to bring him back to the present.

One of the great miracles of sharing our lives with dogs is how they seem to know us so intimately. Many clients down through my years as a vet have said how their dog knows them better than their husband or wife. And I think to a large extent that's true, because a dog allows us to be who we really are, without the distortion of who they would like us to be. As a result, we let them into our inner psyche, our inner soul, to a greater extent perhaps than we would do with a human, because we know they won't tell anyone about our vulnerabilities and sensitivities and won't ever judge us.

However, in this way there is a danger of anthropomorph-ising dogs too much. I have never in my career directly imposed human characteristics upon dogs, though it is a natural thing for us to project humanity onto them. It's one of the ways we try to understand them. But it's really important to recognise that they are beings in their own right and that a dog's perception of the world is different to ours. We should love and respect them as their full, unique doggy selves, and not as small furry humans.

Of course, there is something about that moment when you just know what your dog friend is thinking. When they give you a quizzical look, or are annoyed with something you've done. In that moment, the distance between our species collapses and you know without a doubt exactly how they feel. This immediate empathy is one of the great joys in life and those who haven't experienced it are missing out. But what do they see when they look at us? We know that dogs have the same five senses as us. But the balance between them is very different. Though it's not true that they see in black and white, it's generally agreed that they have poor colour perception when compared to ours and their eyesight is better in low light than ours. They also have a wider field of vision due to the positioning of their eyes but find it harder to judge distances. Their hearing is incredibly acute; dogs are able to hear sounds that we cannot, both in terms of frequency and volume. Their hearing is up to four times as sensitive as ours, with ear flaps optimised to move so that they can maximise the soundwaves entering their ears.

Their sense of smell is remarkable and it is hard for us to understand what the world smells like to a dog. Most dogs have about fifty times the scent receptors we do. Bloodhounds have upwards of sixty times. Some people even believe that dogs have the smell-brain intelligence to self-medicate by eating plants and mushrooms that contain ingredients they are lacking or feel may benefit them. The nose print of any individual dog is as unique as the fingerprint of a human. They can trace scents for more than a mile, tell different varieties of bird by scent, and they can sniff out adrenaline and many different human and animal pheromones from a distance. So, when your dog is sniffing you, they are learning more about you than you may know about yourself.

It is no wonder that smells we humans may perceive as simply unpleasant may to a dog present a rich cornucopia of olfactory delight. To you, you're a smelly stinky mess; to them, you're infinitely fascinating. Perhaps counterintuitively, most dogs' sense of taste is less developed than humans. They have around 1,700 taste buds, which are concentrated around the tip of the tongue, compared to our 10,000. That won't be of surprise to anyone who has seen the things their furry friends eat in the park.

It's so common for us to gaze into the eyes of the dogs in our lives and wonder 'what are you thinking?'

Dogs possess the same brain structure as we do, which means they have essentially the same emotional equipment. They have the same hormones and chemical signals communicating between their neurones as we do. It is not currently possible to know exactly what it feels like emotionally to be a dog, but our best guess is that dogs experience a wide range of emotions like humans do, including excitement, distress, contentment, disgust, fear, anger, suspicion, shyness and love. These canine cognitive processes have even been accurately mapped using specially trained dogs who will sit for long enough in functional magnetic resonance imaging (fMRI) machines. Interestingly, it is currently thought that dogs might not feel shame, guilt, pride and contempt in the same way that we do, however much they might look ashamed when they steal the Sunday roast off the table. It appears that where emotions are concerned, they are literally the best of us.

But, in the same way that the word oxytocin doesn't *explain* the feeling you experience looking at your child when you release this so-called 'kindness hormone', none of this truly explains the mixture of magic experienced emotionally between a dog and their human.

Gavin would look down at Larry looking up at him and he would feel that he really mattered to him. He could tell that Larry knew what was going on and just the fact that there was one being in the universe who saw, who knew and who reached out to him changed everything. He found himself talking to Larry. Not about big stuff. Just chattering away, telling him what he was doing, holding a conversation. And the act of doing that loosened something that had been tied tightly inside his brain for a very long time. He no longer got to the end of the day only talking to delivery people through a window or door. He had Larry to talk to.

But when it was time for the first sleepover, Gavin was nervous. He'd got used to spending hours at a time with

Larry, but this was different. What if something went wrong? What if Larry got hurt? What if he had a nightmare and freaked him out? What if Larry got out and Gavin had to chase after him in the dark? He couldn't do that, he hadn't been outside in so long. The thought of having responsibility for another life seemed too much. It was too soon.

Hugo promised he would sleep in his car outside the cottage in case anything went wrong. He said that Larry didn't have to sleep on his bed if he didn't want to or if Gavin didn't want him to, but reassured him that lots of people had told him that just having a canine companion close by helped with nightmares. That first night, Gavin woke in a lather of sweat, trembling from a nightmare about the things he didn't want to remember, but he could feel the gentle weight of Larry leaning on his body next to him in bed and it was as if he had a guard dog for his sleep now. He stroked Larry and slowly the tremors subsided as a shroud of calm descended around them. The panic attack and sleepless night that would usually follow such a nightmare didn't happen. Larry reached out in his own inimitable way and brought Gavin back from the abyss of darkness. He hugged Larry tight to him and fell back to sleep. For the first time in a very long time, sleep felt safe.

That first night, Gavin didn't go outside. He opened the door, and Larry ran out for a pee and a poo in the overgrown garden and ran back in again. Hugo parked further away out on the street observing, making sure they were safe.

The next day, Hugo came to check in and found Gavin as wide awake as he'd ever been. Hugo asked if everything had been OK. 'It was good,' said Gavin, and he said it so casually that it made Hugo smile. 'Happy to have another night together?' asked Hugo. Gavin just nodded, but Hugo noticed a small twinkle of joy in his eyes.

A couple of nights later, Hugo awoke from a half-sleep in his car to see Gavin in his slippers and dressing gown, holding a torch and furtively looking around for any sign of movement or noise as Larry had a poo. Gavin looked around again, checking and listening, scooped the poo up in a bag and popped it on the side of the overgrown path, barely discernible now in his small garden.

Bit by bit, as trust between Gavin and Larry grew, Hugo pulled back. One night he told Gavin he wouldn't be staying outside in the car. Larry sat by Gavin's feet, looking up at him expectantly. No words were said. It was implicit that everything would be OK. The following day, Hugo told Gavin that he wouldn't be bringing food for Larry and that if he opted to order dog food on his phone, he was sure that Larry would be very disappointed in him. Before long, Larry and Gavin were making the short trip to the local shop, and not long after that, going for walks, where Larry began to meet other dogs, yearning to sniff them. Gavin held him back, pulling hard on the lead, but in the end, he acquiesced and eventually was forced by the furious bottom-sniffing of Larry's new-found Schnauzer friend to at least exchange a few words with the Schnauzer's human.

A dog can feel emotion down the lead attached to their human, like a telepathic cable of both thought and trust. We get it wrong and think the person at one end of the lead is in charge. But I have seen again and again how dogs lead people out of themselves. I have seen non-verbal children communicate with dogs in a way they never have before and certainly couldn't with a human. I've heard countless times how humans lost to pain and trauma are brought back to life by the dogs they love. In my own life, I know that I have communicated with animals in a way I have struggled to with humans. Talking to big crowds or doing events, I'm fine. But put me round a dinner table full of people I don't know and it's like everyone is playing a game I don't know the rules for. I am hesitant and tongue-tied and want to constantly kick myself because I'm so clearly getting it all wrong. But dogs take us out of the self-consciousness of our own heads. By sharing their own thoughts and feelings, they lead our thoughts and feelings to a better place. It is often they and not us who are taking the lead.

Dogs have been alongside us for tens of thousands of years. They have learned to read our tone of voice, our gestures and even perhaps our minds. The benefits to them initially were food and a place by the safety of our fire. To us, a dog may have been a hunting companion. But over centuries of companionship, the lead of trust and understanding between dogs and their humans has strengthened immeasurably. Studies show that our relationships with dogs can reflect the depth and complexity of human parental relationships. In other words, both they and we can feel like parent and child and this is a marvellous blessing. Dogs can break through even the most severe psychiatric disorders and find a point of connection with a human being which proves elusive even to the most highly trained medical professionals. Deep in our collective evolution and memory, we know that dogs belong with us and that we belong with them.

We recognise this incredible and ineffable bond at every level. Biologically, when we stroke a dog, our blood pressure lowers, our heart rate slows and we release oxytocin, that same hormone mothers release when they look at their children. It is called the 'kindness hormone' for good reason, for that's exactly the emotion we feel alongside our canine best friend. We also produce less cortisol, the stress hormone. But, as I alluded to earlier, such biochemical explanations are reductive of the Midas-touch magic of how it feels to stroke a dog. Every fibre of their hair touching our fingers turns what can be a bleak world into gold for the soul. To know, without any doubt, that you are making the world a better place for both of you with such a simple action is incredible.

Socially, we are connected to a being who needs us, who trusts us and who we trust and need back, and in turn this enriches the lives of those around us beyond measure. Studies suggest that humans with dogs in their lives suffer less from depression and anxiety. At a basic level, having a routine to get up, get out and walk with them is transformational for many people. The dog lead keeps many human beings connected to life itself. Studies have even found that contact with dogs can help us learn and retain information better. I can personally vouch for this as Keira sat at my feet, conducting willpower, patience and calm resilience into me with the electrical field of every wiry hair on her fuzzy face while I studied for my specialist examinations which led to my professorship. The bottom line is that dogs don't just make humans better, they make society better.

The profound bond of trust, loyalty, love and companionship that bound Gavin and Larry was utterly mutual. Gavin loved Larry and wanted him to be happy. Larry loved Gavin and wanted him to be happy too. Larry always knew how Gavin was feeling through his lead. If Larry saw a dog with his tail between his legs being sad, or swishing his tail high, ears up with fear, he would always smile, loll his tongue out a bit, hang his ears down in a non-confrontational way and swish his tail happily. Soon Gavin felt this happiness down the lead of trust and he rapidly found that when he met a person with another dog on their walks, if he smiled, they smiled back and sometimes conversations began. Trusting humans again would take some time, but Larry had prompted the beginning of a life-long journey for Gavin, who trusted Larry with all of his heart.

And so, the greatest medicine that Larry gave Gavin wasn't that of pills from a bottle but rather trust carried down a lead. Larry led his human to a better future where trust of another human finally did become possible. That human was me, but sadly it took a massive trauma for poor Larry to broker this unfortunately very necessary deal.

One day as Gavin went to close the gate of his now freshly mowed and tidy lawn, Larry's lead slipped from his hand and he ran across the road to greet a Poodle. Bang.

Straight into the side of an oncoming car. He was carried into my consulting room by Gavin, grief-stricken and terrifyingly traumatised by both the sound of the impact and the state of his friend. He had been driven to his local vet and then directly to me by the kindly driver of the car that unavoidably hit Larry. He stood in my surgery and everything poured out of him. I was made aware very quickly indeed of the importance of Gavin's relationship with Larry.

As I mentioned, I had no idea of the journey I have just explained until much later, but I could see that Gavin desperately needed Larry by his side. What if I had to tell him bad news? What if I had to look in his eyes and tell him that Larry would no longer be in his life? There are times when this weight is especially heavy, and this was one of those times. The news I bring can be outside of my control. All I can do is assess the damage, weigh up the risk–benefit of all possible treatments in the best interests of my patient, and make a recommendation. This might be the greatest news a human can hear, and their face lights up. Or it can be the worst news possible in that moment, and I see them crumple. In such circumstances, I am the one who has to tell any guardian of any dog whether I feel I can broker salvation or whether there is nothing we should do other than allow their best friend to pass peacefully away, if intervention isn't in their best interests. As I have said before, just because it's possible to do something does not make it the right thing to do. No surgeon ever picks up a scalpel blade unless they expect to win.

I examined Larry thoroughly. He was covered in cuts and grazes from the impact of the car. He had a laceration on one side of his face, skin hanging off, his breathing was rapid and shallow, the membranes of his eyes and mouth were pale and I could see he was in considerable shock. I could see that one front limb and one hind limb were clearly broken, bent over on themselves, his gorgeous yellow hair matted with fresh blood. Having given Gavin a hug, my team and I took the utmost care with Larry's sedation. We immediately established that two of his ribs were broken and air had leaked from one of his lungs that had ruptured inside his chest. This is called a pneumothorax and it can be life-threatening. We got rid of this air straight away by using a very large pointed needle to place a long rubber tube between the ribs through the wall of his chest, which was then attached to a one-way valve and stitched to the skin on the side of his chest, where a suction device was held with a mesh vest. We stabilised him on intravenous fluids and appropriate drugs, including heavy-duty pain-killers. He didn't need a blood transfusion just yet and we hoped it would stay that way. We stemmed any remaining bleeding with bandages and he had one-on-one nursing in our intensive care ward throughout the night.

A couple of days later when Larry was stable and out of immediate life-threatening danger, Gavin came to visit and sat with him for a while. It was heart-wrenchingly painful to see him draped over his dear friend on a foam mattress on the floor in one of my rooms. The fear in his eyes was that of a deeply scarred human whose past wounds had been wrenched open and were raw and bleeding every drop of blood from his soul.

The day after that, I operated on both of Larry's legs at the same time. One fracture was compound comminuted, meaning that the shin or tibia bone was smashed in pieces and sticking through the skin. I pulled all of the bone pieces back into alignment using pins sticking through the skin, which were then attached with clamps to a kind of scaffolding outside the limb called an external skeletal fixator. We could dress his open wounds and hopefully prevent infection in the bone ends protected within. The forearm of Larry's front limb, his radius and ulna bones, were also shattered, but were readily put back together and held in place using a couple of plates and screws.

Gavin visited a couple of times more before Larry could go home, where he recovered slowly but surely. It was something of a role-reversal. Now Gavin had to get water and pills for Larry, just as Larry had once done for him, except now, Gavin wasn't afraid for himself any more; he was just afraid of anything he might get wrong in the salvation of the dog who had saved him in so many ways. And so, they led each other to a better future, as dogs and their humans often do.

When Gavin came with Larry for final X-ray pictures and removal of his external skeletal fixator, a tall blond man walked into my consulting room with him.

'Noel, mate. This is Hugo. I wanted you two to meet because . . .' I nodded and shook Hugo's hand.

'Thank you,' Hugo said. 'For looking after Larry.'

'It was an honour,' I said.

Gavin told me that he'd started volunteering at a local charity shop which raised money for dog shelters. He was even thinking about going to university, so he could help people with difficulties like he had. There was no way he could have done that before. In going through his journey with Larry and ultimately in becoming Larry's carer, he had himself become a leader of sorts. Where once Larry had taken the lead, he had since inspired Gavin to lead. I nodded and smiled because I've heard so many times that it's the dogs in our lives that help us make that presentation, get that promotion and really test ourselves. Dogs give us the confidence we need to become leaders. They make us feel that we are capable of anything, because they genuinely believe we are. They lead us. I gave Larry one final scratch behind the ears, gave Gavin a hug and a whispered 'well done, mate', and sent them on their way.

Then I watched with a full heart in the early evening sunlight, as Larry, Gavin and Hugo walked out from my reception into the yard outside, Larry pulling Gavin forward on his lead, into the wonderful partnership of their future.

3

A perfect life

Fairy the Berdoodle and Cheryl

I saw Cheryl's nails before I saw her, long red talons the colour of cartoon blood, curled around the edge of my door. I was furiously trying to finish off the paperwork for the previous patient, plus trying to get hold of one of my engineering colleagues to make a custom implant for a particularly tricky case. I'd been running in and out, checking on our patients in rehab, and must have left the door ajar when those nails came into view.

I soon learned that Cheryl had the almost perfect life. She had the clothes and the hair and the nails. She had the exercise regime and the make-up. She had the chiselled boyfriend. They were paid to go on holidays and, while there, to take artful photos of her standing in the sea looking into the distance. They were sent free outfits and beauty products and gadgets. There was one thing that was missing. The perfect Instagrammable dog.

By this point, I had already met Fairy. She had dragged Cheryl into my consulting room, an utterly irrepressible bundle of fur and energy. 'Oh my God, she'll be the death of me,' Cheryl had said, as her whirling dervish friend spun her and the giant pillar-box red puffer jacket she was wearing around my consulting room. All of a sudden, Cheryl was in my arms as she flailed and I lunged to catch her, coupled with the razor-nails and the slobbering tongue that was desperately trying to lick both of our faces.

'I'm Cheryl and this is Fairy,' she said. 'She's a St Bernard Poodle cross. A Berdoodle. And that was the first disaster – she was meant to be a Cockapoo!'

I was to learn that this was how Cheryl talked. Everything was perfect or a disaster. She had been expecting a neat lapdog. An accessory for the constant stream of images her chosen lifestyle needed her to produce. Instead, already at nine months old, Fairy was more than a handful. I was pretty sure they had the name before they'd met her, as she couldn't have been further from a delicate fairy. She was a galumphing, harumphing force of nature.

I've already mentioned that dogs and their guardians often reflect each other's emotional or physical characteristics, but they can also be polar opposites who fate has somehow thrown together. And so it was with Cheryl and Fairy. Cheryl was petite, meticulously manicured, blonde and composed. Fairy was an undeniably gorgeous but chaotic whirlwind of fur and slobber and joy. She refused to stay in one place, wanting to explore everything. And she kept checking in on Cheryl, and me, making sure we were OK.

Once we were all finally untangled and sitting down, Cheryl took me through what the last months had been like. I found out quickly that she was a very popular social media influencer who had a gazillion followers.

For a start, Fairy wouldn't keep still. Every photograph they'd been able to take was a blur of her running or jumping away. And to top it all, she chewed everything and got muddy footprints and drool everywhere. Everything in the house had been carefully chosen to co-ordinate harmoniously. Cheryl showed me photos on her phone and it looked like a showroom in a shop. Cream or rose gold as far as the eye could see. I tried to imagine Fairy sitting quietly for a photo and I couldn't. I had to suppress a smile. She was just one of those dogs who had to keep moving. The St Bernard in her was clearly desperate to be doing tasks. And most of the time, that involved licking anything within reach. Right now, she was sniffing every inch of the room, then forgetting which bits she'd sniffed and starting all over again. She was having an amazing time.

Cheryl, meanwhile, was not. She had taken off her giant jacket to reveal a T-shirt that read 'Too hot and too cool!'

'So how can I help?'

'Mam likes her . . . but she won't take her off our hands,' she blurted out matter-of-factly. 'And now look at what's happened! Sam wanted a dog because all his friends have dogs. I told him that we should have got a Frenchie. Apparently, she's going to grow about three times that size,' she wailed. 'My friend Gloria has a Frenchie. He's perfect. Sits still for every picture. Loves the attention. People have gone crazy for him. She's going to start him up his own account.'

I promise this book won't be full of lectures, but I do have to deal with something at this point. French Bulldogs are very popular on social media. In fact, they have become the most popular dog in America, surpassing the Labrador Retriever, which remains the most popular in the UK. Cockapoos are the third most popular dog breed in the UK and also highly desirable 'social media assets'. Both Frenchies and Cockapoos are cute, which is why folks love looking at pictures of them. Cognitive ethologists, who study how animals process and respond to information from their environment, have observed that Frenchies and Pugs are more likely to look at humans longer and display traits that appear 'helpless' and more 'infant-like' to humans. Some people even think that they appear to 'smile' and appear to 'be human'! That's probably why they're very popular on social media.

I enjoy working with Frenchies and Pugs because they generally have great temperaments and just want to make friends with me. But one cannot ignore the undeniable litany of genetically associated problems they suffer from. As a vet, I have a moral duty to point this out. The short noses and flat faces that appear so appealing are more correctly termed 'brachycephalic', which is a genetic shortening of the skull. This gives rise to all kinds of problems including Brachycephalic Obstructive Airway Syndrome, which often prompts surgery to shorten their soft palate and widen their nostrils so they can breathe more easily. They have an increased risk of heat stroke, and multiple eye issues; they may be unable to give birth naturally (requiring Caesarean section) and can also often have skin infections and dental problems.

As a neuro-orthopaedic surgeon I often see and treat Frenchies, Pugs and another brachycephalic breed, English Bulldogs, when they present with progressive paralysis of their hind limbs due to intervertebral disc disease, spinal vertebral deformities and even the formation of cystic structures within and around their spinal cord. In fact, vertebral deformities and instabilities so commonly cause problems in these breeds that I have developed a special fusion system called a FUSS plate – Fitz Universal Spinal Stabilisation plate – which is a 3D-printed implant construct based on the dog's individual CT scan. And indeed, these issues are a 'fuss' of our own making, because selective breeding that has largely been aesthetic-based has resulted in major problems for all of these brachycephalic breeds. The Netherlands has banned Frenchie breeding on ethical grounds, and the British Veterinary Association (BVA) has urged people not to buy flat-faced breeds. The guidance from the BVA is to 'avoid imagery of brachycephalic dogs in advertising, marketing materials, and social media to reduce demand and prevent normalisation of the health issues'. The International Collaborative on Extreme Conformations in Dogs similarly advocates avoiding the use of images of dogs with extreme conformations in all forms of public communication that are not directly aimed at protecting their health and welfare. And so, vets have a collective duty to make people aware of such guidelines and recommendations.

Instead of the Frenchie over whom Cheryl felt dog-envy, Fairy was in fact a bewildered Berdoodle who his mum wished was a Cockapoo.

'What had happened' was that while Cheryl and Sam were away being 'perfect', Fairy was charging around in a local park with Cheryl's mother in a very 'unperfect' way and was now lame on one of her hind legs. Of course, this didn't stop her charging around at a million miles an hour – but nevertheless, it didn't take a genius to see she was carrying her left hind leg.

As Cheryl's tale of woe continued, I asked one of my interns to pop into the room to hold Fairy for a physical examination. Then I asked a nurse to come in as well because one person wasn't enough to control her boisterousness. As soon as I felt her knee joint (known as a stifle in a dog), the problem was instantly apparent. I could feel that there was abnormal movement between the thigh bone (femur) and the shin bone (tibia). She'd ruptured her cranial cruciate ligament. In humans this is called the ACL or anterior cruciate ligament. It's a very common ailment and usually treated surgically.

I attempted to explain this to Cheryl with gentle reassurance. But my colleagues and I looked on with both surprise and concern as Cheryl had a full-on meltdown. I asked them to leave the room to give her a moment but she melted further downwards.

'Oh my God, it's a disaster,' she whimpered, her eyes filling with tears. 'Mum is away and Sam can barely look after himself, and I just can't make the time. Can you not just give her some tablets?' As she went on, it appeared that I had become the conduit for more than a little pent-up frustration.

'Do you know what he said to me last weekend?' she asked. I shook my head. 'I asked him if he'd come for a drive to the park with me and Fairy, and you know what he said?' I again shook my head. 'He said . . . "Do we have to do this every Sunday?" And then for good measure he told me that we used to have such fun before she came along. Bloody hell, she was supposed to be fun. I thought if we got a dog, it would bring us together. She was supposed to make us better and now all she does is make us worse,' she wailed.

It did indeed appear that Fairy had driven a big hairy dog wedge between them, but I couldn't help but feel that it was going to need something bigger than the right dog to fix her relationship. I just let her spout off and said nothing. It was clear that the tears were more for herself than for Fairy and I found it hard to summon any sympathy at all as she went on . . . and on.

'Sam and I have this really important trip next week to the Maldives. We just cannot cancel. They're setting up the beach tents and everything for the advert. We just cannot have surgery. Is there not a brace or something you can use?' And then she said it, as if she just couldn't help herself. 'You're the Supervet . . . can't you do something?!'

Well, I could think of lots of things to say, but I said none of them. I felt it best to keep my thoughts to myself at that particular juncture. I advised that she have a think about surgery and, in the meantime, I would give Fairy some painkiller medication and she should keep her strictly on a lead.

As Fairy limped out into the car park and Cheryl wiped mascara off her cheeks, I couldn't help but pity the poor dog.

And then, disaster.

Within a few days, Cheryl's world ground to a standstill.

As did everyone else's world too.

The Covid-19 virus was declared a global pandemic and people had mere days to return to wherever they would spend an unknown duration of global lockdown.

The Maldives beach-tent trip morphed into a trip to a tent in the yard outside my practice (we tried to avoid people coming indoors). Cheryl would not be advertising swimwear or cosmetics but would instead be asking me how long recovery from Fairy's surgery might take. I got to meet Sam too, though 'meet' would be a generous term for the encounter, limited by both the social distancing of Covid and also the fact that he barely made eye contact, spending almost the entire consultation flicking the screen on his phone. He was, I observed, even more self-obsessed than I could have imagined.

Cheryl may have been a little self-centred herself, but I came to realise during this second meeting that she was in fact terrified of everything, but especially of being on her own. Her every movement and thought seemed to be geared towards approval from Sam, while Sam seemed to me to approve of nothing except Sam. I quickly learned that during our initial encounter, what I had interpreted as her thoughtlessness towards Fairy's welfare now appeared to be a manifestation of fear . . . fear about what might happen to Fairy, fear of what Sam's response was likely to be, and, I surmised in that moment, maybe even fear that

Sam might leave her because Fairy was too much trouble and didn't fit in with the 'perfect' life in his head. Or at least that was the vibe I was getting.

Cheryl looked to Sam for reassurance throughout the consultation, which was all about deciding what kind of surgery to have, when to have it and what the aftercare might look like. But as far as I could see, the social media feed on his phone was more important and he answered in monosyllabic grunts. He clearly couldn't wait to leave, and in this case leaving my tent meant a walk of no more than twenty feet to his car. Sam was already in the car, still on his phone, while Cheryl hugged Fairy goodbye. The decision had been made for Fairy to have surgery that very day. Her lameness was getting worse and Cheryl had finally accepted that there was no other good option. This time I got the impression that her tears were real.

It turned out that Fairy had indeed precipitated more than a little crisis in the 'perfect world' of Cheryl and Sam. Her not fitting into their Insta-perfect and TikTok-perfect world didn't just shine a light on what Cheryl didn't want to see in terms of muddy footprints on her beautiful carpet, but Fairy's predicament also shone a blazing beam of light on something else that Cheryl did not want to see – the cracks in her relationship.

It transpired, I heard later, that there had been a fierce row on the way home, with Sam saying how Fairy had been Cheryl's idea and that she should never have brought a dog into their lives. Now they were stuck with the 'bloody thing' and couldn't even leave the house. He absolved himself of all responsibility. It was indeed true that only one walk outside per day was permitted during the initial government-imposed lockdown, but Sam's increasingly irritable attitude to Fairy was forcing Cheryl to take a good long look in the mirror.

Meanwhile, I was taking a good long look inside Fairy's knee. The cranial cruciate ligament had ruptured as I suspected. But, again as I suspected, running around manically had simply been the last straw. In fact, for most large-breed dogs such a rupture reflects a very chronic degenerative process of osteoarthritis within the joint, whereby the ligament frays like a worn shoelace and eventually ruptures. When we operate, we generally don't replace the ligament, but rather take away the load that the ligament hitherto neutralised. If you think about the thigh bone as a truck parked on the hill of the shin bone, what we generally do for dog breeds like Fairy's is take the hill away so that the truck doesn't need the rope of the ligament to hold it in place any more. It's called a tibial plateau levelling osteotomy, TPLO.

Sadly, in Fairy's case, the duration of her wait for surgery meant that the truck had been rolling up and down the hill for a while, grinding up one of the cartilage buffers between the two bones, the medial meniscus. And so, I removed pieces of macerated cartilage from the joint before making a curved bone cut in the tibia and rotating the top part so the femur bone wouldn't slip down the slope of the tibia ever again. The bone segment was anchored with a plate and screws and Fairy went home the following day.

She was a model patient, totally calm and accepting of what was 'absolutely the best thing for her', as I whispered to her afterwards in the wards. I also told her that 'we all loved her'.

Well, I stretched the truth on that last bit. It appeared that Sam just loved Sam, as Cheryl returned to pick Fairy up on her own. I almost didn't recognise her. Gone were the nails, the T-shirt and the bomber jacket, and gone was the façade. She had on a sweater and jeans and no make-up.

Cheryl told me about her argument with Sam and that she didn't know how she was going to cope during the weeks cooped up in the house with him and Fairy. She admitted to me for the first time that since Fairy's lameness had begun, her relationship had also begun to limp, such that now it was on its knees. They had nowhere to go and were running out of ideas to post about from their living room. She said that she was worried for Sam as he had become withdrawn and even more uncommunicative, and she was desperately worried about how they would deal with Fairy's recovery.

People tell me things like this all of the time. It may seem weird that people tell me their innermost secrets and lay their souls bare in my consulting room, but I think that has a lot to do with the portal of truth which is opened by the vulnerability of the unconditional love they share with their animal friend. When that is threatened, everything is threatened. Their fears about the animal they love invariably open other wounds in their life as well and they confess all. They trust that I will do the right thing for their best friend and that I'm a safe pair of ears. And they are right. In this book, most names and circumstances have been slightly changed to protect the integrity and sanctity of this guardian–clinician trust. Many secrets I shall take to the grave with me.

I have heard all kinds of stories, but the particular tale that Cheryl imparted to me on her next visit blew even my mind. It turned out that the wounds in her relationship with Sam were even deeper than she may have thought and that Fairy was the one to tell her about it.

When she had brought Fairy home after her surgery, Sam was asleep on the sofa and was unhappy at being disturbed. He grumbled off upstairs, not even welcoming Fairy home, and so Cheryl had to sort out the cage and everything else herself. I had given her strict instructions – 'Cage rest, collar at all times, no running, jumping, slipping or sliding' – and to her credit, she had ordered a flat-packed cage and set it up in the living room. Afraid to ignore any of my instructions, she tied Fairy's lead to the leg of a chair next to the sofa while sorting out the bed and her feeding bowl in the cage.

And it was then that the epiphany happened.

Fairy lurched forward, inevitably pulled the chair after her and knocked magazines and stuff off the chair in her wake. Cheryl lunged to grab her and they both landed in a heap of clutter. Cheryl couldn't help but smile at her own foolishness. She remembered that I had told her about a lady who had tied her dog to the leg of a table upon which had been her collection of priceless china, which was soon worthless. 'The price we pay for love,' she thought, lying on her back on the floor, with Fairy's big tongue dribbling on her face.

But the frivolity was short-lived.

Beside her face on the floor, the luminescent glow of a phone screen shone through the scattered magazines. Cheryl picked it up, still lying on her back, with Fairy now lying prone beside her. It was Sam's mobile phone. Sam was never separated from his phone, it was permanently welded to his hand. He must have been so flustered by his irritation on their arrival home that for once he let his guard down . . . and what a guard it had been.

The screen flickered with messages from two different women. Their photos were familiar to Cheryl since they were also fairly well-known influencers. Her heart plunged into her stomach as she clicked on one of the messages, and barbed wire seared through her mind as she flicked on another. She lay there paralysed with disbelief, anger and fear, and cried. Fairy licked her tears.

It came to light in the ferocious argument that followed that Sam had accidentally left his phone unlocked when he'd been sleepily 'sexting' these women. It also transpired that his illicit dalliances had been going on for some time. No wonder Cheryl felt insecure in her relationship, was always on edge and constantly afraid of abandonment.

All of this came out in the wash and all of it came out through Cheryl's tears in my consulting room. Sam had left their home to join another Covid family bubble with his father and Cheryl was now all alone. When she brought

Fairy for a check-up and stitch removal, she told me, 'For the first few days I felt so betrayed, but I was so lonely, I really wanted to give him another chance . . . But then it felt like my heart had been ripped out of my chest and all of my life was a sham. I'd tried so hard to be perfect for him, to look perfect and to be with him in all of the perfect places, and all that time he had been cheating and lying.'

Then things got even worse. Cheryl couldn't take Fairy to her mum's house anyway because of Covid restrictions and then her dad became really sick with Covid and had to be hospitalised. There were a couple of days when things did not look good and Cheryl told me that she had been out of her mind with terror. 'If it hadn't been for Fairy,' she said, 'I don't know what I would have done.' Thankfully, her dad made it through and was home a week later. This explained why Fairy had been a week late for her stitch removal.

Now, Cheryl was crying again because, though Fairy had been doing well, she had noticed some swelling in the area where I had placed the plate. Then Fairy began to hold her leg up, not wanting to put weight on it at all. I took one look at the knee and a delayed infection was obvious. More than a decade ago, I published a scientific paper on 1,146 knees in 1,000 dogs on whom I had personally performed a TPLO procedure. Infection occurred in 6.6 per cent. Though this rate of infection has been reduced with recent implant technology, infection remains a risk at this site, which, as anyone who has ever banged their shin will tell you, is quite superficial.

Long story short, I resolved the infection, first by giving antibiotics and later by removing the plate and screws once the cut in the bone had healed, which became necessary because bugs sometimes 'hide' in the nooks and crannies of metal implants in a gloop of disguise that is impossible to penetrate, called biofilm. And in the meantime, I saw the impenetrable gloop of make-up and made-up persona fall away from Cheryl too. In her case, Fairy's love was the cure.

During her many trips to see me, and as lockdown led to further lockdown, Cheryl told me that her numbers on social media had dramatically dropped off because there were no perfect trips to perfect places with perfect people. She had initially tried to make stuff up, but there's only so many outfits one can buy on the internet to pose in around the same house and the same garden before one runs out of money. Finally, she dressed herself and Fairy up in the kinds of outfits that she used to pose in with Sam and mocked up exotic places in her garden or house with a simple prop like a miniature palm tree or a poster of a beach. Still her social numbers plummeted, and any semblance of her self-worth plummeted with them.

Fairy was as mischievous as ever, knocking the plant over, tearing any poster to pieces, flicking off hats and trying to chew them. In the end, Fairy wore her down and Cheryl acquiesced to the inevitability of the mayhem. Utterly bereft of anything to post one day, and with her defences lulled, she posted what Fairy was really doing rather than the perfection she had been aiming for. Cheryl had filled the sink with washing-up liquid to wash mud off Fairy's paws, but while her back was turned, camera still running, Fairy flipped the tap lever and soon the entire camera frame was filled with suds. Yes, you've guessed it — Fairy Liquid! The video went viral.

Once Cheryl stopped trying to make everything appear perfect, threw caution to the wind and broadcast life as it really was, things took a turn for the better. She started teaching Fairy tricks with hoops and balls and doing doggie-dancing. She constructed a kind of parody of her former existence and her Instagram and TikTok took off. Their antics went viral, 'Fairy dust' was scattered through the world and the world revelled in it. Every day a different pillow ripped open, a different cup of tea knocked to the floor.

I got to know a completely different person from the one I first met. Her enforced isolation with Fairy brought about a remarkable transformation. As they grew ever closer, Cheryl became ever more the best version of herself. At each follow-up visit I could see that Cheryl was slowly letting go of her profound insecurity, which had been thinly veiled by her projection of a 'perfect life'. Like a Russian doll slowly shedding layer upon layer of fear of judgement, fear of abandonment, fear of not being liked enough and fear of who she really was, finally I saw a young woman who had rediscovered the essence of her true self.

And Fairy? She was what she'd always been: an irrepressible bundle of chaotic love and freedom and energy. She didn't care about followers; she just wanted to know where her lead was, so you could take her for a walk. You could 'follow' if you wanted, but she was going to go everywhere anyway, given half a chance. When she laid her huge (and getting huger), heavy head on Cheryl's lap, she felt the joy and absolute security of a love that wasn't about hugging you while looking over your shoulder for better options, but was there, present, in the moment. There's a useful phrase I think of often – 'don't let perfect be the enemy of good'. Once Cheryl had let go of a perfect life, she found the lasting joy of a good one.

Cheryl never mentioned Sam again after the day she told me about his departure, so I have no idea what happened to him and his 'perfect life'. What I do know is that Cheryl and Fairy went from strength to strength. I had an email from her some months after lockdown ended. Attached was a beaming picture of Cheryl with a new boyfriend in the Scottish Highlands, a tongue-filled beaming smile from Fairy sitting up between them, their arms around her. Cheryl thanked me for everything I had done for Fairy and she thanked me also for being what she called 'a shoulder to lean on' during a particularly difficult period of her life. Late that night, writing medical reports after a long, bruising day, I sat in the dark of my office smiling. She had signed off her email with 'Life is so much better with paw prints all over it.'

4

More than everything

Teddy the Doberman, Rosie and Ryan

Ryan's girlfriend Rosie rang me. I didn't know her. But I did know her partner. Everybody did. He was a famous bloke in a famous band. And like many famous blokes in many famous bands before him, the sex and drugs were threatening to overshadow the rock and roll. He came from a working-class background and after the gig he was 'all in' for whatever the night might offer. It wasn't quite the '60s, '70s or even the '80s, when what happened on tour definitely stayed on tour, and Ryan was in trouble, as was their relationship. Big trouble. And the press was all over it on both sides of the Atlantic. But Rosie didn't want to talk about Ryan. She wanted to talk about Teddy, who was a magnificent shiny, brown and black Doberman. I gave up thoughts of a sandwich during my only gap in the day, sat back in my chair and told her to start at the beginning and tell me everything.

I had seen the stories. I have been a music obsessive ever since I'd first seen fuzzy black and white television footage of Queen, Black Sabbath and Led Zeppelin as a child. I had a secret radio that I found on a scrapheap, made an aerial out of a coat hanger and secretly listened to a pirate (unlicensed) station called Radio Luxembourg. I'd curl up on a nest of straw in an old cowshed where our farm dog Pirate was chained up, hugging his neck and, in my imagination, building a 'Stairway to Heaven'. Escaping my insular world through the airwaves was possible through my imagination of a literal stairway to heaven.

Aged ten, I wanted to be Brian May from Queen. My aspirations were short-lived, though. When I asked my father for a guitar, I was given a saw to cut horns off bullocks. 'There'll be no guitaring around here . . . there's enough noise as it is.' I guess that was a win for the world of music and a win for the world of veterinary medicine.

But I had always escaped into music, and songs written by heroes of mine like Brian May and Tony Iommi from Black Sabbath were my salvation from bullying and other stuff that went on back then. Alongside my love of animals, music has been my refuge throughout my life, amid all of the ups and downs, the failures and the death, and the insane stress.

I was well aware that Ryan's band had taken its inspiration from bands like Black Sabbath, and I also greatly admired him as an artist and as a musician. But there was no music or animal to save Ryan in his particular predicament. He had jumped head-first into the kind of paranoia that Black Sabbath had sung about. Nobody could save him except himself, and I learned from Rosie later that he had given up caring.

Meanwhile, Rosie cared desperately and talked to Teddy

about all of her fears for the man she still loved. Teddy would curl himself up next to her and gaze up with his dark brown eyes, his velvet ears and his pink tongue all seeking to bring her some respite from her pain. He would race across the fields and then come back to tell her all about it. He would come and find her if she was in a different part of the house and remind her that it had been far too long since she last stroked or scratched or hugged him. Teddy had been her constant companion through all of these shaky times. And sadly, now it was Teddy who had started to get shaky on his feet.

Rosie's life unravelled at every level. The two beings she cared about most had come undone. She had to somehow hold herself together as both Teddy and Ryan were falling apart. She had unceremoniously been dumped by default from the other side of the world. She just read the latest salacious story of the next notch on the bedpost and had heard nothing for weeks. That wouldn't have mattered if she didn't love Ryan so much, and I wouldn't have been involved if she didn't love Teddy so much too. And because the only love she felt she could potentially rescue resided in Teddy, this made his plight even more traumatic for her.

Rehab had been mentioned to Ryan by a couple of people who actually cared, but they were quickly disposed of. As long as the gravy train kept rolling for everyone making money, the pleasure train kept rolling for Ryan, and nobody could tell him any different. Previously he had been anchored by Rosie and Teddy but he was locked in free-fall and it didn't seem there was anything Rosie could do.

All of his demons were out to play and seemed determined to destroy him.

Meanwhile, she was destroyed by Teddy's predicament. Rosie struggled with both Teddy's front and hind legs on a harness with two handles as she got him out of her car. I saw her through the window of reception and ran out to help. He was in a very bad way. So was Rosie. Teddy sat on a rug on the floor of my consulting room as I took on board everything she told me. She was fighting back tears as I asked one of my colleagues in to help me examine the nerve reflexes in his legs. Then we were alone again and I explained what I thought was going on. The positioning reflexes were absent from all four of his limbs (this is called absence of conscious proprioception). I said that he most likely had a badly bulging disc in his neck which had degenerated for genetic reasons and was progressively squashing his spinal cord. He had gone from wobbly to unable to get up at all by the time I saw him. He would need an MRI scan of his neck to be sure and to guide what might be the best intervention for him, but I explained that there would be no way that he'd do well without surgery. Rosie knew this deep down, of course, which was why she was in my room, but she suddenly crumbled in a deluge of tears streaming down her cheeks and onto Teddy's forehead as he looked up at her helplessly from the floor.

My team and I anaesthetised him and whisked him off to the MRI scanner. A disc is like a jam doughnut buffer between vertebrae so that any of us mammals can move our spines in all directions. The dough is a rim of fibrous tissue called the annulus fibrosus and the jam is a pulpy gel called the nucleus pulposus. The MRI scan showed that Teddy was affected by DAWS, Disc Associated Wobblers Syndrome (the medical term is disc-associated cervical spondylomyelopathy). But even worse than that, the bulge of the outer part of his disc, which is called a protrusion, had suddenly ruptured, causing the pulpy centre to explode up into his spinal cord, which is called an extrusion. The cord had nowhere to go inside the spinal canal and was well and truly squashed. That's why he couldn't stand on any of his limbs. This was now an acute crisis and he was headed for total limb paralysis – tetraplegia, in medical terms – which could become permanent unless we acted quickly.

Rosie was knocked flat by life, and so was Teddy. She told me that her 'partner' (she hesitated on this word, the inference being obvious) Ryan adored Teddy and asked me if I could please call him, knowing he wouldn't speak to her in the circumstances. She didn't want to call his manager or the people around him, since she really needed him to understand what was on the line – everything.

I didn't have the full story at this point. She had told me all I needed to know and she filled in the gaps later. And so I called Ryan in the full knowledge that Rosie needed him to pay for urgent surgery on Teddy. I think Rosie hoped that the crisis affecting this dog that Ryan loved would help him realise that his own life was on the verge of blowing up too. Was there a price for that, I wondered? One of the wonderful things about my television show is that even if people haven't watched it, they generally know who I am, and because I have insisted from the beginning that we tell the truth at all times and show life as it really is rather than as some dressed-up reality TV show, people know that I'm likely telling the truth. Or at least, that's what Rosie was banking on. For everyone's sake.

It's not that I take lightly the responsibility in such situations, but I'm generally quite calm when I pick up the phone because I have seen time and again how the truth bubbles to the surface, sublimating all else, when the animal one loves is in crisis.

Whether it was luck or fate, I don't know, but Ryan answered the phone. I suppose he saw it was a UK number and thought he'd better pick up.

'Listen, Ryan, my name's Noel. I'm a vet and I'm calling about Teddy.' He didn't hang up. This was a good start. I was pretty sure he'd have hung up had Teddy not been mentioned straight away.

He was impatient as only a man with a drink or something stronger waiting for him can be.

'Won't it wait till I get back?' he asked rather perfunctorily.

'No, it won't,' I countered with equal pointedness.

'Has Rosie put you up to this?' he sighed.

'No, she hasn't,' I said.

After a long pause, he sighed impatiently again and, in spite of himself, asked, 'Well, how bad can it be?'

'Mr Jones, your friend Teddy is going to die unless you make a decision. And you need to make that decision today. Not tomorrow. Tomorrow will be too late.'

It was as if I had punctured a balloon and all of the air came out at once. The inflated self-importance evaporated as the heat of reality hit him, and within a minute he was sobbing.

'OK, OK . . . can I come see him?' Ryan now sounded like a grief-stricken boy rather than an all-powerful global music icon.

'Well, you can come of course, but I'd recommend that our best chances are if I operate in the next twelve hours, so you wouldn't get here until it's done . . . You know I can't guarantee anything, don't you . . . except that I shall do my very best,' I said.

'I know you will,' he said quietly. 'When will you start if I say yes?' he added.

'Now,' I replied.

Rosie was in the consulting room with me while I was on the phone. Ryan didn't ask to speak to her. His parting words were, 'Thank you. Do whatever you have to do to save my boy . . . please text me when it's done . . . and tell Rosie I'll take care of things.' I assumed he was referring to the finances. Fixing their relationship wasn't within the power of my scalpel blade, and from what I could see, it was probably past saving. I wish I could have told her that he'd asked after her, that he'd had an epiphany and realised what really mattered in life.

But I did the only thing in my power – instruct my team to get the operating theatre ready, and get gowned and gloved as quickly as I could.

Teddy lay on his back on my surgical table, his neck outstretched. I cut down under his neck, moved the trachea, the oesophagus, the jugular vein, the carotid artery and various other bits and pieces that keep us all alive to one side, and drilled down into the disc that had bulged and exploded, garrotting the spinal cord, which is the cable powering life itself. I spent about an hour trying to scoop out all of the disc material that was squashing the spinal cord. Some of the exploded pulpy centre was easy enough to scoop out, but the bleeding was like an erupting volcano, because the ventral venous sinuses had been ruptured. Every time I poked around for more material, fresh blood bubbled uncontrollably from the hole I had made under the spinal cord as I stopped and started, started and stopped. Each time I tried to scoop out some more material, the fibrous strands of the ruptured bulging annulus fibrosus stubbornly refused to be plucked out, much like trying to grab the flailing rubber of an exploded car tyre from the inside out. I knew I'd never get enough material out to alleviate his pain and the compression preventing him walking and now he was in danger of critical blood loss. He could die or be paralysed forever, which would undoubtedly lead to euthanasia.

I had faced this situation before. I needed to settle for what I had managed to get out and then push the vertebrae apart with a spacer, so that the 'flailing rubber' wasn't squashing the spinal cord any more. There was one hope . . . a new technique I had invented a decade previously. I had ultimately lost a patient of mine who had been affected by the same condition because the technique we had at the time for trying to push the vertebrae apart to create more room for the spinal cord and nerves wasn't very good. I ended up euthanising the patient when his vertebrae collapsed after the surgery, and I was profoundly sad. As I drove home in the snow, I pulled into a layby and cried. I saw a man pushing Christmas trees into the back end of a horse-box. The trailer was full, but the man had one last tree in his hand. He pushed the tip of the tree amid the tightly crammed bases of the other trees. He pushed and shoved, and because the branches of a fir tree are shaped like a wedge, of course it compressed the branches of the other trees and, ultimately, in it went. And so, the Christmas tree-shaped intervertebral spacer was born, which I called a Fitz Intervertebral (dis)Traction Screw (FITS).

Luckily, I now had all different sizes of FITS devices in a box in my office. I sent a nurse to get the box, chose a size as if picking from a box of biological chocolates, autoclaved it on a flash cycle to sterilise it and set to work. I screwed the spacer in between the vertebrae, pushing them apart and stretching what was left of the compression of the cord, much like pulling tentpoles apart, whereupon the tent collapses. The bleeding stopped immediately. I had also invented a new plate, which was shaped like the saddle of a horse. I'd asked my colleague to sterilise one of these of appropriate size also, and then I bolted this titanium saddle beneath the two vertebrae, anchoring it with large screws which locked firmly into the bones and also firmly onto the FITS spacer device. I took some bone marrow from the top part of a humerus bone underneath one of Teddy's shoulder joints and transplanted it around the spacer. The implants immediately pushed apart and stabilised the adjacent vertebrae, and within six weeks, fusion should become permanent because transplanted marrow grows into solid bridging bone. Within two hours, the procedure was done. Teddy's spinal cord was free of compression and he was waking up.

Whether Ryan might ever be free of the depression caused by his self-destructive behaviour and whether he'd ever actually 'wake up' and get sober was another thing entirely. The irony was not lost on me as I picked up my phone to text him as he had asked, after I had spoken to a very tearful Rosie, who had clearly still not spoken with him, though it was hours later. I guess he hadn't been brave enough to call her while the life of the being he cared about more than any other was balanced quite literally in my hands.

I have observed over the years, having treated plenty of patients whose humans are well known, that those in the public eye often form an especially strong relationship with the dogs in their lives. In my consulting room they're the same as everyone else. In fact, often they're more devastated than most by the thought of anything happening to the animals they love so much.

I think that when you are any sort of celebrity, you are constantly confronted by how often people want something out of you. Maybe it's those around you who need you to earn the money, a list of people that only gets longer the more famous you get. Or it's the people who have an image of you that they need you to be. So many performers craft a persona that they then have to fulfil. Or maybe it's the ego that develops when everyone you ever meet calls you a genius, or tells you things they think you want to hear. Dogs don't believe any of the hype or the bullshit. Perhaps it's just because it's hard to believe you're a rock god when you're picking up a little bag with their poo in. Though most people don't delight in this particular part of the 'dogs and their humans' equation, interestingly I have had a few very famous performers who have told me how this act alone snaps them right out of their indulgences and anchors them to what's really important – a home, and a friend with whom to share love, who loves you for who you really are rather than who people want you to be.

When you're with a dog, you don't have to pretend to be someone else or behave in a certain way. They don't want anything from you except love and joy and it's a fair two-way exchange without agendas. Of course, performers do what they do out of love and passion, but sometimes applause might fill a gap in their lives too. Dogs are like a constant standing ovation. Just for being you, they're applauding wildly with every sinew of their bodies, whether you are Taylor Swift or just singing in the shower into your hairbrush.

For those used to being on stage, dogs are an emotional green room, the company in which they can truly be themselves. You might be Billy Big Bollocks when you're at a hotel in LA with a massive entourage, but your dog doesn't care about that. They see you. They love *you*. You don't need to change to make them happy. You don't need to buy a big house or a car. Or wear the right kind of clothes. You don't need to take them for fancy meals and take photographs of what you eat, or have the perfect body.

You just being you is enough. We intuit that there is a purity to a dog's love because it doesn't come with any strings. A constant succession of sycophants and groupies is like junk food for the soul. You can survive on it, but you're going to get sick eventually.

There's a special lineage of dogs and rock stars. In the Led Zeppelin song 'Bron-Y-Aur Stomp', Robert Plant sings about a 'blue-eyed Merle', which is a reference to his friend Strider. When he sings the song live, he changes the words to shout out Strider's name. Ozzy Osbourne and his wife Sharon share their lives with eleven shelter dogs; Gene Simmons of the band Kiss with four rescue dogs. 'Martha My Dear' was famously written about Paul McCartney's beloved Old English Sheepdog. When Eric Clapton wrote 'Layla', a song about George Harrison's wife, Pattie Boyd, George returned the favour by writing a song about Clapton's canine friend in 'I Remember Jeep'. Elton John's home is shared with more than twenty dogs. When he married David Furnish, Arthur the Cocker Spaniel was best man.

You only have to look at the number of celebrities' dogs who have their own social media to see how many people in the public eye return home to dogs as a cocoon of calm and understanding where they can be themselves, a security blanket for their souls when the security of their entourage has evaporated. As both a passionate advocate for the bond of love between a dog and their human and a passionate music fan, I have gone so far as to say on national radio that if Noel and Liam Gallagher from the band Oasis were by some quirk of fate in my waiting room, each worried about a sick dog, barriers would evaporate in the presence of this raw, vulnerable love – which invariably makes us realise we have far more in common than ever drove us apart – and Oasis would reunite in a heartbeat. Who knows? Maybe it was exactly this kind of love that finally brought the brothers back together in the summer of 2024.

I know in my own experience that I have shown parts of myself to Keira, and now Excalibur and Ricochet, the cats I share my life with, that I have not shown to any human. Partly this is because they emit only positive energy when I'm feeling low. I was an actor in a former life. It's a long story, but for a short interlude for a few years after vet school, I went to drama school to learn how to communicate, translate, interpret and hopefully eventually use the stage and the cameras to change the world for the better for our animal friends and for all of us. I was shy, and I didn't know how to communicate, and I am forever blessed that I had that training. I vividly remember one particular teacher of improvisation who breezed around wafting the faint aroma of alcohol in her wake. Improvisation is the art of being in a state of heightened communication where you engage completely with yourself, your character and the character of others – off script. This requires trust and throwing caution to the wind, jumping all in. In improvisation there is a principle referred to as 'yes and', which means that you are only ever positive and build upon what the other performers are doing. If they begin an improvisation, you should never challenge its premise but rather build upon it. Dogs are the ultimate 'yes and'. To them a hedge is a gateway to a magical kingdom, a tennis ball an object of infinite possibility. Every time an aperture opens or a ball is thrown, the miracle occurs again.

In that miracle of communication with an animal, there is innate trust. We jump all in, completely and absolutely, because that trust is built on the foundation of unconditional love. There is no judgement. Whenever I have felt the pressure of owning a business, or studying for endless exams and degrees, or preparing for academic lectures, or being that vet on the TV, I have escaped to my relationships with animals, and it is this purity of communication without words, this being in the absolute present, that has allowed me to escape the pressure. Strangely, though I never forget the importance of what I'm doing when I operate, that is a space I can escape into also. The operating theatre may be a scary place for patients, but this particular theatre of performance is my safe place, a place where I can be completely at ease, completely in control and completely in harmony with biology, my constant mistress and arbiter of my success or my failure. I know the rules there. I know how to do what I need to do. And all of this is anchored by my profound love of animals. So often, being a human is a messy, complicated business. Our love for those animals we share our lives with is a much simpler place.

The following morning, Ryan pulled up at my practice in his blacked-out Mercedes, having flown back to London on the red-eye. I couldn't see his eyes as he was wearing shades. He said very little to me, just hoped I was well and thanked me for operating. When he saw Teddy, I heard his voice break as he said, 'Hey, boy.' My team and I carried Teddy from the wards to my consulting room and gave them some alone time. Teddy was still lying on his side, with none of his limbs working yet, but he was also doped with as many Class A drugs as his dad had ever been. I was a little worried about him lying on one side for too long and I came back into the room a little too quickly, before Ryan had popped his rock-star shades back on. He had been crying, not something he was accustomed to doing. Teddy would be staying with us for a few days at least and Ryan said he'd be back tomorrow to see Teddy again. Teddy was straining to get to Ryan with every fibre of his being. It was as if he could tell there was something wrong with his human and he wanted to help. With one final whisper in Teddy's ear, Ryan popped his shades back on, got up, nodded at me, said, 'Thank you for doing your best,' and left the room. He got back into his blacked-out Mercedes and it drove away.

Rosie came too, but later that day. She and Ryan were ostensibly still leading separate lives. It turned out that Ryan didn't visit the following day. We had a call from an assistant saying that he wasn't feeling well. But Rosie came several times over the following days and, within a week, Teddy was able to stand following intensive rehabilitation. Within two weeks he was able to walk and had begun hydrotherapy. Then Rosie brought him home to cage rest and harness-only walking, performing physiotherapy exercises with him as I had demonstrated for her. Over the following weeks, with occasional trips back to our physio and hydro centre, he made a full recovery.

For the six-week check-up, Rosie brought him in to see me personally and I was overjoyed to see him walking normally, a spring in his step. She said Teddy was back to his old self. Bounding about and exploring the world, putting his nose into everyone's business and barking at anything that moved. She seemed more buoyant too, and as I signed him off, she asked if I would mind coming out to the car. Ryan wanted to say hello.

'Oh, he's here?' I said.

'Yeah, he's a bit out of sorts at the moment . . . he didn't want to come in,' Rosie replied. 'Rehab. You know how it is,' she added.

I didn't but I nodded anyway. I had earnestly hoped that I hadn't seen Ryan since that first encounter because he may have been undergoing his own intensive rehabilitation. I went out to the car, which was parked round the back of the practice, where there was a bit more privacy. The chauffeur got out as I approached, acknowledged me, tapped on the window and opened the back door of the Range Rover. Ryan got out. He was in a tracksuit, no shades and no façade. He reached out and gave me a hug. 'Thank you, bruv,' he said. 'Thank you . . . for everything.'

Ryan looked pale and thin. But there was something different when I looked in his eyes. When I had last seen him, he had seemed disconnected somehow. It struck me how often drink and drugs are ways to numb the world. To avoid feeling pain. Perhaps the same can sometimes be true of a life on the stage. While you are there, you can be someone else. Someone who doesn't carry around your past.

To be on stage, then drunk or high when you are off it, then pass out — if you did that, perhaps you could avoid feeling at all. But the problem then is that you would never get to feel the good stuff either. The joy and the elation and the love. It is the knowledge that we die which ultimately makes the love of those we share our lives with while we're alive so important. To feel great love is to risk great pain, but that's the deal. If you're brave enough to take it.

It turned out that once Ryan had felt this love swelling up from within him because of Teddy's crisis, when he was forced to make a decision about surgery, he was also forced to make a decision about life. Apparently, seeing Teddy after surgery and realising that he had almost lost what really mattered was the only tipping point that could have ever got him into rehab. And so, he saved Teddy's life by saying yes to surgery and Teddy saved his life by saying yes to life. I had picked up a scalpel to cut away Teddy's disease, and Ryan had realised he had to do the same to the people and things in his life that caused his disease too.

I thought of that little kid growing up in Ireland who dreamed of the life that Ryan lived. I thought of Ryan's red-rimmed eyes behind sunglasses. I thought of what life would be like without the feeling I am blessed to experience in doing what I do. And I was so very glad that my life's training had turned out as it had, in allowing me to save Teddy's life and so much more.

Rosie came up behind me with Teddy. She gave me a hug and got in the other side of the car, Teddy leaping in beside her. Ryan turned to get into the car. Then he stopped and beckoned the driver to get in. Ryan put his right hand on my left shoulder, looked me straight in the eye and said, 'Without you I would have lost everything, man . . . Nah,' he smiled and added, 'I would've lost more than everything . . . You know?' And I nodded.

I did know.

5

But will he love me again?

Bertie the Pomeranian and Cynthia

Cynthia had had a rough couple of years. She'd been through an acrimonious divorce after her husband of more than twenty-five years had fully inhabited the cliché and left her for a woman half his age. She told me this almost as soon as she'd sat down, entering my consulting room in a cloud of expensive perfume as she held out an exquisitely mani-cured hand. As I've mentioned, people often enter a confessional mode in my consulting room. Sometimes, I suppose, to explain the crisis of your animal friend at the centre of your world, you have to explain the rest of it first. Cynthia told me she had been crushed, at first. She felt like she'd wasted the best years of her life on him. What was she going to do now, start again?! She thought she might never stop crying.

Luckily, in the divorce she had kept Bertie. There was no chance he was going with her ex-husband. Bertie hated him and always had. But now, Bertie was her rock. Every time she had cried on the sofa, he had come and comforted her. He was her loyal and absolutely constant companion whatever she was doing. She knew she had to feed and walk him, so she didn't stay in bed with the curtains closed, which is all she felt like doing because depression had hit her hard in spite of her normally bubbly character. But Bertie could always sense what she needed and he would follow her around, checking in on her. Bertie was a perpetually perky Pomeranian. At only 1.8 kilograms, he was indeed tiny, but his massive tufts of tan-coloured hair stuck up like the spines on a playful porcupine, from whence his ever-pert ears and ever sticky-out tongue protruded, ready for anything and grabbing every moment of every day as if it were the last.

At night, Bertie would curl up on her pillow and drape himself over her head. He'd wake her up in the morning with licks of love. He'd shout out in joy when he saw her if she'd been away for even a few minutes. Cynthia knew she had to keep things together for Bertie. And Bertie patrolled alongside her, barking warnings to other dogs, as well as people and trees, that he was her guard and that no one should even consider hurting his mum. She had thought on occasion that maybe that's why he never liked her ex. He must have always suspected something was awry.

Gradually, Cynthia began to see the upsides of being single. She was able to see friends and family whenever she wanted. She realised that her ex had actually been a weight around her neck, stopping her from doing things she wanted to. And anyway, she was sick of his constant moaning, his refusal to ever fill the dishwasher or put petrol in the car, the way he tightened the lids on jars so she couldn't remove them and always left the recycling drawer open. Come to think of it, she had resented him quite a lot for quite a few years. Their daughter was already nineteen, but as Cynthia walked Bertie in the park, she remembered how it was only she who gave up her successful career as a head-hunter to look after their daughter, whom she loved deeply of course; only she who would watch their daughter throw dough balls in Pizza Express, while he was always at some work dinner or event. Their daughter was now at university and her life was well and truly under way, but Cynthia wondered if she would ever find any human to love her again. Then she'd look down, pick Bertie up, cuddle him and know for sure that there was one man who would always be loyal and would never ever leave her.

Cynthia realised that she could do what she wanted with her time. She took evening classes – life drawing and cookery. She realised that people liked her. They found her funny and interesting. She even went on a couple of dates. Nothing serious. A couple of glasses of wine, the odd meal. For the first time in a long time, she'd had fun. But there was no one special enough to bring back to meet Bertie. She wondered how Bertie would react. He was so protective of her, she wasn't sure how he'd deal with someone new in their life.

And then Frank came along. Frank was a wonderful, kind, funny man. And it was clear within a couple of weeks that he was crazy about her. There was none of that teenage wondering if you should text them stuff. They both immediately and mutually decided that they should see as much of each other as possible. They went out for long meals and talked about everything. They made each other laugh. It was as if they'd known each other for years. Things began to get more serious surprisingly quickly and that was when it was time for a frank conversation with Frank. 'There's another man in my life,' said Cynthia one evening over dinner, 'and if you want to stay in my life, he comes too. We're a package deal.'

'I know,' said Frank, surprising her.

'What?' she asked. 'I mean, how?'

'Well, we've had the kids conversation and I thought it was unlikely you were checking the security camera in your house for burglars,' he quipped. 'So, when do I get to meet him?'

Frank arrived in the drive and Bertie started barking immediately. When Cynthia opened the front door, he ran outside, still barking.

Frank knelt down and put his hand out for Bertie to gently sniff. Then Bertie slowly raised his head to be tickled in his proffered spot. It was like smoke over St Peter's Square – Bertie had spoken and Frank was OK. Bertie kept an eye on him warily. And he sat between them on the sofa like a chaperone. When it was time for bed, he even tried to go up with them, but Cynthia put him firmly in his own bed. Bertie was astonished. He hadn't slept in there for two years. He yipped for a while but eventually acquiesced to the happiness of his mum. Gradually they settled into a rhythm, the three of them, with Bertie relaxing into Frank being there. He even stayed overnight at Frank's.

And then one night when Frank was away on a long business trip, Bertie was immediately back in Cynthia's bed, curled up at her head as before. But in the morning, she woke up and Bertie wasn't in his usual place. She looked all around the house and finally found him hiding down by the side of the sofa, hunched up in a ball.

'What are you doing down there, you silly sausage?' She went to bend down and he bared his teeth at her. She flinched. She was shocked and stood back up quickly. This had never happened before. She decided to go and make his breakfast and call him in. He came in, eyeing her carefully, but didn't go to his bowl. She stepped back a few feet and only then would he eat, but keeping one eye on her. The rest of the day was the same. He kept a wary distance, refused to let her pick him up, seeming happiest when he was furthest from her. That night, Frank was still away, but Bertie didn't even try to get into bed with her, but instead went and slept in his own bed. She hoped that she'd wake up and it would all be a horrible dream. But the next morning it was exactly the same. She truly did not understand Bertie's sudden aversion to her and any hope she had felt for a return to his normal behaviour had now curdled into disappointment. If she came near him, he'd growl. She'd back off and he'd calm down.

After a week, with Frank still away, she went to see the vet, who politely ushered her out the room. So, she tried another one. Then another. Each took temperatures, listened with stethoscopes, poked and prodded, but nothing. One even took X-ray pictures but they couldn't find anything.

Another prescribed tablets but they didn't do anything. She was desperate. Money was no object. She'd been to see two behaviourists and they couldn't work it out either. They asked if Bertie could perhaps be in pain, since it seemed as if he was exhibiting a fear of imminent discomfort.

'I don't know, I don't think so. He just woke up one day and started hating me!'

By the time she was sitting in my room, Cynthia was at her wits' end. A friend had recommended me when her own precious companion hadn't been able to walk. She said Cynthia should come to my practice, to see if I could help.

She was sitting there, ostensibly a perfectly normal, rational woman in her early fifties, with not a hair out of place and wearing elegant, understated and obviously very expensive clothes. But emotionally she was a wreck.

'I can't take much more of it,' she said. 'I just want my old Bertie back.' She explained that she had been able to get through her divorce because of Bertie. But how was she going to get over *Bertie* dumping her?

By this point, Frank had come back from his trip. He had come straight round to comfort her. And Bertie ran straight into his arms. It was like something out of a film, as if 'Take My Breath Away' was playing in the background of their embrace. He was acting as if Frank was his saviour, that he was rescuing him from this awful woman. He'd gaze up at Frank with those shining brown eyes, as if he was in love. Then she'd come too near and he'd start growling. As she explained all of this to me, she began to cry, mascara running down her cheeks like a kind of treacle of despair she was wading through.

'I love him so much,' she wailed, 'but I don't know how to make him love me again. I don't know what's wrong with him. It's as if I have done something absolutely awful, for which he'll never forgive me.'

'Does Bertie sleep in the bed with you?' I asked. That set her off again.

'He used to!' she cried. 'But the first night Frank was back, he jumped into bed with him. Then I tried to get in and he growled so loudly, I slept in the spare room. I've been there ever since!

'It's horrendous. I'm even thinking I might have to end things with Frank. It's too in my face, for Bertie to love him so much. It just reminds me how much he hates me now. I can't bear being the *other woman* with my own dog.'

She was so upset, but I had to work very hard not to smile. It was indeed a very unusual clinical history-taking session. We medical folks call this taking the signalment, but during this time, I let Bertie wander around the floor of my consulting room so that I could watch his behaviour as if I *wasn't* watching his behaviour, if you catch my drift. I didn't want him to be spooked, but rather to do whatever he wanted. And in so doing, the single most important piece of the puzzle clicked into place for me with a flash of intuition.

'Has he been holding his head down like this for long?' I asked. Cynthia replied that this had indeed been his posture for the past couple of weeks. She explained that she thought that it was because he didn't want to raise his head to look at her. I said, 'I think he may have neck pain. Do you mind if I have a look? This might hurt . . . I'm sorry.'

I asked one of my interns to pop in to hold Bertie since it was very clear from his growling and baring of teeth that he didn't want his mum to hold him, but it was also abundantly clear to me that he did indeed have neck pain.

'When was the last time you slept together?' I asked, quickly adding, 'I mean you and Bertie.'

'Well, that was the night before he hated me,' Cynthia answered.

'I see. And you said that he hadn't been sleeping in your bed for a while before that?'

'Yes, that's right,' she answered.

'Is there any possibility that you could have rolled over on Bertie during the night?' I probed.

'Well, I do move about when I sleep. My ex-husband always said it and so does Frank. Both of them are such heavy sleepers. They're still as a statue.'

And now the cogs really began turning in my head. 'Thanks,' I said. 'Sorry to get personal, but I think that he has a problem in his neck and maybe . . . just maybe . . . he got caught for a minute when you rolled over in bed.' Poor Cynthia was mortified as she signed the consent form and went for a walk, and I took Bertie off for an MRI scan of his spine.

Sure enough, half an hour later, there it was, as I suspected: atlanto-axial subluxation. It was clear as daylight on the scan. It's where the connection between the atlas (which I call the 'yes' bone because we nod with it) and the axis (which I call the 'no' bone because it's this bone that our skull pivots on when we rotate our heads) vertebrae had come apart. Pomeranians can be genetically predisposed to a condition whereby the ligaments that hold these top two vertebrae of the cervical or neck spine together don't develop properly, such that sometimes the axis tilts relative to the atlas, driving the pointy bit on which the skull rotates – the dens – up into the spinal cord like a spear. It was immediately apparent that the spinal cord was squashed within about a third of its diameter and not only was poor Bertie in severe pain, but he was also on the literal 'spear-edge' of complete paralysis of all four limbs if this vertebra tipped any further. No wonder he was head-hanging and more than a bit angry.

Piecing the evidence together like some kind of biological detective, which is what my job often feels like, Cynthia must have rolled over on top of Bertie with a jolt that had likely jarred apart the latent separation of the two vertebrae to the point that he felt severe pain. The straw that broke the spinal cord, so to speak. She'd probably been asleep, oblivious, while Bertie lay there stunned in excruciating pain for a few hours. Then he'd pulled himself together and crawled as far away from her as possible. Now he associated her with probably the worst thing that had ever happened to him. Meanwhile, Frank had suddenly gone from an interloper to a valued ally in the battle against the bringer of pain and terror.

I rescued Cynthia from her pacing in the car park, brought her in and showed her the scan. She was flabbergasted, as anyone would be if the vet just told you that the love of your life was on a spear-edge of possibly permanent paralysis. She sat down trembling as I explained the enormity of the diagnosis, but tried to reassure her that it really wasn't her fault and had been an accident waiting to happen at some point with the least nudge. She just happened to be that unfortunate nudge herself. She was beating herself up terribly and I felt very sorry for her, but there was really only one thing I could do and that was to explain how I could potentially fix her little pal.

I explained that down through the years I had used many techniques for stabilisation of these two vertebrae relative to each other, which is called atlanto-axial stabilisation. I had used various kinds of plates, screws, wire, pins and cement, either by going in underneath the spinal cord, bypassing the dog's larynx and all the vital structures under the back of the skull, or by going in on top of these vertebrae from behind the skull. There were many challenges, however, especially for a tiny dog like Bertie. His bones would be super-tiny and super-fragile, in some places so thin that one could actually see through the bone, in my experience. Therefore, it would be very challenging not only to get them back into alignment, but also to secure them in alignment with implants. And we were operating just behind the brainstem from which all life and movement flowed, and so he could die during the surgery. But left as he was, he could die anyway from respiratory arrest or need to be put to sleep because of extreme pain and permanent paralysis. Cynthia and Bertie were between a rock and a hard place, but I resisted the analogy to his head being trapped by her as the precipitating cause of his crisis. She cried bitterly.

I gave her a moment, and as she pulled herself together, I explained that in my opinion the best option would be an invention that I'd only used twice before. It was, like all of my inventions, born of frustration with previous failures and an effort to do better every single time I picked up a scalpel blade. Using many years' experience from the placement of pins and screws with or without guidance from a CT scan, I had designed an implant that could go on top of these two tiny delicate vertebrae like a grappling hook, with hooks and screws that, if placed in the right spots, would tip the axis back into the right place relative to the atlas, releasing the pressure on the spinal cord and holding the vertebrae secured. I explained to her in detail the risks of death, of things not working. She nodded along, stunned. I knew that it would be a very challenging surgery on eggshell-thin bone. I advised a CT scan that would give us the bony dimensions with which we could manufacture the custom implant. This was obtained and I could see that some of the bone was just a millimetre thick. 'Challenging' was an understatement.

As she picked Bertie up carefully in her arms to take him home – where he would be on medication and strict cage rest until I could make the implant, which would take a few days of work with my engineering and machinist colleagues – she sobbed with fear and remorse and other unnamed feelings. It all came tumbling down upon that particular moment, as it often does for those who love a dog in crisis. The rest of their trauma comes toppling down upon them like a stack of cards that had been propped up by a paw.

I asked if she had any further questions related to the risk of the procedure, because the very next time I saw her we would be operating and there was no way back – it would either work or not. The die would be cast. I was expecting some kind of technical question, but, looking up at me, Cynthia asked, 'What I need to know is, will he love me again?'

I had absolutely no idea. I am often asked to give certainty where there is none. But even for me this was a new one. I looked down at Bertie's fox-like spiky fawn-coloured face, his little tongue sticking out with noticable apprehension as he was almost visibly sidling away from Cynthia and back towards my hand. I settled on, 'You can never say never.'

Two weeks later I found myself and my surgical instruments feeling our way around eggshells, pulling back one of many muscles here and packing a dab of collagen on a bleeder there. Finally, we were down to bones . . . very tiny bones . . . One slight false move and the brainstem was dead. My anaesthesia team was fantastic, my surgical assistant was fantastic, my theatre team was fantastic, and I did my best. With much delicacy and more than a little bit of cursing, I managed to get my implant in place. It's called a FitzAASS, Atlanto-Axial Stabilisation System, and it sure was a pain in the a★★★ to get in place. I was more apprehensive when taking the post-op CT scans than I had been on possibly any other occasion in my career. For instrumented bone surgery like this, a surgeon can immediately be judged by the position of the implants, which is very different to soft-tissue surgery, the effect of which one cannot generally see on scans or radiographs. It wasn't *perfect*, but then I had known that during the op, because the bones hadn't moved as much as I wanted them to and there was nothing at all I could do about it given the bone was so delicate. So, in this case, *good* would have to suffice. Now I would have to wait until the spinal cord and Bertie himself would tell me whether all of my effort was in vain – and Cynthia would have to wait to find out whether or not he would love his mum again.

Poor Bertie had one-on-one nursing in intensive care for forty-eight hours because there was a real risk of sudden respiratory arrest, him going blue and dying. Gradually, though, he perked up. And yet, even seven days later, he was still not walking. But he had recovered enough neuro-logical function to be able to urinate, and so he could go home. Cynthia came in and I showed her how to perform the physiotherapy exercises for all four limbs. Frank came too. He let Frank hold him as he kneeled in front of him on our physio mat and pushed his manly beard up against Bertie's tufty forehead, which had been shaven so he looked like an Ewok from *Star Wars*. Cynthia was, so far, as relieved as she could be, but she looked at Frank and, half jesting, half serious, said that she couldn't believe how cruel I had been to give Bertie tufty hair envy of her 'perfect partner', whom he now had even more reason to love than before!

And then the miracle of love came to visit, as I have seen it arrive so very many times in my career.

I had instructed strict cage rest, strict physiotherapy and absolute support at all times. And yet two days after Bertie returned home, as I tried to balance the needs of an emergency case halfway across the country along with a hundred other things, I got emailed the scariest but most extraordinarily exciting and anxiety-relieving video that I have ever been fortunate enough to receive. It was Bertie, lips wide with a beaming smile, actually running. I reiterate – running! Not walking, not on a lead, not in a cage, but running towards an elated Cynthia and scrambling up into her willing arms, throwing his paws around her and licking her face joyously.

Mum had absolutely not followed my post-operative instructions, but gosh I was pleased with my fabulous FitzAASS miracle. And it really did look like he loved her again!

6

The Queen, the King and I

Willow the Corgi and Elizabeth

The main thing I remember is how much she made me laugh. I was nervous. Who wouldn't be, going for lunch with Her Majesty Queen Elizabeth II and Prince Philip? Even though it was as informal as things get for them, when you grow up on a farm, you don't exactly learn which one is the salad fork. And to be in Buckingham Palace, a building soaked in three hundred years of history . . . But both of them had such a sharp sense of humour behind that gravitas and dignity. And of course, we were always going to have lots to talk about because of our shared devotion to animals. The Queen's eyes shone as she talked about Emma the fell pony and the many Corgis she had loved.

Corgis had first entered Her Majesty's life in 1933, when she was six years old. Her father King George VI bought her and her younger sister Margaret two Corgis. On her eighteenth birthday, she was given Susan and it is from her that all the Corgis in her life were descended. But for hundreds of years before this, the royal family have had a deep connection to dogs – from King Charles and his love of Spaniels in the seventeenth century, through to Queen Victoria and Albert, who shared their lives with Dash the Spaniel, Eos the Greyhound, as well as Dachshunds, Pugs and Collies. King Edward VII had Jack and Caesar the Terriers and his son George V had a childhood companion Heather the Collie and loved yellow Labradors his entire life.

We talked about Willow, one of the Queen's older Corgi companions, who suffered from osteoarthritis. Willow had featured in the 2012 James Bond London Olympics sketch. Her Majesty wanted to know which medication was best, whether to give it morning or evening, and also about the stem cell revolution that was just beginning at the time. Nowadays we treat many dogs affected by severe arthritis with a cocktail of fat-derived anti-inflammatory stem cells, platelet-rich plasma and a viscoelastic lubricant, much like changing the oil in the joint every few months. I explained this and Her Majesty was intrigued. I definitely have concerns about some of the much overpriced and uncon-trolled biological and pharmaceutical mixtures that are available for joint injections in dogs. My great hope for this area of veterinary medicine, which, like veterinary implants, is largely unregulated in the UK, is that those desperate to alleviate the pain of their beloved friends should have full transparency regarding what they are paying for and be given exact price comparisons. There are huge differences between the various methods of isolating and culturing cells from the patient's own fat to create anti-inflammatory stem cells, and between the various methods of preparing the platelet distillate from blood. But sadly, most people don't even know to ask.

Her Majesty asked lots of questions and was deeply interested in the concept of One Medicine, where human and veterinary medicine might share techniques, implants and information, so that we can phase out animal testing with modern alternatives to try to create a kinder world. Currently, diseases undergoing study for human patients are inflicted on healthy animals, which are then sacrificed. But such diseases are naturally occurring and could be studied in animals already affected by these diseases. There is no existing formal infrastructure for such cross-pollination of ideas and joined-up thinking with studies in animals and humans at the same time. The function of all such research animal experiments is to create drugs and implants for humans, but while these drugs and implants may have applications for dogs, human drug companies generally don't pay for a clinical dog licence, so my patients often don't get the drugs and implants for which their species die to give to humans, or at least not for many years thereafter until patents expire.

The irony that disease is induced in dogs and other animals in research experiments to develop treatments for humans, which are then not available for animals affected by the same diseases, is a very difficult pill for me to swallow. Dogs are collateral damage in human medicine and very little of the information gleaned from naturally occurring diseases that could improve treatment for dogs and their humans is shared in either direction. This seems utterly crazy to me and my central life goal is to change this paradigm and create a fairer world for animals, while also taking care of humans.

Her Majesty was an inimitable conversationalist – smart, joyful, insightful, playful and witty. She listened intently as I explained the premise of One Medicine and nodded sagely, adding her own observations here and there, mainly with regard to how difficult it is to change the minds of those who do not wish to change, even in the face of overwhelming evidence contrary to their opinion. She was also very interested in bionic limbs and how research on such implants and on joint replacement implants in my patients could help human patients. We had first met a few years previously, when she opened the School of Veterinary Medicine at the University of Surrey, which I helped to found and where I showed her how implants like these could help both humans and animals. She was particularly intrigued by the mechanism by which the bone grew onto the metal rods and plates in amputation prostheses and how the skin grew onto the metal mesh of the implant, which I explained I had called the dermal integration module, the DIM, much like how skin grows onto the antlers of the deer that roamed her estates, I mooted. Endearingly, she said, 'Not so dim at all!' That's how witty and charming she really was.

I told her of my wish that, one day, we would find a way for the parallel tracks of research on human and animal implants and drugs to help each other. I know that the human healthcare industries are full of good people, trying their very best to help human patients. They are operating within their own well-established paradigms and have both integrity and good intent. However, I believe that increasing human appreciation of the value of the life of a dog in all parts of human and animal medicine would help everyone. Sadly, I have lectured at more than one human medical conference where, as I alluded to earlier, really good people with good intentions still say to my face, 'It's only a dog!' I would really love to change this perception in my lifetime. We just have to be brave enough to do it. I believe that it would be a tide that would lift all boats, animal and human. To treat dogs as well as their humans with more care and more importance, and to try harder to achieve compassionate unity of human and veterinary medicine for all beings, would create a virtuous cycle. I realised at one point I had been talking with such passion that my soup had gone cold.

It struck me as I spoke to Her Majesty how important dogs are in anchoring us to the here and now. How, para-doxically, they keep us connected to the human within us. Here was a woman who had been head of state for more than fifty years, whose reign had begun with Winston Churchill as her prime minister, who had seen so much change. Though Churchill might be intrinsically linked to the Bulldog in most people's minds, it was two Poodles to whom he was most devoted. Rufus slept on his bed and sat on his lap in his car. He was master of all he surveyed at Chartwell, Chequers and 10 Downing Street and is rumoured to have once tried to join his best friend in the Cabinet Room only to be told, 'No, Rufus, you haven't joined the War Cabinet.' He had a habit of barking along if Churchill raised his voice. He died after being hit by a car in 1947 and Churchill was heartbroken. At first, he didn't think he could bear sharing his life with a dog again. But he was given another Poodle, whom he also named Rufus, and he would introduce him to people saying, 'This is Rufus II – but the II is silent.' Rufus II wasn't a well dog; he had digestive problems and his teeth fell out. He had halitosis that was once described as 'like a flamethrower'. He would sulk all day if Churchill didn't give him enough attention. When Churchill went away, he would howl mournfully for hours. But he would eat with the family, in a special chair next to Churchill or on his lap. They were once watching the film *Oliver Twist*, where Bill Sikes kills his Bull Terrier. Churchill put his hand over Rufus's eyes saying, 'Don't look now, dear. I'll tell you about it afterwards.'

When Rufus II died, he was buried next to Rufus I at Chartwell. I don't know about you, but when I read the stories about Winston Churchill and his Rufuses, I felt as if I suddenly understood him in a way I hadn't before. As soon as you start to look into dogs and their indelible relationship with their humans, quite quickly you end up down a rabbit hole in which many great people in history seem to have had a great dog standing next to them.

Alexander the Great loved his dog friend Peritas so much he named a city after him, according to Plutarch's *Life of Alexander*. Mozart's father Leopold wrote a symphony that calls for dogs to perform as part of the piece, barking on cue to symbolise a hunt. Leonardo da Vinci made a series of beautifully detailed studies of a deerhound's left forepaw and many other drawings of animal anatomy that weren't bettered for more than a hundred years.

Charles Darwin was surrounded by dogs, including a beloved Terrier known as Polly, who he once described as loving 'with all his heart'. He was fascinated by their behaviour, especially the bond between humans and dogs. He was an early advocate for the regulation of experiments on animals. And of course, Darwin is a fellow human with whom I intensely relate, since many of his fervent beliefs were not commonly accepted until well after his death. I guarantee it shall be sadly thus for me too.

Karl Marx was rumoured to love the dogs in his household and commented how he was constantly taken aback by their intelligence. Sigmund Freud fell in love with Jofi the Chow Chow when she entered his life in his early seventies. She sat with him, ate with him and comforted him when he was ill and in pain. She even sat with him in his therapy room, to calm patients. He once wrote: 'Dogs love their friends and bite their enemies, quite unlike people who are incapable of pure love and always have to mix love and hate in their object-relations.' Charles Dickens had a huge family of Newfoundlands, St Bernards and Bloodhounds when he moved to the countryside. Mark Twain once wrote: 'The more I learn about people, the more I like my dog.'

One of the best stories I was ever told was about Napoleon Bonaparte. Famously the love of his life was Josephine. But the love of Josephine's life was a Pug named Fortune. Napoleon's initial suggestion that they find somewhere other than the marital bed for Fortune to sleep was met with short shrift. So, he got ready to try and share. The only problem was that Fortune was incredibly possessive. So much so that at the first opportunity, he bit Napoleon on the leg and left a scar. Several years later, in the midst of his defeat at the Battle of Trafalgar, he was brought the news that one of the boarding party seizing one of his key vessels was the ship's mascot, a Newfoundland. He was reported to cry out, 'Dogs! Must I be defeated by them on the battlefield as well as in the bedroom?'

According to legend, Isaac Newton shared his life with a dog named Diamond, who once upset a candle and set fire to all of his experimental notes. However, anyone who has ever watched a dog look up at a sausage on the table knows that dogs are firm believers in the laws of gravity.

George Washington, known as the 'Father of His Country' in the US, was also one of the founding dogfathers of the American Foxhound. He was given French Foxhounds by the Marquis de Lafayette in 1785 and his journals mention more than thirty dogs he shared his life with, including Sweet Lips, Drunkard, Tipsy and Tipler. Thomas Jefferson shared his life with several dog friends, including Briards, a Bull Terrier named Pete, a Pekinese named Manchu and a St Bernard named Rollo. Franklin D. Roosevelt shared the White House with a German Shepherd dog called Major and a Great Dane called President, which must have been confusing if there was a mess on the carpet and they were trying to work out who was responsible!

John F. Kennedy shared his life with Charlie a Welsh Terrier, Wolf an Irish Wolfhound, a German Shepherd dog called Clipper and an English Cocker Spaniel named Shannon. He and his wife were also famously given Pushinka by the Soviet leader Nikita Khrushchev. (Pushinka was the daughter of Strelka, who survived being sent into outer space aboard Sputnik 5 in 1960.) Barack Obama welcomed two Portuguese Water Dogs, Bo and Sunny, into their family. Joe Biden welcomed Major, the first rescue dog ever to live at the White House. Donald Trump did not share the White House with a dog. In her memoir *Raising Trump*, his ex-wife Ivana Trump remembers that 'Donald was not a dog fan', and how her dog Chappy would 'bark at him territorially'.

I believe that dogs reveal who we really are. Because they can't talk, our behaviour towards them reveals how we treat those who cannot speak behind our backs. Some people are very good at being nice to those who are useful to them and treating those who are seen as 'below' them badly. Dogs challenge us to be kind, in the invisible, unheralded moments that matter most. Loving a dog reminds us that giving a gift is better than receiving one. This is why therapy dogs are such a powerful force for good in medicine for the mind, especially for children. Dogs take us out of the moment we are in, however painful it is. I have seen with my own eyes how that magical wand a dog waves with their playful tail or a cheerful twist of their head can actually heal a human in pain. This canine elixir opens a portal for any human willing to enter to escape from their suffering for a moment and maybe for longer. You just need to be willing to jump headlong into the pool of doggie love and let go of your inhibitions. Trust me when I tell you I have never met anyone who regretted that jump, no matter how scary it seemed at the time.

As I have mentioned, I have found time and again that presidents and politicians, rock stars and famous actors may struggle to be true to themselves in the midst of what their public persona needs from them. But dogs don't care if you are the president of a country or of your house. For your dog, you are always the Queen or the King, no matter what you may think of yourself. Most importantly, the dog who loves you allows you to be truly yourself, which in turn allows you to be everything you need to be for everyone around you – and indeed to fulfil your own ambitions and dreams, whether they're for the whole of the world or a small part of it. The only world that matters to a dog is the one they share with their human, and that human is so very lucky to have the place of truth and sanctuary that a dog provides to return home to amid the madness of the outside world.

If you have a job that forces you to operate at a super-human scale, this love, support and companionship is even more important. I once operated on the dog companion of an incredibly high-powered figure. He was in charge of his nation's armed forces and I knew from the news they were literally gearing up for war. The lives of thousands of people were in his hands. But he was in pieces over an injury to his best friend, who was on my consulting room table. My personal opinion is that the love he felt for his dog was likely to make him a more humane leader and perhaps even help him to make better decisions. The love of a dog is an earthing kind of love, the kind that allows you to be the best version of yourself for everyone around you and for everyone over whom you have a duty of care, whether that's your human family, your workplace, or, in his case, an entire army in extraordinarily difficult circumstances.

It is also a tragic fact that when you share your life with a dog, you are forced to confront death. You are reminded on a daily basis how important each moment is. The dogs I have loved have imbued within me a keen sense of treasuring every moment of life. This is a blessing for all dogs and their humans. Every day that I miss Keira, I am profoundly grateful for the time we spent together. Every time I am sad that I will never again see her face light up when she sees me, I recognise that her light remains and will be within me forever. For me and for many of the clients I have been blessed to serve, the legacy of loving a dog far transcends their earthly existence and permanently illuminates the lives of us lucky dog parents. Dogs are a perpetual reminder of what matters. The here. The now. The eternity of true unconditional love. Everything else is just background noise. When Willow died in 2018, Her Majesty was said to have been heartbroken. But no matter who you are, where you come from or what your circumstances are, we are the fortunate ones, because the dogs we have loved have taught us that light and love, when shared unconditionally, are eternal.

In one of those strange quirks of fate, the same week that Her Majesty was mourning Willow, I was looking after a dog named after the King of Rock and Roll.

Elvis was a vivacious black and tan miniature smooth-haired Dachshund. As I later learned, he was the fulcrum around which not just an extended family, but an entire village revolved. Everyone loved Elvis, and he was the life and soul of every day for everyone he met. No village hall meeting, fete, Sunday dog-walk club or event of any kind was complete without his presence.

By any measure Elvis was the king. My favourite bit of his 'act' was when he would burrow under the deepest parts of a blanket or a heap of clothing and pretend not to be there. He used one of his little front legs to lift the fabric just enough so you could see his snout and a single eye peeking out from beneath, and as soon as he had caught your attention, he'd promptly lower the cloth again over his head, daring you to come find him. And oh, when you did find him, tummy tickles were ecstasy for all – the giver and the receiver. His currency was the abundant joy that flowed from his inimitable excited yipping and the perpetual gyrations of his shaking and wriggling hips, just like Elvis Presley himself. He had a toy with a little bell in it which he chased endlessly, and so he literally shook, rattled and rolled! Elvis lived his life in the service of others, bringing beaming smiles wherever he went. He was an electrical conductor of effusive love; everybody loved Elvis and he really was the king of entertainment.

Well, everybody loved Elvis, except Gregory. Gregory tolerated Elvis. Sometimes. It was the price he paid to see his only friend, Rachel, at the assisted living residential home where they both lived. Gregory was a former ship-builder from Govan in Scotland. A hard job and he'd been a hard man. But Gregory was beginning to be more and more confused. And when he got confused, he got angry. He'd shout and swear at the care team and the other residents. Dementia is a tragic disease that can steal not only one's thoughts, but sometimes also one's peace of mind. It was only Rachel who Gregory would stay calm for; only Rachel who seemed able to pick up what jigsaw pieces were left of his mind and put him back together for a while. She knew the right words to mutter to him, the right way to stroke his hand and bring him back when he started to feel lost. And there was no way you could see Rachel without seeing Elvis, who was Rachel's best friend. So gradually and grudgingly Elvis worked his magic on Gregory. He'd never admit it, but sometimes the nursing team would secretly catch him talking to Elvis. A rumour went about that Gregory was keeping his Saturday sausages to feed him.

Then Rachel died.

Amid everyone's sadness there was the practical concern – who would look after Elvis? As I've emphasised, everybody loved Elvis, his swagger and seduction, and everybody could feel the absence of his light when Elvis had left the building. But Rachel had got special permission to have him at the residential home and none of her family could look after him.

One day, when the senior nurse came around to the communal sitting room, Gregory stood up and cleared his throat. Elvis sat by his slippers, gazing lovingly up at him.

'Elvis is living with me,' he said. 'And that's the end of it.'

When I first met Elvis, he was three and a half years old. Gregory, his care assistant Clara and Elvis came to see me because, overnight, Elvis had gone from his usual boisterous self to his hind legs being paralysed. He couldn't feel them and he was dragging himself around. A disc had exploded in his spine and knocked out the conduction in his spinal cord. About a quarter of all Dachshunds will get intervertebral disc disease in their lifetime as they are genetically predisposed to the drying out of their discs.

What I have referred to earlier as the 'jam doughnut' of a disc had dried out and ruptured, sending the jam exploding upwards into the spinal canal, knocking out the signals from the brain to the hind limbs to a variable degree. Grade 5 is the worst degree, which is what Elvis was affected by. He couldn't feel either hind foot when squeezed; he was what is known as deep-pain negative. His spinal cord had been badly damaged by the impact of the exploded disc and only about half of such dogs ever walk fairly normally again. Everyone in the care home and the village was devastated.

As Clara held Elvis in her arms, I held Gregory in mine. He wept unearthly tears, drops that came from somewhere deep within that transcended the human form; tears that came from a well that cannot be rationalised or understood, even by himself. He leaned on my shoulder and whispered in my ear, 'If Elvis doesn't make it, I don't want to make it either.'

I hugged Gregory, my heart bleeding for him, and I bundled little Elvis into my arms. For me and my team at Fitzpatrick Referrals, this circumstance is an everyday occurrence, and we spring into action in a very rapid and coordinated way. Within half an hour, Elvis was anaesthetised and in our MRI scanner, which identified, as expected, that all of the intervertebral discs in his spine were degenerate, as they are for most Dachshunds over a year old, because it's an endemic genetic problem that humans have bred into them over hundreds of years. The price for long backs and short legs, so-called chondrodystrophism, is a life-long risk of spinal disease, just like for poor Elvis. As I mentioned with regard to Frenchies, it is my moral responsibility as a veterinarian to emphasise again that humans have caused this by selective breeding, and that we should do our best to advocate for responsible breeding and avoid advertising aesthetic characteristics above welfare concerns.

Once the site of the disc extrusion, as it is known medically, was identified, it took about twenty minutes to get his spine clipped and get him wrapped up in a blanket of hot air to keep his temperature stable while he was prepared for surgery in my operating theatre. My assistant draped the table and laid out the surgical kit that I always have on standby for this frequent operation. I scrubbed, gowned and gloved, and was in theatre within half an hour of him exiting the scanner. I draped the surgical site, picked up my scalpel blade, cut down through skin and muscle and then cut a window in the side of the vertebrae, which is called a hemilaminectomy. This involves removing a bit of the lamina or roof of the vertebrae where the disc explosion has occurred so that the pulpy jam can be removed from squashing the cord. Many years ago, I invented a series of little metal scraping devices like toothpicks, which are called Fitz-Excavators. I used various sizes and shapes of these small instruments to first remove all of the extruded material and then to cut a hole in the side of the disc and scrape out all remaining pulpy jam so that no more could come out and cause more damage. This is called nuclear extirpation. Then I cut a hole in the side of the disc on either side of this exploded one, which is called a fenestration, from the Latin for window. Through this window I scraped out their pulpy centres too in order to decrease the risk of them also exploding in the future. And then I stitched him up, all in under half an hour of surgery time.

And so, within ninety minutes of admission, Elvis was the king of our wards, being waited on hand and foot by a team of nurses. His outcome would now be determined by how much damage had occurred inside the spinal cord at the time of impact, and that was anyone's guess. The disc material hitting the cord is much like bashing a plastic-coated electrical wire with a hammer; one cannot see the damage inside the covering, which for the spinal cord is called the dura. We needed to wait quite some time to see if the king would ever shake, rattle and roll again. We would take care of emptying his bladder, performing physio-therapy on his hind limbs and making sure he wasn't in pain, and this was how it would be for at least two weeks.

During that period, Gregory came a couple of times, sat with Elvis on his lap, slipped in and out of lucid thought, cried and smiled, as I held them both.

And then a miracle. About two weeks after his operation,

Elvis began to recover feeling in both hind legs. We started hydrotherapy for him as soon as his surgical sutures were removed, and he went from strength to strength over the next two months. Because Gregory was both mentally and physically incapacitated over time, we took care of all of Elvis's recovery. But then on the most joyous of all joyful days, about six weeks after surgery, I volunteered to take Elvis back to the residential home.

It was extraordinary. As soon as I walked into the 'gathering room', as the residents called their sitting space, every single one of about thirty elderly people and about twenty carers squealed with joy. Elvis nearly jumped out of my arms as I handed him to Gregory, who was sitting in the middle, now in a wheelchair, his eyes bright and his smile broad. He looked happier than I had ever seen him. And then because the king does whatever the king wants to do, he jumped off Gregory's knee and ran around, albeit with a little more swagger than before in his hind legs, greeting everyone in turn, sniffing for a biscuit here and probing for a kiss there. The room was the most incredible stage of excitement and unfettered joy that the King of Rock and Roll could ever have wished for. The king was most definitely back in the building!

And so, it really doesn't matter if you're the monarch worried about your beloved Corgi friends, or a shipbuilder worried about your king, this amazing transcendent love is the same. And, as I've mentioned, with great love sometimes comes great sadness. But I'd rather know people who have loved and lost than never loved at all.

If you never try, if you never risk, you'll never fail. But you won't have lived. Dogs teach their humans all they ever need to know about the true joy of a life well lived. One only needs to stop just for a moment and listen to what they are telling us.

I was reminded of this when I spoke to Her Majesty and we came on to the subject of other people's opinions. I had been stung by an accusation from a fellow vet that a procedure I had carried out was not in the best interest of my patient and that, in their opinion, euthanasia would have been preferable, which was of course anathema to me, because I always make every effort to do the right thing. I wanted to understand how someone whose entire life had been lived in the glare of public opinion dealt with criticism born of lack of understanding, when one is only doing one's best. She listened, thought for a while and then said, 'Isn't it rather like dogs barking? One listens sometimes if it's a bark that should be listened to; but much of the time, one hears it but doesn't listen at all. It is most vital to know the difference.' And she was right, as she was about so much.

I treasure the time that I spent with her. When I went to Windsor to pay my respects to her as her funeral cortège passed, I peered over the railings beyond the crowds and there was Emma the fell pony, standing in between the thousands of bouquets of flowers on the Long Walk at Windsor Castle, with one of Her Majesty's headscarves draped across her saddle as the coffin passed by. When the procession reached the castle grounds, there were Muick and Sandy the Corgis to accompany her for one final walk. Her animal friends stood there with love, respect, dignity and integrity – all one could ever wish for in a life well lived.

I don't think it is any coincidence that this wisest of women surrounded herself with animals. She knew that they are the finest way of remembering what matters. Kindness, care, duty and generosity. She had those qualities in abundance and the dogs and other animals in her life knew it. And now, when I hear that someone who doesn't know me has been saying that what I do is wrong, I remember what she said about the barking of dogs, and I also remember that other great English dog lover, Winston Churchill, who once said, 'You will never reach your destination if you stop and throw stones at every dog that barks.'

I am determined to reach my destination of making things better for animals in my lifetime and beyond, without stopping to throw stones at barking humans I'd be best off ignoring, preferring instead to listen to the barks of dogs, which 'should be listened to', as Her Majesty put it. As for any important pursuit in life, it is indeed 'most vital to know the difference'.

7

The right thing to do

Xīngxīng the Chow and Anton

Anton's right arm was blown off by shrapnel from a Russian bomb. After five days of diving into a trench to escape the constant bombardment, this final time he was too slow. In the months since Russia had invaded Ukraine, Anton, his wife, their two children and Anton's elderly mother had gone to bed not sure they would wake up again in the morning. It was this fear which drove Anton to do whatever it took to protect his family. This was his family's home and he would die to defend it. It was the right thing to do.

As he lay in the stench of smoke, sweat, urine and rotting wood in the trench, he tried to work out why his arm wouldn't work when he attempted to get up. It was their faces he thought of. He had to get to them. He felt himself lifted up and carried to the back of a van. The pain was starting now. He blacked out.

Those of us lucky enough not to know war at first hand are insulated from it. We go about our days, we have our worries and our concerns. We watch the news, we read the headlines. Thousands dead. Millions displaced. But every single one of those numbers on either side of the conflict is a person and they have a family.

When I first heard Anton's story, I lay unable to sleep, thinking about what he had gone through. I am surrounded by animals. But I don't see that as an escape from being human but rather an example of the very best of what it means to be human. It is only when we see others as less than human, as beings different to us, that we can do such terrible things to them. Humans 'other' people all the time and for all kinds of reasons, but the act of sharing your life with an animal, of choosing care, empathy and compassion when you don't have to, is the greatest antidote to man's inhumanity to man that I know of. I sometimes imagine the love I see between an animal and their human friend radiating out into the world like some kind of force-field from the Marvel or DC comics I love; an Animal Love Field – ALF – turning everyone it touches into the best versions of themselves. In my mind, the ALF can wrap around us like a comfort blanket of kindness, truth and endless possibility.

Anton knew he had to get his family out of Ukraine. Without his arm he felt unable to protect them, or himself. A week after the surgeons patched him up at the local hospital, using whatever they hadn't already run out of, they set off. No one wanted to leave their home, but they all knew that it was a case of leave, be driven out or die. They all wept.

The journey from Ukraine, through Moldova and into Romania in their old Toyota, took Anton and his family several days. His youngest child was only two years old and became very ill en route. His wife drove, because Anton couldn't change gears with only one arm. Anton had distant family in Romania. He knew that they couldn't stay long in his cousin's meagre house, but he was grateful even for a few days' shelter while he tried to get to England.

Before the invasion, Anton had been a computer programming guru, whose talents had caught the attention of a company in Manchester, in the north-west of England, for whom he'd worked on some contracts.

I received a call one day from a dog charity based in Bucharest. They told me Anton's story. There was a scheme in the UK which allowed UK nationals to sponsor Ukrainian refugees and their immediate family members and so Manchester was Anton's destination, where he had a job sponsored by the company he had worked for remotely in his former life. The problem was he had no money for the journey. Through the lady at the dog charity, who knew his cousin, Anton had been introduced to a client of mine who lived in Bucharest called Roy. Roy was a great guy. He had done well for himself in construction. I had met him, his wife and their two lovely children a couple of years before when I had operated on their German Shepherd dog. Family was the most important thing for Roy and I knew that if he was getting involved, I would help in any way I could.

I get requests from all over the world for access to various procedures that either other surgeons cannot perform or do not have access to the technology to perform. The first question which must be answered in all cases is whether it is ethical to transport the animal and to perform the procedure. I can't operate in a vacuum. I need my support team of imagers, nurses, care assistants, junior vets and all the technology to solve any biological challenge. I can't simply fly that around the world. It's not just about money, it's the care infrastructure that is essential to success.

Roy had said he would pay for a car for Anton and his family to drive to the UK, but on one condition. He needed to take a dog with him. The charity would take care of all the necessary paperwork, certification and vaccinations and Roy would replace Anton's Toyota, which had broken down twice, with a spacious Renault minivan, which would have a cage in the back of it for a rescue dog called Xīngxīng. It would also be an automatic vehicle so that, with a bit of adjustment, Anton could drive it.

I saw a photograph of Xīngxīng when she was rescued and she had been very obviously near death. But in the most recent picture of her massive yellow ochre-coloured fluffy head, sticky-up ears and lolling tongue, she looked much better, having been very well taken care of by the animal charity. Xīngxīng was a mixture of several breeds. To me she looked like a Chow Chow crossed with a Husky, which would have made her a Chusky, but she might have been something else like a Chow Chow mixed with a Labrador, which would be a Chabrador. Xīngxīng means 'Star' in Chinese and they named her that because in spite of her crushed pelvis and dislocated hip joint, which nobody felt they could fix, in spite of all the terrible pain, suffering, emaciation and persistent constipation, this amazing dog shone love and light out into the world.

She was too weak and incapacitated to be allowed to travel on a commercial flight and was in constant pain from her crushed pelvis. She had been one of many dogs piled on top of each other in cramped and filthy cages. There was no food or water. Some died and their bodies lay in their own urine and faeces for days. The cages were in the back of a lorry heading from Hebei province in northern China to the city of Yulin in Guangxi province, where they would all be slaughtered and eaten. This is a year-round practice in this part of the world but the conveyor belt of stolen dogs and street-napped dogs ramps up considerably at the end of June during a dog meat festival where over 10,000 dogs are eaten.

Folklore would have it that dog meat brings good luck, good health, can ward off diseases and can heighten men's sexual performance. Though the Chinese government has officially recognised dogs as companions and not livestock, up to 20 million are killed for human consumption every year. Chinese law enforcement usually ignores dog and cat thefts; it is said that they take more notice of the theft of a pig or a bicycle. The pictures I have seen of both cat and dog slaughter are too horrific for words.

Xīngxīng was one of a cohort of more than fifty dogs saved by activists who stopped a truck headed for Yulin and paid the driver off. Allegedly he didn't care as long as he was paid. Every one of these dogs made their way out of China through acts of selflessness by a series of people because they truly believed it was the right thing to do. I was told that Xīngxīng and some other dogs had been transported in a van across Kazakhstan and would have gone through the very region in which Anton and his family lived had it not been for the war. Instead, the van drove through Russia, Georgia, Turkey and Bulgaria to get to Romania.

Despite the serendipity of the arrangement, it wasn't immediately a marriage made in heaven, as Anton was reserved when it came to dogs. I didn't know why until much later, but he was very cautious about a possible journey to the UK with Xīngxīng in tow when the idea was first proposed. There was no doubt that his desire to get his family to safety and some semblance of security had been thrown a lifeline by the generosity of Roy and the dog charity, and truth be told, Roy could probably have been persuaded to help Anton and his family anyway, but the reality was that Roy would never have been introduced to Anton without Xīngxīng. It was the dog charity who told me that Xīngxīng meant Star. And it's certainly true that without this guiding star in the shape of a skinny, injured, fluffy ball of love, Anton didn't have the money or means to get to safety. From the day that Anton finally agreed to the deal – he got the car and the dog got transportation to the UK – everyone called her Star. I learned later that Anton had spoken to his wife and mother saying that he was worried for the well-being of his young children in a closed space with an unpredictable dog. But Star would be in a cage in the back. The safety of his family was at stake and eventually Anton was persuaded. It was the right thing to do.

Three days later, a minivan parked outside my practice and a lady from a UK dog charity met them there and then came into reception. The family didn't want to come in except to use the toilet. I was told that they felt self-conscious that they couldn't speak English and that it wasn't their dog anyway. The charity would take Star into their care and the hope was that I could fix her. Roy had already paid for the scans that I'd proposed as a starting point.

It was love at first sight for me. Star was the most glorious fur-erupting volcano of love one could imagine. Though there was a makeshift sling under her belly to help take the weight off her hind legs, though her legs buckled under her and though she was clearly in extreme pain, she greeted me with a huge smile and a lick on my hand which said all at once, 'I feel so lucky to be here' and 'please help me'.

I knew Star's injuries would be bad, I just didn't know how bad. I never cease to be amazed by how much dogs put up with in silence. Many times, I have seen dogs with injuries like Star's that would leave me in agony and unable to get out of bed. No wonder the poor dog couldn't defecate properly. I examined Star and I had already seen the rather poor-quality X-ray pictures provided from Romania, where the attending vet had been doing the absolute best they could with the equipment they had. Her pelvis had been crushed down such that there was barely enough room for a third of the size of her normal colon. Her hip socket on one side had been decimated by implosion fractures, which had tried to heal but of course couldn't, and both hip joints were dislocated.

I spoke to the charity lady, Emer, and then took Star in for sedation and imaging. My team and I performed radiography and a CT scan of her pelvic region and hind limbs. When I called Emer back into my consulting room to discuss the situation, I was very surprised to also meet a mother and a six-year-old boy, who had clearly decided to come in after all. Emer explained that Katya did not speak much English, but that her little boy, Dmytro, had grown very fond of Star on their long journey and had sat with her whenever they had stopped for a break. On the final night, Dmytro insisted that Star be allowed to sleep by his bed. It turned out that the boy had a speech impediment and was normally very shy with people. Since the war had broken out, he hadn't been to school and he hadn't been able to play with other children.

His mother explained in very broken English what was already clear from Emer's cursory overview, that Dmytro had found a companion in Star that he had not found with humans in his life to date. His little sister was only a toddler and was sick all the time and his mother and grandmother were permanently terrified and worried. I didn't need to be told the detail. It was obvious. As soon as a nurse coaxed Star back into my consulting room, supported on her sling, Dmytro was immediately down on his knees. She stumbled towards him, still under the influence of the sedative drugs, and licked his face. He laughed and wrapped his arms around her big fluffy neck, his face lost in her loving fur.

I kneeled on the floor with them and just waited for a while. I stroked Star's head and I nodded at Dmytro, trying to be as reassuring as I could without any words at all. I could see that Star had been this boy's first real solace since his dad left to be a soldier and since his little house in his little town had become a prison surrounded by big explosions. I could see that Star had also been in a prison of man's making and that she somehow sought peace in his arms too. Their impediments had drawn them together with a language that did not need words, and in their embrace, they were each released from the cages of their minds by just being held by the other.

I have often seen how children with social and learning difficulties and even physical and mental impediments are drawn towards animals.

As Dmytro and Star hugged on the floor and as Katya looked on concerned, I tried my best to explain as tactfully as I could what was wrong using drawings. Emer understood absolutely. She was wise and pragmatic and had told me from the outset that if I truly felt that it wasn't in Star's best interests to proceed from an ethical perspective, she and her friends in Bucharest would understand. In fact, that is a caveat I insist on for all referrals with severe pathology like Star. Heartbreaking as it is, I never have and never will operate on a patient just because of the feelings of their guardian, but rather only if I can truly determine through my knowledge and experience that it is the right thing to do ethically. Importantly, I must also weigh up the risk–benefit ratio – what the patient must go through to get to the end point and whether I have a good chance of success. There is a line in the sand of life that I never cross, and that's if a patient is suffering beyond reasonable hope of redemption in a reasonable time frame. Even if considerable effort has already been expended, euthanasia may absolutely be warranted in such circumstances.

At that point there was a knock on the door of my consulting room. I opened it and Anton walked in. He had the look of a man who was accustomed to being in control, but having lost an arm he was visibly self-conscious and I sensed that he also felt more than a little self-conscious about the situation that had evolved. He was very respectful but also very worried. He explained in broken English with Emer's help that he understood his son's feelings, but there was just no way that this dog (I guess he couldn't bring himself to say her name out loud) could stay with them, either fixed or not fixed, since they were at the mercy of whatever housing could be provided by their sponsor in Manchester. He wanted to make this clear so that I could understand that he meant well, and he was very grateful for the financial help with his journey, but it was always the plan that 'the lady from the charity' (Emer) should take the dog.

I nodded and then asked Emer to step out of the room with me. Out of earshot of the family, I asked what her view of the situation was and she confirmed that was indeed the plan, but that Star had no definitive home as yet and it was their intention to find a home for her if I could fix her. If I could not fix her then perhaps it was best to euthanise her now.

As we walked back into the room, Dmytro looked up at

me wide-eyed, his arms still wrapped around Star's neck, who was now prostrate on the floor. It's hard for me to find words to express the feelings that came silently from his eyes into mine. A cry for help, a bottomless pit of desolation, a prayer to a God he didn't know, an unfathomable loneliness, a yearning for reassurance from the only person in the entire world who stood between life and death for his new-found best friend. His look was all of that and more.

His look ripped my heart out of my chest, and yet I could not act for him, but only for Star. I had the moral responsibility of doing the right thing for Star, whatever myself and my colleagues deemed that to be. She had travelled about seven thousand miles by land and had shone her light for all of her fellow travellers along the way, but that very day I had in my power the law-given right to snuff out her star and to quench any light from Dmytro's heart too.

Anton slowly peeled his little boy's arms from the fur of Star's neck with his one remaining arm, tears welling up in his son's eyes. As Dmytro left, he looked at Star and only Star. He had done all the looking he needed to do at me. He kissed her nose and went back to the car with his parents. I gestured for a receptionist to sit with Star for a minute while Emer and I went out to the car. I could see that an older lady who I later learned was Anton's mother had remained in the car holding a sleeping child in a blanket in her arms. I nodded kindly at her. I watched as Dmytro and Katya got in and I purposely held out my hand to Anton. He shook it forcefully and said thank you. I said,

'No . . . Thank *you* for giving hope . . . to your family . . . and also to the dog!'

He nodded back, hastily got into the car and made a speedy departure, as if he might feel guilty at staying a second longer. I can still remember Dmytro's haunted eyes as he stared through the side window, his little hands gripping the door as if he might rip it off its hinges and run back into the building to rescue his friend, who he knew he would not see again, even if his heart told him otherwise.

I had a professional 'job' to do. There are no shortcuts and there is no rule-bending on compassionate grounds for human beings. Their feelings and my feelings do not matter as part of my oath. My oath and my regulatory and legal responsibilities are to act only in the patient's best interests, and euthanasia for animals is still recognised as an entirely valid 'treatment'.

The truth was that I was fairly confident that I could fix Star. She was not neurologically compromised, so all I had to do was straighten the pelvic bones, weld them back together using custom-made plates and screws based on her CT scans, put in two new hip joints, one of which would also be a customised system to fit her deformed pelvis, and with a bit of luck, all could be well. The implant system I proposed would involve making a new hip socket out of a device that looks a lot like an ice-cream scoop, the handle of which would be screwed to the wing of the pelvis, the ilium. In fact, that's where the idea for this AceFitz came from. The femur side of the joint would be reconstructed using a 3D-printed titanium stem and neck bolted to a long, specially contoured plate called a FitzFAR – Femoral Augmentation Reconstruction plate. A cobalt chromium head would articulate within a polyethylene liner cup bonded with cement into the scoop bit of the AceFitz.

First, I needed to discuss her clinical situation with my colleagues to obtain consensus of ethical approval that it was indeed the right thing to do to operate, since my opinion alone hasn't stopped detractors from doing what they do and saying what they say about my motives, as they see them. They have hitherto complained to my governing body and hauled me through tribunals for trying to help stricken animals for whom they felt the best 'treatment' and the right thing to do was euthanasia, as I mentioned in my conversation with Her Majesty. Then I needed to meticulously plan the surgeries with my engineering colleagues to design and manufacture the implants. And then two major, very long, staged operations with a huge team of people and with considerable aftercare and a twelve-week recovery period.

But, thankfully, the miracle happened, coaxed along by the team I am blessed to call colleagues, and after three months of intensive physiotherapy and hydrotherapy at our rehabilitation centre, biology finally smiled upon us and Star was walking reasonably normally and without pain.

Emer and her colleagues at the charity were tremendous throughout and looked after Star when she didn't have to be at the hospital. Roy was also great. We sent photographic updates and he paid all the bills. About three months after her first surgery, as I took Star through the hospital on her walk to freedom after follow-up CT scans, at least a dozen of my colleagues hugged her, patted her head, stroked her glorious ears or even had a face lick from the dog who lit up our hospital with her light and her joy for living. They each wanted to say goodbye and they each loved her in their own way. Indeed, her name was very apt, as Star would illuminate the path for other dogs who would benefit from similar implants thereafter.

In trying to fix the ailments of my patients, I always insist on follow-up for all of the advanced implants I deploy. Nothing challenges one's perception of how great one is as a surgeon like follow-up. How does a surgeon know if they have succeeded if they never check long-term function? Perhaps the guardian just didn't bring the patient back in spite of complications and that patient was put to sleep. How does one know if one doesn't ask the difficult question? And how can one recommend any treatment without evidence-based, ethically well-founded follow-up? In my career of thirty-plus years, I can say hand on heart that I have seen significantly more harm done by the sale of unregulated implants which are implanted by well-meaning vets, but without enough training and with suboptimal judgement, than I ever have from a highly specialised surgeon executing a highly specialised surgery. I encourage my profession to look at this as a matter of urgency as the number of complications I am asked to treat sky-rockets.

Meanwhile, I continue to perform long-term follow-up free of charge for advanced surgeries, many of which are world-firsts, as were some of the implants used for Star's repair. Because it's the right thing to do.

A minority of vets consider that some of the surgeries I perform are 'experimental'. I fervently contend that the entire edifice of science and especially medicine is experimental – small or large steps forward from where we were before, born of necessity. You could have said the same of hundreds of situations over the history of medicine. Before there was anaesthetic, the kindest thing to offer a patient was a glug of brandy, a stick between the teeth and a surgeon's blurred hands. The moment we invented anaesthesia, the previous paradigm quickly became barbaric. Blood transfusions, organ transplants, plastic surgery and antibiotics – the history of medicine is the history of our increasing willingness and capacity to treat conditions that cause pain, disability and death. What was left to luck and the gods becomes something we can do something about.

But in veterinary medicine, I am concerned that we could become complacent about the status quo and not give enough consideration to ethically well-founded change. As I have said, euthanasia is still deemed a 'treatment' in veterinary medicine and it can be very difficult for vets to navigate the subjective judgement of clients in this regard. Vets are trying to do their best in the circumstances in which they find themselves. But, in my own practice, while there is a time and a place for death and a time and a place for salvation, technology and experience have moved the dial regarding the 'right thing to do'. For Star, thankfully, the scythe of death was subdued by the scalpel of life.

As planned, I saw Star at six months after her operation. Emer dropped her off with one of my intern colleagues and I said that I would see her out after her final CT scans and chat to Emer then. Star was doing tremendously well. She was fit, healthy, happy and bubbling over with effusive energy, a joy to behold. And her CT scans revealed that everything had gone as hoped for.

But even more joy awaited me as I walked into reception with Star to greet Emer, to tell her the good news and to thank her for all her efforts on Star's behalf.

Dmytro ran towards Star and threw his arms around her. I can honestly say that this was one of the very best surprises of my entire career. I had absolutely no idea he was there and I was thrilled by what greeted me. Katya smiled as she stood up with Emer by her side and Anton stepped forward and held out his hand. I took it, we shook, and then I pulled the big man in for a Fitz-Hug. I was close to tears I was so happy.

It was immediately apparent of course that, for whatever reason, the family had decided to adopt Star after all. Star licked Dmytro's face as he laughed and spoke to her haltingly but without a notable stutter. I was beyond whatever the 'over' in overjoyed means. I was ecstatic.

It transpired that within just a month of working in Manchester, Anton had done so well that he had already been promoted and had secured a nice rental property with a garden. Dmytro had talked of nothing but Star, Star, Star, Star . . . and so it came to be . . . a guiding Star would light their path for many years to come. The lady in Bucharest, Emer and Roy were all delighted.

Anton beckoned for me to step to one side. I beckoned in return for him to pop into my consulting room. We left the fur-cuddling group of happiness in reception. Once inside my room, Anton said he wanted to thank me for everything I had done for Star and for his family. He said he wanted to give me something. He reached inside his pocket, and then hesitated for a moment. He was a big guy, and he always emitted an aura of control and strength, but all of a sudden, his eyes became waxy with the thought of what he was thrusting into my hand.

It felt like a small photo frame wrapped in newspaper. As he put it in my hand, he said, 'I am sorry . . . I almost didn't bring her . . . I was a coward . . . the pain was too much . . . this was my dog . . . and when she died, a part of me died too. I am sorry . . . thank . . . thank you so much for bringing me . . . alive . . . for bringing my family life.'

I have never met someone less of a coward than Anton. He had put his life on the line for the family and the country he loved and ironically the only thing that brought him to his knees was love itself – the unconditional love he had shared with the dog of his childhood. I opened the paper and inside was a black and white picture of a small boy hugging a big hairy black and white dog in a very old wooden frame. It turned out that his painful memories of losing this dog were the reason for his hesitancy about transporting Star. I had only been part of the journey to bring Anton and his family renewed life. The light of a dog called Star had decisively led the way.

Isn't it amazing how easy it would have been and how nobody would have noticed if the light of Star had never been saved from a stinking putrid cage, if people who cared desperately hadn't somehow got her to a vet in Surrey, and if that vet hadn't chosen to give her light a chance?

I look at that picture every now and then to remind me that no matter how strong we can be for ourselves and those we love, sometimes we need saving too. And I have never met a greater saviour than the light and hope of a dog called Star. We should most treasure this light, because it might just save everything we treasure most. It's the right thing to do.

8

He saved me from myself

Bob the Staffordshire Bull Terrier and Dave

Dave didn't want Bob to begin with. But then Bob wasn't even called Bob back then. He was just a shape that Dave swerved to avoid one night, a glint of eyes in the hazy orange streetlight. Dave crashed his bike into a cluster of dustbins. Shaking his head in a 'what just happened' moment, he came to his senses with this dog looking down at him. He was a scruffy, tousled-looking mutt. A mixture of lots of things by the look of him but with a big dollop of Staffordshire Bull Terrier. You could see it in the set of his shoulders, in the curious eyes. Even now he was sniffing intently at the pizza boxes that had fallen out of Dave's bag.

'Hey. Leave it.' Dave made mock kicking movements, then nudged the dog forcefully out the way with his foot. He checked to see no one was about and bent down to recover the small packets of white powder from the boxes and left the pizza on the floor, while the dog began to happily eat the pepperoni. He picked his bike up and swore as he saw the front wheel was bent. He walked off down the street. The dog abandoned the pizza and followed him, looking up at Dave expectantly, as if he might make more pizza fall from the sky. I laughed when Dave told me that. He was one of those people who is good at telling a story. When he came into my room, I had the usual thousand things on the go but, as ever, I made sure to focus, to listen to everything that a dog's human needed to tell me.

So that's how it began. Truth be told, Dave loved dogs, he had done since he was a child and a dog called Jimbo had turned up in his house. Initially Jimbo had slept by his bed and then eventually in his bed, when the shouting and the bangs and crashes downstairs and outside got too loud. And then one day Jimbo and the man who came with him were gone. His mother didn't seem to care; men came and went, and what did it matter if a dog went with them? But Dave really didn't have time for a dog now. For the first time in his life, he had the chance to be someone. And those little packets of white powder were the key to it.

It had been Billy's idea to use the pizza. Billy had been ten years old when he'd started running drugs for the county lines. And by the time he was twenty, he had made a name for himself. They called him 'The Eel', because he always seemed to just slip out of the hands of the police. He had it all – money, girls, cars and the thing he craved the most: respect. He was looked up to in Woking, in Surrey. He was 'The Man'. The fact that he had to carry a knife, wear a Kevlar vest everywhere he went and had three guns stashed in various places of quick access, including his nan's house, was a price worth paying. The Eel had set up the pizza place with a couple of 'friends'. Standard menu: pepperoni, ham and pineapple, cheese, and Class As.

Billy had noticed Dave and interviewed him. Well, if you can call drinking vodka on a park bench an interview. Billy said that Dave was bright, hungry and handsome. The customers would love him. Soon Dave had the customers eating out of his hand – and snorting and shooting up too. Dave wasn't just delivering pizzas with his big fourteen-year-old smile, he was delivering smack, crack, blow, beans and special K. Ordering drugs was literally as easy as ordering pizza. Or, in this case, both at the same time.

Then someone managed to grab hold of The Eel. Specifically, he got caught with 400 pizza boxes, with the added condiment of a sachet of cocaine glued inside the chunky cardboard corners, not that those receiving the boxes really wanted the pizza anyway. This led detectives to the stashes of heroin and ketamine . . . oh, and the small meth lab downstairs at his nan's house. His nan swore she knew nothing and didn't actually know what meth or amphetamines were. 'Mash and beans,' she and Billy used to call them as they laughed about it on a Friday night. Billy got sent down for seven years.

Everyone was questioned. Everyone did the same as Nan and said nothing. Everyone went into hiding, Dave included. Except Dave was bright and still hungry, very hungry. Plus, he had begun to 'become someone'. He didn't want to let go. He wanted to keep feeding the pizza to the many hungry mouths. Six months later, when the fuss and the fuzz had died down, Dave went to visit Billy in the clanger and that's where the street-talk stopped.

Billy was a shadow of his former self. He spoke in a whisper and told Dave to get out – at least out of town. And not to visit him again, because people were watching … or more specifically, the pillars and trees had eyes and ears. Dave didn't listen. He tried to pick up where Billy had left off, a contact here or there on both sides of the fence – supplying and receiving. And soon he was back on a bike with a delivery company logo on his bag.

He asked to visit Billy several times, but the next time Billy consented was half a year later. Dave walked in, a new-found swagger in his step. Billy knew immediately what was going on as they sat on either side of the small table. Dave had no idea what was going on with Billy, though, because Billy was a changed man. He was no longer gaunt and dishevelled. There was light in his eyes. 'The chickens,' said Billy, 'I get to feed the chickens.' He and two other inmates had been selected as suitable for working on the smallholding inside HMP Guys Marsh, and in his daily interaction with the chickens, he found himself not only developing genuine affection for them, but also an appreciation of how he'd never really liked himself. He had filled all the gaps in his emotional life with chemical dependency and then dependency on the proceeds and the persona the drugs afforded him. Inside he was empty. But while 'on the inside', he had finally come to see the light and the error of his ways. He was no longer the angry young man, and was becoming the repentant, self-reflective young man. Dave was on the other side of that journey. Billy knew it and he told him; Dave didn't want to hear and told him so.

But Dave couldn't get the look in Billy's eyes out of his head. And that night he crashed his bike, as he went to the addresses on foot, delivering the packets and apologising for the absence of pizza and the presence of a dog who wouldn't stop following him no matter what he did, he might have laughed in his head at the simplicity of Billy's transformation through chickens, but in his heart there was something about the particular animal at his heels that he could neither understand nor shake. The recipients mostly didn't seem to mind that there was no pizza. The dog continued to follow, and Dave didn't seem to mind either. Finally, back at base, he took pity on the canine waif and let him in. They both woke the next morning entangled on the sofa of Dave's dingy flat.

Dave told me this story when he came into my consulting room quite a long time later. He was pale and thin. He looked so much older than his twenty-one years. His face was weathered, his voice croaky. 'Please,' he said. 'Please, mate. Help him.'

Every patient matters. Everyone gets the same treatment, whatever their background and story. But you only had to talk to Dave to know he'd had an especially rough ride; to see what Bob meant to him, how high the stakes were. I took his hand and told him I would do everything in my power to help Bob.

Dave told me that he owed Bob his life. How that first morning, the dog didn't seem to want to leave. Fair enough, you can sit there while I work, he thought. The dog sat under the kitchen table biting at an old tennis ball he'd found somewhere, while Dave set about yet another day of mixing powder, making calls. He popped down to the pizza shop to check on the lads. They were doing what they were told, and they were enamoured with Dave's new canine friend, who was all over them. They asked what his name was. Dave just said, 'Oh, he doesn't have one . . . he'll be gone tonight.' The lads didn't argue.

But that night, Dave found himself buying a tin of dog food from the corner shop and putting half of it in a bowl. The stray tucked in, muttering and snuffling contentedly to himself, then came and sat on the sofa while Dave watched telly. He pawed and pawed until Dave let him up beside him, and he laid his heavy head on his leg. Dave just ignored any inner feelings and, as his hand brushed gently over the dog's ears, he told himself it was just a momentary distraction.

The next day, Dave was getting twitchy on the way home. He always got twitchy when he needed a fix. He got home and set the gear up, ready to shoot up. He desperately needed to escape, mainly from himself. Lots of things had happened when he was a kid that he didn't ever talk about, even to himself. Too painful. No dad and eventually no mum to care what happened to him. Nan had looked after him for a while and then the drugs made all that stuff seem less important anyway. But this time round, the dog was here. Dave felt a pang of shame, but only for a moment – it was only a dog. He'd chuck him out later. He set about heating the heroin on some kitchen foil over a makeshift flame and picked up his tube to inhale. But the dog knocked the foil off the burner. Dave was furious. He grabbed him by the scruff and chucked him outside the flat and onto a long cement walkway that led along a row of a dozen flats.

Dave just carried on and lost himself under the spell of the dragon. That evening, he half awoke to a sound at the door. In his stupor, he grabbed a knife and eased the door ajar. The dog was still there, pawing the door. And before he could shut it, the dog came right back in again. Dave was too drugged up to do anything about it. The next morning, they woke up on the dingy ragged sofa together once again.

It wasn't like some fairy story. It didn't happen instantly. There were plenty of times when the dog would chew up Dave's new trainers, or knock stuff over when he ran around the flat like a maniac and Dave would shout at him. Threaten to get rid of him. Kick him out. But the dog would always be there, scratching at the door, waiting to come back in. He'd forgive Dave immediately and sit with him, mumbling in pleasure as Dave scratched him behind his ear.

'He wore me down, mate,' was how he put it that day. 'With love.' And gradually the scales tipped. The fact that he had the dog to look after began to change everything. And at some point 'the dog' had become Bob. The name came from Dave's frustration at the way the dog incessantly bobbed up and down at the door until he was let in or by the sofa or bed until he was allowed up on them. This was according to Faye, who helped to manage a refuge for homeless people. Faye had watched my TV show and reached out to see if I might be able to help when Bob developed a problem that the local vet couldn't treat. Dave had watched my show at the refuge too but didn't dare reach out himself. Apparently Bob was also a fan.

As time went by, Dave had one big reason not to take drugs. Bob. Of course, his drug addiction didn't disappear overnight, and there were plenty of relapses. But as the drug of Bob's constant presence, constant looking up at his dad with unadulterated hero-worship, began to take hold, the need for other drugs slowly waned. People were beginning to annoy him anyway; what did he need their respect or attention for? It was all hollow; they'd stab him if they had to, he finally figured out.

A drug-fuelled life was all that Dave had ever known from his early teens. He didn't know how to be anyone else or do anything else. But he decided he needed to stop using because when he was out of it, he invariably woke to Bob gazing down at him with that 'look' in his eyes – a look that somehow said, 'I know you can be better than this mess, Dad!' Dave didn't understand this at all, but gradually the feeling of coming down after the high by Bob's side made him feel more ashamed than anything that any high could provide. And that meant he had to stop dealing. There was no way he'd be able to stop using if he was still dealing. But that meant no more money from the dealing. He lost the flat, and at first a couple of mates let him sleep on their sofas but they ran out of patience. They weren't mates anyway because he had no gear to oil the wheels of their so-called friendship.

So, then it was the streets. Dave gave in to temptation more than once. It was really hard out there. Cold and hard. For a couple of weeks when he started using again, he spiralled downwards. Then some days he had to choose between a fix for himself or food for Bob. Thankfully he gradually started choosing food for Bob.

It wasn't easy. For everyone who gave money because of Bob as he begged with a sheet of cardboard on the pavement, there were ten more who didn't, who thought it was cruel to have a dog when you couldn't even look after yourself. And some hostels and shelters didn't take dogs. There was no way Dave was going to leave Bob on his own. So, they'd sleep at the back of shops, wrapped in cardboard and blankets, Bob pushed tightly against Dave's chest. Both of them started awake every time someone stumbled by in case it was some drunk who thought it would be funny to piss on them, or worse. But Bob was always there, curious and friendly. He never let life get him down. Every time he made Dave smile, it was as if a miracle had occurred. Bob was mischievous and did all he could to make Dave smile, pawing at his cap full of coins when he needed him to buy a can of food, gnawing at his toes when his socks ran bare and, on one occasion, running off and finding a sock in some undergrowth, dropping it delightedly by Dave's feet and looking up at him as if to say, 'It'll be OK, I'll look after you, Dad.'

There were many low points. On one occasion Dave developed such self-loathing and depression that he ended up on the side of a cliff, which was a well-known suicide location not far from the seaside town where he had relocated to the refuge. He stood there, full of pain. Then he looked at Bob, and he thought about what would happen to him. He thought about never getting woken up by him grumbling and licking his ear. So, he sat down on a bench nearby. Bob sat by him; Dave stroked his ears as Bob nuzzled his chin and they looked out to sea. Then Bob led his human, Dave, back down from the cliff.

Bob also led Dave off the streets and into the refuge by befriending Faye. The refuge was a communal housing project for recovering drug addicts and Bob paid particular attention to Faye when she was on her street rounds, as she called them, talking to various homeless people to see if she could help and if they'd be willing to give the project a try. In return for doing various carpentry, clothes mending, bag making and gardening jobs, they could have a room and two meals a day. Faye fell in love with Bob's charming eyes and even more charming demeanour as he flirted with her and smooched his head against her legs. So, she got special dispensation for him to become the communal dog at the refuge. Soon he had all of the residents eating out of his paws – and him eating out of their hands whenever they'd let him.

Bob was so gentle. He'd say hello to everyone and everyone said hello to Bob. He was like a 'smile vacuum cleaner' on four legs wherever he went, sucking smiles out of everyone he met on life's journey, no matter how dirty their mood might be. Every night, he slept curled up in Dave's bed under the covers until he got too hot and would come out panting. Then he'd get too cold and grumble to be allowed back under the covers. Every night the same thing. 'Come on then,' Dave would say, smiling in the dark. 'You silly boy.' Dave made sure he had a never-ending supply of old shoes from charity shops for Bob to chew on. They'd go for long walks and Bob would chase bees and butterflies with the same unrelenting optimism every time: maybe I'll get this one. Dave found himself talking to Bob about everything. About things he'd never told anyone. Things from his childhood. Things he'd locked away in shame and fear. And Bob responded to everything with more love. He would turn his head sideways and look up at Dave and make him feel like there was nothing he could ever say that would change that. For the first time in his life, Dave felt like he was worth something and that being in the world might be for him after all.

And then one day, Bob started limping. When I had first seen Dave in my consulting room, Bob had been limping for a few weeks and the local vet had felt it was likely due to a ruptured cruciate ligament in his knee. Bob had always been so full of energy, racing around. It broke Dave's heart that Bob might be in pain, unable to enjoy life to the full.

Dave had no money to pay for any treatment. But just as when he had led Dave into the refuge, Bob somehow found a solution. Though my practice remains proudly independent, that doesn't mean I can ignore financial considerations completely. I borrowed all of the money needed to build the practice and I have had a few periods of financial difficulty. Though I am not bound by the monetary gain demanded by shareholders, I still have to pay the wages and the bills, maintain the scanners and the operating theatres. I can't just take on hundreds of cases for free, though I wish I could. Luckily, every now and then, an altruistic individual, usually someone who I've met with their animal companion, will help towards the bills of those less fortunate, and almost as soon as Dave's friend Faye reached out about Bob, I showed a picture of Bob to one such person, who stepped forward to help. Bob had beckoned a guardian angel into his life somehow. Such is the wonder of the world sometimes. If you put out love, maybe love really might come back towards you. The philosophy of Bob.

When I first heard about Bob, I thought that I'd be able to fix him with relatively simple knee surgery if it was a ruptured ligament, and that's what I relayed to both Faye and the kindly donor. However, when I laid eyes on Bob for the first time, I knew that the situation was disastrously worse. I took a radiograph then obtained a CT scan. Cancer was eating the bone of his femur away . . . and not just any cancer . . . one of the worst kinds, a highly invasive and destructive (osteolytic) osteosarcoma. The only viable treatment for his pain was to amputate the entire limb.

Dave wept uncontrollably in my arms when I told him. I held him and said that there would be some comfort in always doing the right thing for his best friend. Through his stuttering sobs he whispered in my ear, 'I will have no comfort . . . He's the only real friend I've ever had . . . There for me no matter what . . . Saved my life he did . . . And now you're telling me I can't save his?' No, I couldn't. Even after I would have taken his leg off, the cancer would have certainly already spread elsewhere in his body at a cellular level through what is called metastasis and he would likely not live long. The median survival time for osteosarcoma in dogs is generally acknowledged to be just under a year.

Dave and I spoke many times, first after the surgery and then because chemotherapy was administered every three weeks for five cycles. And that's when he told me this story. He told me that it didn't matter how loud the shouting was in his head. However much he wanted to leave the world because it was too painful, he'd feel the weight of Bob leaning against him. He'd look into Bob's blue eyes shining up at him, and he would realise that this was the deal. Without feeling the pain, you wouldn't feel the love. That he couldn't bear the thought of not living every moment with Bob. He couldn't bear the thought of Bob looking for him, circling, lost, not understanding why he wasn't there. He couldn't bear the thought of people who didn't know the exact way Bob liked to be scratched behind the ears. Or of them shouting at him for chewing their shoes. There was just no way that he could abandon the best friend he'd ever had.

With chemotherapy we had got Bob through fourteen months of life, and then the metastatic spread of the cancer meant that he was in too much pain, gasping for breath, unable to get up without support from Dave. As I've observed before, with great love comes great pain in the end.

Dave asked if he could come to the practice and if I could help Bob on his way. We sat near a bench in the field out the back of my practice. Dave was already shattered inside and out, but he tried to make some conversation as we settled Bob's weak and heaving body on a rug I'd brought outside. Since I had last seen him, poor Bob had shrunk and become a shadow of his former self. 'Seems like my whole life has revolved around benches,' said Dave. 'A bench where I became a drug dealer, a bench where I nearly said goodbye to myself and now a bench where we say goodbye to my boy.' I didn't say anything. I didn't know what to say. I called a nurse who had hung back nearby and we put a cannula in Bob's vein and taped it in. The nurse then respectfully departed.

Dave lay on the rug with Bob and held him, whispering into his ear, his tears melting into his soft fur as he told him how much he loved him and how grateful he was, calling him his bestest boy. He said that where he was going there were piles of shoes everywhere, the best chewiest kind. And there were big fat bumblebees, the kind he liked the best. I cried too as I held Bob's paw and as a gentle blanket of mist descended around us, the faint glow of dusk holding us for a moment in its cocoon. Just as night follows day, our responsibility was to allow Bob to pass away peacefully.

Without really noticing, Dave and I each rested our head against the other's, as I gave the final injection. Dave said he'd see Bob again one day and they'd go on long walks and watch the butterflies. And then Bob's chest stopped rising and falling and he was gone on the wings of his spirit to the other realm. We held his body as life ebbed away, his lingering light infusing both of us with its comfort. We had done the right thing, in spite of the pain.

We sat there for a while, our hands around Bob's paws as darkness closed in and the final fingers of daylight crawled away from the clouds behind us. Dave told me that Billy had come to see him the day before. Bob was too ill to walk by that point. But he and Billy had gone for a walk up on the cliff, where Dave had once contemplated the worst.

'He's a really good dog, mate,' said Billy, patting him on the back.

'Yeah,' said Dave, his voice catching. 'Yeah, he is.'

They sat on the bench looking out to the flat line of the horizon where sea meets sky, in silence, knowing how close they had both come to flatlining. Then Dave walked down the steep hill away from the setting sun, away from Billy, away from his past and back towards home, or rather the place that Bob had made home.

Now, as I scooped Bob up in the blanket and into my arms to bring him inside, Dave put his hand on my shoulder, looked deep into my eyes from his own, which were swollen and red. 'Thank you for saving him from pain when you first met him and when you last met him,' he said.

'It was an honour,' I said.

As we walked back across the field towards my practice, Bob in my arms and Dave beside me, he went on to say,

'Thank you for giving him the final injection . . . He saved me from my final injection when I met him first, you know.'

'Yes,' I said, 'I know.'

'And from jumping off when he showed me why I needed to stay around,' he said.

'Yes,' I said.

We walked back inside, I laid Bob on the table in my consulting room and Dave and I embraced for the last time.

'Look after yourself,' I said, tears in my eyes.

'I'll do my best,' he replied as he shuffled out into the night. 'I shall have to . . . He saved me from myself.'

9

There was a hole in my soul, which he filled with his love

Thor the Pyrenean Mountain Dog, Natalie and John

Natalie hadn't wanted a dog. She hadn't wanted much of anything. In fact, she couldn't imagine wanting anything ever again. Their baby had been born prematurely and had died. Her partner John watched as every day she drifted further and further away. Like an astronaut floating into space. John was in pieces too, of course. But he knew they had to try and find ways to live. But she couldn't. She couldn't do anything, each day seeming worse than the one before. She had lost touch with herself and any reason to go on. She didn't call her friends, made excuses not to see them, so that eventually they just left her alone. Natalie never wanted to smile again, as if to do so would somehow be disrespectful to Lily's memory. She lost her job, became agoraphobic and just trudged from bedroom to kitchen. She didn't even want to puncture the quiet of her sadness with the TV or radio. And there was nothing John could do.

I sat listening to their story, as the light faded on a damp autumn evening. The last appointment of a busy day, in a busy week, in a busy month, in a busy year. But I was utterly focused on them. I have learned how much people need this stage, to tell me the background, so that I understand just why coming to see me is so very important. And in that moment, as I have said before, they are the only client in the world. Usually the totality of the story doesn't unfurl until later in our collective journey with the animal they've brought to see me, but on this occasion, I sat back in the chair of my consulting room while John and Natalie poured their souls out.

John told me that one day his colleague Simon came to their plumbing supply business with a giant floppy-tongued, floppy-eared, bounding fluffball Pyrenean Mountain Dog puppy. Rory sped like a tornado around the office, jumping up on everyone's knee, bashing into the waste-paper bin, sending it flying, and trying to lick anyone's face who bent down to say hello – and even some who didn't. Pyrenean Mountain Dogs, as you can probably guess, were bred for running around mountains. And with their thick fluffy coat that blends their head and neck into their chest, they almost look like a cross between a fox and a polar bear. John couldn't remember the last time he'd laughed so hard. Then Simon fed Rory, and he slept for an hour and a half before starting all over again. It was an extraordinary distraction but also an extraordinarily life-affirming day for everyone who got to bask in the reflected light of Simon's canine friend.

As John bid farewell to Simon in the yard outside at the end of the day, he quipped that he hoped he wasn't bringing Rory into work again tomorrow, because he had been so distracting.

'I couldn't get a thing done,' John smiled.

'Oh, don't worry,' said Simon, 'Sally will look after him tomorrow.' Sally was his wife. He continued, 'How is Natalie?' already knowing the answer. He regretted asking when he saw the familiar look on John's face.

'The same.'

Simon just nodded.

As he opened the back of the car and Rory leaped in, he blurted out, 'You know that Rory has a brother that nobody has taken on yet!'

John just looked at him, not knowing what to say. An awkward silence. Then, 'Thanks, pal . . . see you tomorrow,' John replied as he got in his car.

But all the way home, John couldn't get out of his head what Simon had said. When he got home, he pulled into his drive, and just sat there in his car, his hands frozen to the steering wheel. He couldn't bear it. The person he loved more than anybody or anything in the world was inside a prison and he didn't know how to get her out. He had come to dread seeing her with so little joy for life. He felt as if a chasm was opening between them and every day it got a little bit wider.

He thought of how much she'd have once enjoyed the puppy he had met that day. How much she'd have laughed as it skittered around, distracted by how interesting everything was, wanting to smell and lick and touch everything. He thought of her meeting that puppy now. It just didn't feel possible.

'Madness, pure madness.' He got out of the car and trudged towards the front door.

John cooked dinner and they ate in silence again. As Natalie rested her hand on the table, he reached out to touch her. She recoiled. He was at breaking point and felt like walking out and not coming back. The whole situation was tearing him apart. He couldn't stand the pain, the what-ifs and the grieving that neither of them could process or speak about. They had tried counselling, but that just made it worse, rehashing every moment of the pain.

'I gotta take a walk,' he said, already on his way out the door.

John felt like going down the pub and drowning his feelings, but he knew tomorrow would be the same. He loved Natalie beyond words, but he couldn't bear to see her like this and he hated himself for feeling so helpless. He walked down the lane from their house not knowing where to go or what to do. His mobile buzzed in his pocket.

'All right, mate?' said Simon as he picked up the call.

'Yeah,' John said half-heartedly, desperately not wanting to burden his friend.

'So, listen, I'm down having a cup of tea with Rory's breeder . . . His brother is still here, matie, what do you think?'

'I can't. I just can't, bro, I'm sorry,' said John.

'Why?' asked Simon pointedly.

'I have too many problems already,' answered John.

'But that's the whole point, isn't it, mate . . . I don't want to interfere, you know that, but you're not gonna solve the problems if you keep doing the same thing. Excuse me for saying, mate, but you're going round in circles. It won't end well. You can't undo the past. You gotta stop beating yourself up. Natalie does too. It's not your fault. It really isn't. I know this is a horrendous thing to say, because it might sound disrespectful, but you have to start living again at some point . . . You have to get out of this routine, and if there's one thing that disrupts a routine – it's a puppy!'

More responsibility was the last thing John felt like he needed. But, even worse than that was not doing anything at all, and the only other options that occurred to him were destructive. And so, the following day, scared out of his mind, he again sat in the car in his drive, only this time he was forced to smile as a big bundle of fluff called Thor bopped him on the head with his huge bear-like paws.

'We've been calling him Thor,' said the breeder. 'But you can call him—'

'No,' said John. 'No. Thor is perfect.'

The whole way home, Thor sat on the back seat looking around excitedly, his safety harness attached to the belt buckle as the breeder had instructed. At traffic lights, John would turn around to check he was OK and he'd strain against the harness to try to lick John's face. He could feel Thor blowing away the cobwebs of sadness.

He was beyond scared as he put the key in the front door, knowing that Natalie would be in her usual state inside. Thor hammered the door right open with his paw and in he bounced. Natalie ran screaming into the bedroom, where she shouted at John through the door, berating him for bringing more trouble into their home.

'How could you? How dare you, without consulting me? Take him back to where he came from! You're a total idiot!'

'I'm sorry, darling. I thought it was for the best. Please just come and say hello,' said John. Then silence. Nothing. Nothing at all. After fifteen minutes, John was getting worried. 'I'm not going anywhere – and neither is Thor,' he said through the closed door. Still nothing. Another ten minutes passed, not a sound from within the bedroom, but plenty of noise from the kitchen and living room, where Thor was making his presence felt by playing with cushions and anything he could lay his paws or jaws on that seemed soft enough to chew. John didn't know whether to take him for a walk to try to get rid of some energy or just to play tug-of-war with a cushion. Natalie would not approve. She loved that cushion. John hadn't thought far enough ahead to buy any dog toys.

And then the door opened. A tiny crack at first, and then a bit more, and a bit more . . . just enough for Thor to see another room to create mayhem in. He lolloped over, hurled the door open, and within a couple of seconds, Natalie was lying on the bed with a very large bear-pawed puppy slobbering the tears from her face. Thor was like a furry bolt of lightning. Once he was satisfied that Natalie was at least smiling now, Thor ran around the house, going into every room. He jumped in the bath, sliding around and then lying on his back. As John watched him running around the garden in circles, Natalie came and stood with him.

'You're a total idiot,' she said, but gentler this time.

Over the following weeks, Thor blew through the house like a thunderstorm. And he lifted away the heavy, humid air of grief. It was scarcely believable that any being could have so much energy. He lived life at a sprint, lurching from adventure to adventure, and John and Natalie had to pick up their pace just to catch up. Natalie found she began to look forward to waking up in the morning, opening the door so he could come and jump all over them in bed, John groaning to let him sleep a while longer. While John was at work, it was just the two of them. She began taking him for longer and longer walks. They would walk for hours and Natalie began to remember what the wind felt like on her face, the smell of rain. She began to feel part of the world in a way she hadn't for months. Thor was incredibly protective, as Pyreneans were originally bred to guard livestock in the mountains. He would constantly come and check on her. If she was in the house and ever felt sad, Thor would know and come and sit with her, ask her if she wanted to come for a walk. He would patrol the garden, eyeing squirrels with suspicion, and Natalie realised that the threat she'd felt that the universe could just reach into your life and take the most precious thing in it, whenever it wanted, began to recede just a little bit. And now when John came home, they would tell him what they'd done, what they'd seen, who they'd bumped into on their walks. Thor drew people to him and they'd talk to Natalie, ask her how she was. At work, he and Simon would compare stories of life lived alongside beloved bundles of fur.

'I can't thank you enough, mate,' said John. 'Thor has changed everything.'

Hour by hour, day by day, week by week, John could feel Natalie being brought back to life, inch by inch. There were still times when she would sit with him at the dinner table, silent, gazing off into the middle distance. At these times, he could tell she was remembering. But there were more and more occasions when it felt like they were moving forward together, the three of them.

By the time I met Thor, he had been wobbly on all four of his legs for a few months. At first, John and Natalie put it down to him being clumsy, his huge paws and galumphing personality. Perhaps they'd just overdone the walk the day before. But gradually his condition became increasingly pronounced.

They were referred to see me and I knew as soon as I saw him walk what was likely going on, because I'd seen it many times before. He was affected by Wobblers Disease, which in his particular case was caused by a genetically predisposed overgrowth of the junctions between the roofs of the vertebrae in his neck called the articular facets. It was as if the roof over the spinal cord was expanding downward, squishing the spinal cord itself, which had nowhere to go. The spinal cord was a passenger in a series of train carriages crushing down upon it. This type of Wobblers was quite different to what Teddy the Doberman had, but the

result was the same in that both Teddy and Thor had neck
pain and the spinal cords in their necks were being inex-
orably garrotted – rapidly in Teddy's case and more slowly
with Thor – towards progressive paralysis of all four legs.

With Wobblers, the patient suffers squashing of both the
spinal cord, which makes them wobble, and pain from the
nerves to the front limbs that come out through holes in
the side of the spinal column (the neuroforaminae). Affected
dogs often squeal. They say 'oaw' frequently, and so when
I christened this particular form of the disease OAWS –
Osseous Associated Wobblers Syndrome – it seemed to fit.
The technical term is osseous-associated spondylomyelopathy. Poor Thor was in significant pain and could hardly
walk. When he tried to accomplish anything more than a
slow plod, he crashed down face first and tumbled over in
agony. This face-planting was pitiful to watch. Natalie and
John were in bits. As they told me their story, it became
clear just how much their grief following their daughter's
death had been tangled up in their feelings about Thor.
Now, it was as if they were being forced to confront two
lots of grief, the one amplifying the other, opening old
wounds that had never properly healed.

I almost had to hold Natalie up physically as we hugged,
tears streaming down her face, while four of my team, each
with a sling-handle for one of Thor's limbs, held Thor up
and brought him in for scanning. John didn't know what
to do. He felt completely helpless.

MRI scans are best for showing what happens with the
spinal cord itself while CT scans delineate the bone best.

Both types of scans told me the worst possible news. Thor's spinal cord wasn't just squashed at one site – which would have been relatively easy to fix by grinding away the compressing bone – but rather he was compressed at all seven intervertebral junctions of the spinal column of the neck, and on both left and right sides. There is no known treatment for this and, without a miracle, Thor would soon have to be euthanised due to progressive paralysis of all four legs. Needless to say, Natalie and John were beyond consolation. As I was sitting at my screen explaining everything, they were holding each other and sobbing their hearts out.

I have had to put to sleep several dogs affected by OAWS over the years. When steroid medication failed to control their pain and deterioration of the function of the spinal cord, and if several sites were compressed such that simple bone removal wouldn't work, euthanasia was deemed the kindest option. And it still is by many. But not by me.

Because not only did we have FITS intervertebral distraction devices shaped like Christmas trees, but by the time Thor came to see me, my engineering colleagues and I had figured out how to put two FITS devices side by side in place of the discs in between the vertebrae of giant-breed dogs, and more importantly how to link all of these spacers together. The spacers would push apart the overgrown bone between the vertebrae, making more room for the spinal cord and nerve roots, thus alleviating both the progressive paralysis and the pain.

Then the titanium plates I designed based on the saddle of a horse would be linked to each vertebra and to the spacers. But the key to success was to link all of the plates together underneath the vertebrae. I would do this using a series of rods shaped like dumbbells, with a sphere on each end that would not collapse when clamped to each plate using a special mechanism. Each rod could be curved to the exact shape of that pair of vertebrae and so on from just behind the skull to the entrance of the chest. And so, the FITS-Fitzateur construct was born, and in this way, I would fuse solid Thor's entire neck – his entire cervical spine. To keep the vertebrae fused forever, I would harvest bone marrow from the top part of his humerus bones just underneath his shoulders (cancellous autograft), mix it with chips of donor graft from deceased dogs (cortico-cancellous allograft) and pack it all along the underneath of his entire cervical spine as biological mulch, which would hopefully fuse the vertebrae together. Permanently.

I had never fused solid the entire neck of a dog before, let alone a giant dog like Thor. It was essentially unknown how he would respond. But the technology was proven and I'd used it many times for two or three sites affected by the same condition. I discussed the ethics and risks with Natalie and John. Sadly, there wasn't another viable surgery option, so it was a situation of try one's best or allow him to pass peacefully away. They decided to try.

Within six weeks, the construct had given Thor his life back and had given Natalie and John back their saviour. By week twelve he wasn't just running around a field without pain and without collapsing, but you'd hardly know his entire neck was fused at all. A life reborn. They were back to their long walks and Thor could pick up large fallen tree branches and bring them back as gifts for his mum and dad, which was one of his favourite things to do. This time Natalie cherished every moment with him even more because she realised how precious a second chance at life really was. She remembered how it had felt when she thought she might never be able to spend time with Thor again and she was deeply grateful for every moment. They had their lightning bolt back again.

At his final sign-off CT scan, Natalie and John were effusive with gratitude.

And that would have been that. But, as I have explained, part of our clinical practice when we develop new techniques and procedures is the provision of check-ups and scans two or three years later, since I don't think it's ethical to deploy new technology without undertaking follow-up. And as long as there is no regulation of manufacturing standards or absolute requirement for formal training when deploying any type of new implant technology in dogs or cats in the UK, such follow-up is unfortunately not offered everywhere.

As I have also mentioned, nothing challenges your perception of success like follow-up. If clients don't complain or come back, one can't simply assume everything is OK. Many patients have come to see me for revision surgeries after suboptimal techniques have been deployed for spinal fusion and many other bone surgeries elsewhere. Often nobody appears to be accountable for anything in these cases, even though I believe that vets are doing their best with their training and available implants, as I have said before. However, from my perspective, this is not an optimal standard of care and I know with all my heart that none of the other techniques available would have saved Thor's life.

We have proven and published in a scientific journal how use of the FITS-Fitzateur to treat OAWS leads to the bone regressing from overgrowth around the spinal cord over time, and that it can provide a robust construct and great quality of life for many years. And yet people still accuse me of 'experimentation' and 'going too far'. Tell that to Thor and to Natalie and John. Tell them that trying really hard to change things for the better doesn't work!

And so, Thor came back for a follow-up two years later. He was doing great. His entire neck was fused solid and you'd never know this if you saw him carrying a stick in his mouth or charging around a field. A CT scan showed that his spinal cord and nerve compression had resolved and, as in our publication, the overgrown bone had gradually regressed over time due to the stabilisation. But none of this science matters a jot without the beating heart of the dog it serves.

And on that glorious day I was truly blessed to be introduced to another beating heart. Baby Cillian was just six months old. He was giggling and punching his little fists in the air as Thor nuzzled his carry-cot. Natalie and John were very proud parents to one little baby boy and one very big fluffy boy. I was overcome with admiration for this family, who had managed to drag themselves from the darkness and were now standing in the light.

Natalie flung her arms around me with heartfelt gratitude. She looked at John and then at me as she picked up Cillian's carry-cot and John held Thor, who was straining on the lead to nuzzle his little brother. She explained that she had lost a part of her soul when their little girl had died, but that Thor had found it and filled her loss with his love. When they kept hope alive through what seemed impossible for him during his surgery and recovery, they were somehow also inspired to keep hope alive that maybe they should try for a baby again. As they left my room, Natalie turned to me and said, 'There was a hole in my soul, which he filled with his love. I shall be forever grateful to you for mending my family . . . because he mended us. Thank you.'

10

Everyone deserves a second chance

Lucia the mongrel and Sheila

When Sheila retired early after a car accident, at first she was worried how she was going to fill her days. She was worried about keeping active. The accident had left her so down and she couldn't face the thought of all those empty hours. Even now, as she came into my consulting room many years later, she had a pronounced limp. But she was a warm, effusive woman, who filled the room with her presence. One day, she was on one of the walks her doctor had recommended, when she was distracted by something moving through the chain-link fence around some waste ground. She went right up to the wire fence, grabbing it with her fingers and straining to see through the weeds and junk strewn around. Then she saw it – first a little tail sticking out from behind a rusty rain barrel and then a timid nose peering round, two pin-prick dark eyes looking straight back at her. There was a dog, no more than a puppy, a scrap of fur among the rubbish. She managed to squeeze under the gate and, slowly but surely, in response to her gentle coaxing voice, the puppy crept towards her.

Sheila saw immediately that the pup was crawling, as if unable to stand up straight on either front leg. She remained completely still, her hand outstretched. After a few minutes, she was able to run her finger delicately across the puppy's muzzle, which she could now see belonged to a little girl. Finally, she reached down and wrapped her to her chest, using her coat as a blanket. She felt her tiny heart pattering the whole way home.

Sheila called around to see whose responsibility it was to look after abandoned dogs in her area. And every answer came back the same. There was no room. Services could barely deal with the dogs they had. She looked down at this bright-eyed flicker of life who had been abandoned, and she knew she couldn't abandon her again – in spite of her obvious deformities. And that was how Lucia came into her life. Lucia means bringer of light.

She was a small hairy mongrel. When Sheila brought her to see me, it was clear from my clinical examination and from subsequent X-ray pictures that poor Lucia suffered from congenital elbow luxation, where the three bones of the elbows, the humerus, radius and ulna, didn't link together properly during development inside the womb. This was the likely reason she had been abandoned, possibly chucked out of a car near the waste ground where Sheila found her.

Sheila didn't have much money, but she asked her vet to refer her to see if there was anything I might be able to do to help. There were the usual pleasantries of introduction, and even during a brief history-taking, it was clear that though Sheila had only known her a short time, she was already in love with Lucia. And she wasn't the only one. Sheila told me that she hadn't only taken on the care of Lucia, but also the care of her father, Arthur, who suffered from Alzheimer's. She told me that she hadn't seen Arthur smile for many months before she brought Lucia home, but as the puppy played around his feet and tugged at his thick socks, he laughed his head off. Lucia was most certainly a tonic for Arthur. He adored her from the first moment and Sheila explained to me how it was so much easier to get him out of bed and to get him to eat or interact in any way, because his entire day now revolved around the antics of this little fluffy bringer of light. So, Sheila was desperate to see what might be possible to help Lucia, who couldn't walk and was in considerable pain. Just as I was heading off to sedate her for radiography, lifting Lucia from her lap, Sheila touched me on the arm gently, and said softly, 'Everyone deserves a second chance, don't you think?'

It was a tall order for a short dog, though. Even before I sedated Lucia for radiography and a CT scan, I could see that not only were her elbows dislocated, but so too were her wrists, which in a dog are called carpi. She was suffering from horrendous deformity of both elbows and wrists of her front limbs. At the time, there was no mention in the published literature of anyone attempting to fuse both joints in both forearms, which in a dog are called antebrachia, and I hadn't either. Fusion of joints in medical speak is called arthrodesis. I explained to Sheila how difficult it would be, but she asked me to try. And so, I did.

Because Lucia was so crippled, I did something I would normally never contemplate: I performed major surgery on four joints at the same time. My reasoning was that if I operated on one front leg only, not only would Lucia be totally lop-sided with one normal-length leg and one collapsed, but she literally wouldn't have a leg to stand on. And so, with Lucia on her back, I drilled out all of the cartilage from all joint surfaces of her elbows and wrists and packed bone graft that I had harvested from the wings of her pelvis into all the gaps to facilitate fusion. One can effectively chop off the front part of the wings of the ilium bones of the pelvis of a dog and morselise this bone into tiny pieces using a bone mill, producing what is known as cortico-cancellous bone graft. These are the bits of the pelvis that hold up a human's trousers. Dogs can give this bone freely and usually with no side-effects, plus they don't need to wear trousers.

Her limbs were so deformed and her bones so skinny that conventional off-the-shelf plates were not appropriate for holding everything together, in my view. In any case, even if strong enough internal plates could be used, there would be a 'stress-riser' focused between implants in the elbows and the wrists such that the forearms may well snap in the middle. And also, money was very limited. So, I used a series of various thread-ended pins drilled at right angles to each of the bones in the humerus, radius, ulna, wrist (carpus) and palm (metacarpus) bones. Then I used these pins as levers to rotate the elbow back into alignment and also to pull the forearm and paw into alignment, whereupon I attached all of the pins together on the outside of the limbs with clamps on carbon fibre rods, constituting an integrated external skeletal fixator. My hope was that this would hold the bones together while the biological gold dust of the transplanted graft did its magic of making new bone (osteogenesis), inducing new bone (osteoinduction) and conducting in new bone (osteoconduction) to fuse the joints solid.

Even I was taken aback by Lucia's lust for life and for her second chance. The following day after we weaned her off the heavy-duty painkiller drip, she not only wanted to walk, but run. It was incredible. She was a healing machine and her little bones fused like willing strips of Velcro, but, ultimately, they'd not be strong enough to support her body weight, so when I removed the frames six weeks later, I applied short, small plates with screws in both elbows and both wrists for some added strength to make sure they stayed solid forever. I kept her in the hospital for a week after each of these procedures and got to know Arthur quite well on his and Sheila's visits. He called me 'the veterinary', which was an honourable name, as he and I had both come from farming stock, and I'd been called the same when I started out as a vet in 1990. I rejoiced in his second chance as much as he and Sheila did in Lucia's. I loved our chats – because there was something about Lucia and the smell of my veterinary practice that brought back Arthur's memories of the vet visiting his own farm many years ago. And so, Lucia brought with her some moments of lucidity that we all treasured.

Four years later, Sheila sent me a video of Lucia still running around with her stiff front-leg 'stilts', creating mayhem and bringing light wherever she went. She thanked me so much for the extra two years she had with Arthur and for the joy that our collective journey had brought to her father. She remembered telling me at the time of the operation that everyone deserves a second chance and she thanked me so much for giving that chance to both Lucia and Arthur. Sheila had chosen to take something bad in her life and transform it into an opportunity for generosity and kindness. And it is people like Sheila I choose to focus on, rather than those who allow harm to come to dogs or indeed to their humans. It is those guardian angels who reach down and pick up the ones who are helpless and vulnerable that truly inspire me.

Everyone deserves a second chance and dogs teach us this every day we are fortunate enough to have them in our lives. Second chances are what most lives are made of. Every success I have ever had as a surgeon stands on the shoulders of my failures. Troubles come all the time. Converting challenges to opportunities, problems to progress and false starts to new beginnings is the only way to keep going. When mistakes are made, and life punches you in the face, you can lie down, cry, not get up, bemoan your misfortune, or you can wipe the blood from your eyes, get up and keep on fighting. For if our canine friends teach us anything at all, it's that everyone falls down sometimes and it's the willingness to get back up again that allows you a second chance.

Every single day in my consulting room I see dogs who keep on going no matter what. I have seen dogs waddle in with joints exploded by horrifically painful arthritis, tails wagging, making the best of the cards they have been dealt, and I have seen dogs recover from the most horrendous injuries with tenacity and bravery that's incredibly rare in humans. And so, the greatest lesson I have learned from dogs and their humans is that while many humans complain and moan about life, most dogs just get on with life and rejoice in every single second they are allowed the blessing of being above ground.

The dogs I see have often come a long way to be in my consulting room. It is a fact of my vocation that I come up against not just bad luck or an accident, but the product of abandonment or even active cruelty. Dogs are abandoned on the streets, by the side of the road, in gardens, in rubbish dumps, in warehouses and railway sidings, in fridges and binbags, tied to lampposts, kicked about and thrown in rivers. I have met abandoned or 'street' dogs from all around the world. In so many ways these are the very lucky ones. If they have found their way to me, it's likely they have left the cruelty behind and have found a new family who will love them and try to give them a second chance at life. The RSPCA estimates that a dog is treated cruelly every hour, every single day of the year. And it's getting worse.

When times are hard, as they undoubtedly are for so many, unfortunately dogs take their share of those hard times. At one end of the spectrum, pet insurance is one of the first things to go unpaid when times are tight. At the other end, dogs are abandoned entirely, or are kept in conditions unfit for purpose.

There was Hebe the beautiful Whippet, who was found bleeding heavily in the snow with hypothermia, who we discovered had been shot repeatedly with an air rifle and was suffering from a broken leg and a collapsed lung. We were able to sort her lung, remove the lead pellets, realign her bones and, after several surgeries to treat infection and repair her fractures, Hebe was able to walk again. She was ultimately rehomed with a family determined to make up for all that cruelty with love.

There was Honey, a gorgeous Terrier who had been rescued from Vietnam by Trevor and Sue. She had been attacked with a machete, had lost one front leg and sustained massive injuries to her other front paw. They brought her to me because the wrist on the remaining front leg was collapsing. We were able to fuse her wrist and palm bones with a pancarpal arthrodesis, or full wrist fusion, much like that performed for each of Lucia's legs, using a plate and screws, and before long she too had a second chance at life.

There was Shadow, a German Wirehaired Pointer, who had been abandoned on the streets of Prague. He was skinny as a rake and covered in scratches and scars when Linda and Tim found him dragging himself along on his hind legs, and he was so-called because he was clearly a shadow of his former self. When they finally got him to safety, they couldn't take him for a walk because both hind legs were in such a bad way. It was clear that he'd been hit by a vehicle and just left to die on the side of the road. I assessed his injuries. One hind limb was relatively straightforward to fix by drilling out the cartilage in all of the dislocated bones of his hock or ankle joint and fusing them together with transplanted bone marrow and a plate and screws, again with an arthrodesis.

Shadow's other hind limb was an altogether more challenging situation because his severe trauma had ripped out the bones and blood supply of the arch of his hind foot, the metatarsus. His digits were hanging on by some tendons, nerves and blood vessels, while his metatarsal bones that hitherto connected the tarsal bones of his ankle to these digits were gone. Luckily for Shadow, though, he had a very long tail. I cut off his tail and dissected the vertebrae out, each consisting of a small cylinder of bone. Then I threaded them like kebab chunks on metal wires skewered between his toes and his ankle bones that were inspired by the comic book character Wolverine, of whom I was a fan as a child (more of which later).

I then built a very special external fixator frame using aluminium rings attached with further wires to his ankle bones and toes. Between these rings were turnbuckles called linear motors, which I used to oscillate the bones around the tail vertebrae up and down cyclically with a special rate and rhythm that I had developed years earlier. In this way, I pumped blood through the transplanted tail bones allowing them to integrate. And so, I turned a tail into a foot. The technique is called DCOI, Distraction Compression Osteointegration. But apparently it isn't possible; I have been unable to get it accepted for publication in a scientific journal thus far, even though I have given half a dozen dogs a second chance in this way. Sometimes second chances don't happen because people don't want them to happen, because they just do not believe it's possible and it contradicts everything they think they already know. Shadow knows different – and he is now no longer a shadow of his former self, but a vivacious go-getting ball chaser grabbing every moment of his second chance – with no tail, but certainly a tale to tell.

I have seen second chances become real life for many dogs and their humans down the years, in spite of the disbelievers and nay-sayers. Fumble was a gorgeous, joyful and boisterous Border Collie who was hit by a truck. His back was broken in the middle and his spinal cord was severed, so I made his human mum and dad aware that he would never walk again. If he couldn't urinate, and if implanted electrodes for this purpose weren't a suitable solution for him or his family, then euthanasia would be recommended even if I were to repair the vertebral fractures. Fumble's family believed in him so much that they wanted me to try. So, I realigned and repaired his vertebrae using pins and cement, even knowing that his severed spine would likely never conduct to his back end again.

Now, a couple of years later, Fumble can urinate, but will never walk again, as we'd known from the beginning of his treatment. But he runs on the promenade along the seafront near where they live in a canine cart, without a care in the world, right beside a sixteen-year-old boy called

Noah, who is also in a wheelchair. Like Fumble, Noah was paralysed by an accident.

Of course, no vet can know what goes through the mind of a dog whose hind limbs are paralysed, but from what I could tell, Fumble just wanted to get on with his life. I have seen this with many dogs on wheeled carts over the years. What I know for sure, because Noah's parents told me, is that because Fumble embraced his second chance, it was 'as if he made Noah's wheelchair disappear'. Noah had been profoundly depressed after his injury, as was completely understandable. His mum and dad had been at a loss as to how best to help him. But Fumble's bravery and optimism is transformative and gives Noah the strength and courage to get on with his own second chance at life every single day.

Noah's parents told me that they would not have given up on Fumble any more than they would have given up on Noah. I recognise that this perspective on the value of a dog's life isn't appropriate for everyone, and I don't judge guardians for their choices, having put to sleep many dogs with broken spines in my career, but Fumble and Noah's journey is awe-inspiring nonetheless.

Crystal and her family travelled from Sweden to see me. She was a sweet and gentle Tibetan Terrier who was very sadly affected by erosive polyarthritis of her wrists and her knees due to an immune-mediated disease. Sometimes the immune system of an animal or human gets confused and attacks the organs of the body itself, and the trigger for this might never be discovered. Crystal was in terrible pain because these joints had collapsed with severe cartilage destruction and were rubbing bone-on-bone. But her family would not give up on her being offered a second chance, even if every vet they spoke to already had. In staged surgeries, I replaced both of her destroyed knee (stifle) joints with FitzKnee replacements. These are customised implants 3D-printed from CT scans that we have developed to replace the bottom part of the thigh bone (femur) and the top part of the shin bone (tibia) when all of the knee ligaments are beyond repair. The implant components are linked to the bones with titanium plates and rods, while the articulating surfaces are replaced with a super-smooth metal called cobalt-chromium and a plastic spacer made out of polyethylene. The top femur bit is linked to the bottom tibia bit by a pivoting hinge that allows the knee joint to move more or less normally, but cannot dislocate. When her knees were sorted, I also fused Crystal's wrists solid like Lucia's.

Crystal could then run without pain and did so for many years. She was the companion of their young son, Frederick, who developed severe obsessive-compulsive behaviour and physical tics almost overnight, and most doctors sent them away, believing it to be some kind of behavioural abnormality. But his parents didn't give up and finally they found a specialist in PANDAS, or Paediatric Autoimmune Neuropsychiatric Disorder Associated with Streptococcal infection, which by either fate or coincidence is also an immune-mediated disorder: Frederick's immune system had attacked parts of his brain after being wound up by a bacterial infection. Since being properly diagnosed and treated, Frederick's life has been transformed, just because someone was willing to look at his world through different eyes and never give up searching for a second chance.

As I've mentioned, I have seen many instances where dogs and their guardians suffer similar physical and emotional ailments, each helping the other through their crises. In fact, sometimes a dog and their human appear linked at an almost metaphysical level. That's how I felt about our farm dog Pirate when I was young. He was misunderstood by most people and chained to a wall, and I felt misunderstood by most people and chained to some bad things that happened in my childhood. Pirate and I gave each other a second chance in life.

Later on, I knew that to really make something of this second chance, I needed to see the world through different eyes than I had seen it as a child. So, I escaped to America as soon as I could. A year after getting the grades in my secondary school exams to get into vet school at University College Dublin, I applied for and won a scholarship to study at the University of Pennsylvania School of Veterinary Medicine in Philadelphia. I was nineteen years old and I ran away as fast as I could from all of the things I needed to leave behind from my childhood in Ireland.

I was at this vet school in inner-city Philadelphia when a uniformed police officer came in with a beautiful German Shepherd dog. He was distraught as his friend, who he told us was called Dust, hung limp and appeared almost dead in his arms. The clinicians ran to reception and told the police officer that it looked as if she'd been poisoned. While the imaging people were taking radiographs, the surgeons were deciding whether to operate to remove foreign material they had seen in her stomach on the X-ray pictures, and the internal medicine people deliberated over what drugs to give, he stood there saying, 'Who does that? Who the hell does that to a dog?'

Dust was beautiful. Sticky-up fluffy ears, a glorious spiky-haired face and deeply kind eyes. But she was lifeless and could barely lift her head.

I was of no use to anyone as they tried to figure out what to do for the best, so I went and found Anthony, the police officer, in the waiting area and took him a cup of vending machine coffee. We sat in silence.

'Is she going to die?' he said after a while.

'She's in the best possible place she could be,' I said. 'They're doing absolutely everything they can.'

'You're Irish?' he asked.

'Yes.'

'My grandfather was Irish,' he said.

'*Sláinte*,' I said, touching my plastic cup to his. I had zero experience talking to 'clients' and there was no training for compassion in vet school.

'I love that dog,' he went on, staring straight ahead, his eyes shining and his voice wavering.

'I know,' I replied. And then there was a long pause. He looked at his coffee. I felt like I should just leave him be, but something deep inside me, some kind of instinct, kept me sitting there, not knowing where to look. It was after midnight and there was nobody else around. I looked at the badge on his police uniform pledging protection to the people he served, and yet I felt that he was the one needing looking after at that moment.

'Why is she called Dust?' I asked, not quite knowing why.

'That. Is a story.'

I looked around, gestured that I was here, he was here, and he carried on.

'I was still married to my ex back then. Just about. We were screaming at each other. And then she left me for another cop. A friend of mine. My partner, in fact. Took our daughter with her. That was tough. I lost both my partners the same day.'

I nodded, though at that point in my life I hadn't ever even had a girlfriend.

'I never really drank before that. I must have been the only Irish cop in Philadelphia who didn't. But I didn't want to go back to the empty apartment, so I started going to the bar. Then I started taking beers home after the bar. Then it was whiskey. Then it was a bottle a night. It got so I couldn't sleep without it. Then I couldn't go through the day without it.

'Then one night, we're out on patrol, a domestic disturbance. I remember all I could think was how badly I wanted to get out of there so I could have a drink. And on the way out I hear this whimpering sound. And there was this dog. This beautiful dog. And she's trying to move but she can't. I tell my new partner to go on and I wrap her in my coat. I take her to the vet and he patches her up.

Fractured leg. He'd put a plate in it, bless him. And then he says the animal shelter is full. So, I take her back to my place for a few days. And I remember, I'm sitting there, drinking, and she wakes up and calls out and I sit with her on the floor. She sniffs my hand and decides I'm OK.'

By this point he's wiping away tears with the backs of his hands.

'And that's when I called her Dust. 'Cos they put her in a dustbin. And I took her out.'

Anthony said it wasn't an overnight thing. He said he couldn't even look after himself, let alone a dog. But something about the way that dog had looked up at him meant that he knew he needed to get better, so he could look after her. He took the empty bottles and pizza boxes out. He stopped only thinking about the next drink and started thinking about what made sense for Dust. And it turned out that was a pretty good rule. He cut down his drinking. He started seeing his daughter again. She loved to come and spend time with Dust. Then he stopped his drinking.

'Two years in two weeks' time,' he said with a grim smile. 'But this.' He gestured around. 'This is really *really* making me want a drink.'

He'd taken her for a walk in the park. She was on the lead, he'd looked away and she'd been eating something. And by the time they were leaving the park she was sick. Really sick.

We sat in silence, listening to the distant sounds of people moving around the building.

'Mr Lynch?' One of the veterinary nurses was standing

there. He stood up suddenly. And that was the look I will never forget. That look of hope and sadness and desperation. Of his whole universe coming down to one moment.

'She's doing well.'

He hugged her. Then he hugged me.

Humans and dogs find each other. And just because it is a regular miracle doesn't mean we should stop seeing it as a miracle.

The nurse went back into the treatment area, saying that Dust would need to stay the night on a drip, but that she was out of danger. They had indeed operated to remove from her stomach a bit of meat that someone had wrapped in gauze and put poison in. Nobody knew why. Some people are just wrong for whatever reason. But the nurse said she was on the right drugs, so she should be fine. He could go home. Then she nodded farewell and went back inside.

Police officer Anthony Lynch held out his hand in the empty night-time reception of the University of Pennsylvania vet school. I shook it. It was the first handshake I had ever had with 'a client', and it felt good. It felt like I'd done something good, even though I hadn't done anything at all. I had just listened.

'Hey,' he said. 'Thank you. One day you'll be a really good veterinarian.'

I took his handshake and his belief in me to heart. I wanted to be a really good veterinarian one day and I wanted to save animals and perform miracles like those who have been my mentors, to whom I am deeply grateful. But every day is a school day, and if there's one thing I've learned from the dogs who have been among my greatest mentors, it's that if you get your act together, put in the effort and try to do the right thing every day, we really can change, and everyone deserves a second chance. Second chances save lives and also make a life worth saving.

11

Unspeakable things

Mabel the Cocker Spaniel and Mark

As long as he could remember, Mark had always been a fighter. One day, when he was five, his dad had gone out for cigarettes and never come home. Mum said everything would be OK, but at night when she thought he was asleep, he heard her cry. Mark had a lot of anger inside him. He picked fights at school, and then on the streets some guys picked fights with him. One day he bumped into the wrong guy and later he woke up in hospital to the sound of his mum crying. He'd gotten into a fight and hit a guy over the head with a bottle. The guy hit back. Mark said it was in self-defence when I spoke to him years later. I believed him. He had that careful way of holding himself I had seen in some men who were no strangers to violence. He limped into my consulting room one lunchtime and I sat transfixed as he began to tell me his story. The trial judge had given him community service, and he recommended that he get a 'change of scenery' from the various bad influences in his life. As Mark walked out of the court, he stood by the lifts, his heart pounding with what might have been. He could have been sent to prison.

On a shelf to one side, he told me there was a small British Army poster with some leaflets sitting next to it. The words of the judge echoing in his head, he took a leaflet, more as a distraction than anything else, feeling the eyes of those standing in the foyer fixed firmly on him.

His community service involved building an extension to a dog shelter with some other guys. Mark had always wanted a dog, but he was still living at home and working odd jobs at odd hours when he wasn't just getting in trouble in spite of himself. His mother had enough on her plate and, back when Dad was still at home, having a dog was impossible because Dad hated dogs. Maybe that was another reason for Mark's long-standing loneliness and isolation. Mark could remember whenever he was with his dad and they saw a dog, Mark would try to run towards the dog and his dad would often give him a slap on his arm or leg and say something like, 'Dirty things, dogs, stay away from them,' or 'They'll bite you. You know that. Stay away, Mark.'

Mark had never believed his dad and now he knew he had been right not to. It was the best job he'd ever had because he got to see the dogs at the shelter on his lunch-break. He even volunteered to walk them after work. These were usually dogs who had been abandoned. Many of them had suffered cruelty. Mark had always felt he had to appear hard and tough with other people, but with these dogs he could be gentle. He could show them that not all people were hard and loud and cruel.

One particular dog he got to walk was called Mabel. Mabel was a blue roan Cocker Spaniel. She was very cute with big floppy hairy ears, but also pot-bellied and skeletally thin from malnutrition. She had been abandoned, tied up in a dirty shed where she had been used as a breeding bitch.

I wish I could say this was a rare occurrence, but I've seen it time and again where unscrupulous breeders keep dogs like Mabel tied up and pregnant as often as they can be. Their puppies are advertised on various websites and unsuspecting people fall in love with the cute puppies and never think for a second where they have come from. Sometimes they pay a deposit online and the breeder or someone working for them meets them at a motorway service station, saying that they will save them the journey all the way to wherever the 'kennels' are. Of course, invariably, one look at the cute puppy and there's no way that person isn't going to hand over the rest of the money and take the dog home.

Some disreputable breeders have even more sophisticated scams. They set up a litter of puppies in a respectable house somewhere with a presentable polite person there to greet would-be buyers. They even have a fake mother dog, who is in good health and running around the garden of the house, because she has never actually seen the puppies. It's rare that someone goes to pick up a puppy and doesn't instantly fall in love, most not bearing to leave without that puppy in their arms, not realising that they might be funding organised crime.

Mabel was scared of everything when she had arrived at the shelter, especially men. But she wasn't scared of Mark.

He had befriended her with regular visits and sweet-talk outside her cage. She growled at first but finally acquiesced to letting him inside the cage, and eventually, with Mark's humility and persistence, she let him give her a little food from his hand and eventually stroke her chin. Before long, they were walking in the field outside the shelter, each bringing immeasurable joy to the other with the occasional utterance of 'Ruffff,' or 'Mabel, look . . . the primroses are out. How exciting.'

Mark had never been in love before, but one Wednesday afternoon on the day before his court hearing, sitting under a lop-sided tree surrounded by primroses, he looked in Mabel's big amber-coloured eyes and he fell in love with her. He began to daydream of a different life. He didn't really like being a labourer. The only good thing about the job was getting to see Mabel. Maybe he could adopt her and she could live with him and his mum. He could try a different job or a training position. He had no money and no instinct about what he might be any good at.

He walked through the door and found his mother sitting at the kitchen table. He could see that she was pushing down tears. She had received the results of the tests she'd been having at the local hospital. She had breast cancer and it was bad. She would have significant surgery and then prolonged chemotherapy. She cried. Mark held her.

He knew there was no way he could even think about adopting Mabel. It was out of the question and he couldn't possibly discuss it now. Mum had enough to cope with and the doctors had told her that immune-suppression would go hand in hand with the chemotherapy, so she would need to be careful about who and what she came into contact with. Animals were dangerous now.

The next day he sat down by the same tree, leaned against nature and told Mabel everything about his own nature that he hated – the ins and outs of self-loathing, despair and complete helplessness. How he had just lurched from one crisis, one addiction, one rage to the next. How he was sick of hurting people, of hurting himself. She just looked up at him and listened. Then she sat down, put her head on his outstretched legs and listened some more as he stroked her beautiful big furry ears. 'What would you have done if you weren't chained up and tortured? What would you do now? If you could choose?' Mabel barked. And Mark took that to mean 'I would do my best with my life.'

He knew he needed to be strong for his mum because his father hadn't been and he needed to prove to her he was still someone that she could be proud of. His sister was there too as they sat with their mum in the admissions bay of the hospital that morning. She was pregnant and had her own stuff going on. They both hugged their mother and then each other and as she went off to have both of her breasts and many of her lymph nodes removed, they cried.

Again, Mark went straight to the dog shelter and to Mabel. By now they were the best of friends and her waggy tail and excited eyes dried his tears momentarily as he took her for a walk to explain things. The volunteers at the shelter were always only too happy for Mark to walk Mabel. So far all of their efforts to find her a home had failed. They sat in their usual spot. The primroses had long since withered and some weeds had sprung up in their place. Mark wished he had the time or resources to clean the field up, but he had neither. And neither did he have the wherewithal to adopt Mabel.

He sat there, his arm around her neck, her making gentle 'ruff' noises, and he explained as best he could, with tears streaming down his cheeks, how much he loved her, how much he felt safe with her, how much comfort she had given his soul, and how desperately he wanted to stay by her side, but he couldn't. And soon he would have to go away. He didn't think she understood anything of his soul-baring as he brought her back to her kennel. He kissed her on the forehead, something that would have been unthinkable just a few weeks earlier. And he wiped his tears away before saying goodbye and thanks to the folks at the shelter. He said he'd come back if he could, but he had stuff to deal with. He wondered if they might keep him informed about how Mabel got on and if they found a suitable home for her. He left his email address, but didn't have high hopes of any communication.

Mark had no clue what receiving real love looked or felt like outside of his relationship with his mum, which had been difficult because he had kept getting in trouble since his dad left. So, as he left the shelter that day, he told me later that his heart was broken for the very first time. He told himself it was stupid and that he should know better, but he didn't, and for the first time in his life, he allowed himself to feel the pain of unconditional love . . . raw, searing pain of a broken heart.

That same day, Mark went to the Army Careers Centre in a neighbouring town. He sat in a chair by a desk while an officer took him through things. He left with even more questions than answers, not because the brief hadn't been good, but because he didn't know if he was strong enough mentally or physically to face it. He wasn't particularly strong, he was scrappy. He wasn't particularly bright, he was wily.

He went to the hospital where his mum had woken from surgery and was doing OK. She asked how his day had been. He told her. She said that she would go through the chemo and he should go and do something with his life. Two weeks later Mark found himself in an army assessment centre. He had plucked up all of his inner courage to apply online and now his assessment would take two days. He had a medical examination, various physical and mental tests, as well as exercises to see how well he might work with other people.

Just over a year later, Mark had done well in his training, had excelled in the field and, aged twenty-two, he was deployed to a war zone. His mother had lost all of her hair but was in remission from her cancer. He looked at a picture she had sent without her habitual headscarf and he missed her. He looked at a picture that one of the shelter people had taken of him and Mabel under the lop-sided tree and he missed her. He looked at a picture of his sister and her baby. He put all three in the pocket of his army fatigues as he boarded a military flight to Afghanistan in the spring of 2006.

Within days of leaving, Mark was in the middle of what he called 'butchery'. He whispered it to me all those years later in my consulting room. 'I saw unspeakable things.'

Mark was shooting at people in a war he didn't understand. Confusion reigned during some of the battles in Helmand province. Mark didn't remember stepping on the improvised explosive device. He slowly regained consciousness in a battlefield hospital. He looked down and he had no right leg. There was an army doctor by his side saying comforting words, none of which Mark heard. He had no leg and it was never coming back. The life he once knew was never coming back. The morphine kicked in again and as he drifted in and out of consciousness, he didn't want to come back either.

The one dream that held Mark together, however, the one dream that kept him from tipping over the edge of darkness, was that maybe one day he might see Mabel again. When he was deployed in active service, he had been forwarded an email through official channels. The team at the shelter had heard that Mark had become a soldier and had been posted to active duty in Afghanistan. They told him how proud of him they were and how they each took turns looking after Mabel, but that she still didn't like any men, and didn't let any men near her. Three very kind ladies were looking after her.

But that was just a single email and it would be nearly a year on from his deployment before Mark was well enough to return home. Still, Mark couldn't help thinking about Mabel and how maybe he had been the only man she ever trusted. After his dad had abandoned them, he himself had never trusted a man until he was in active combat and he had lost one of those he trusted most. He beat himself up for being alive, because he was second in line when his squad was attacked. The previous day he had been first. It should have been him and not Danny. Another soldier in his platoon had committed suicide shortly after getting home because he just couldn't cope with 'normal life' after what he had seen and heard on the battlefield.

The day he got home, Mark sat at the kitchen table, holding his mother's hand, both crying that they were together again and both crying for what they had lost.

Mark couldn't help himself. He rang the shelter, his voice quivering. On the one hand, it would be wonderful if Mabel had found a loving home and was living her best life, and on the other, what if she was still there?

She was!

The lady remembered him of course and was delighted to hear from him. He went to see Mabel. He was worried she wouldn't remember him, wouldn't recognise who he was now. He felt like a different man. The things he had seen had changed him, on the inside. His leg too. She was such a nervous dog. How would she react to that? She saw him from across the field as he opened the rickety wire gate. Her ears pricked up in that cutest way and she immediately started running towards him. He ran towards her too as fast as he was able, still tentative on his prosthetic leg. As she got to him, she jumped up into his arms, almost knocking him over with the whirlwind of their embrace, limbs flailing. She licked his face and he was laughing and crying simultaneously. For the first time in a very long while, it was as if the sun had come out from behind a cloud and he knew that, whatever happened next, he could never let her go again.

I know all of this because Mark told me. And these discussions became possible because Mark's friend, who had driven him to see me, had inadvertently left the door of my consulting room slightly ajar. I was too concerned with what Mark was telling me about Mabel to notice. Or maybe an all-seeing 'God' or 'Dog' from on high stuck his/her/their foot in the door? I don't know. But as a result of this overheard conversation, a miracle followed – as I will explain.

I met Mark two years after he had come home from Afghanistan. His friend carried Mabel in his arms. I could immediately see that Mark was limping on a stump-socket prosthetic leg. Through my work with human and animal amputees in trying to help develop skeleton-anchored amputation prosthesis implants, I have met quite a few service personnel whose injuries included amputation of one or both of their legs or arms. I didn't blink an eyelid.

Mark shook my hand and sat down. Of course, I knew nothing of the detail of his story at that first encounter; all I knew was that Mabel had been scared by a group of men shouting after a football match, had slipped her lead and been hit by a car. The attending vet said that both front legs were broken, but she felt the left front limb was unsavable and would need amputating. She sent Mabel and Mark to me to see if there was anything I could do. I acknowledged the situation and took a quick look at the leg before admitting Mabel for further assessment. As I gently took her from the arms of his friend, Mark tapped me on the arm, and with moist and pleading eyes piercing through me from his shaven head, looked straight at me and said, 'I miss my leg . . . but I'd miss her leg more . . . Please do what you can for my girl.'

Mabel had a really bad shearing injury of the bottom part of her left front leg. It's called a degloving injury because it's like taking all the skin off like a glove, horrific as that sounds. She also had severe crushing of her paw, meaning that her palm bones, the metacarpals, were all crushed and splintered, her wrist (carpal) bones were sheared off on the road under the skidding tyre, her toes were hanging off and her forearm was fractured. Her paw was quite literally hanging on by a few threads of blood vessels and nerves and I was by no means confident that the blood and nerve supply would hold up, even if I could fix the bones and soft tissues, and that was a big if. Amputation of the entire limb was not the optimal option because she had also sustained injuries to her right front leg.

When I came back, I explained to Mark that one front leg had broken bones but could readily be fixed, but that I did not know if the other front leg was savable. The prognosis was grim. Mark cried a bit. I offered him a tissue. He waved it away. His friend tried to comfort him. He declined that too and asked if his pal might pop out of the room for a minute so that he could speak to me in private. It turned out that the friend wasn't really a friend as such, rather a well-meaning neighbour. Mark shook his head as if to steady himself in what he was going to say next. 'Listen, doc,' he began, 'I've got to be honest with you . . . I love that dog more than my own life . . . but if you can mend one and have to chop the other off then you got to do what you got to do . . . and I know I'm asking a lot . . . but could you give it your best shot?' I nodded and said that I would, but that ultimately, I'd have to do the right thing for Mabel. He said he understood, but added, 'The other thing is . . . and I'm really embarrassed about this . . . but I'm on disability benefit from the army, so I can't afford much.'

As I explained earlier, I can't achieve limb- and life-saving surgeries without a huge team of people, a state-of-the-art surgical facility, advanced diagnostic imaging and a myriad of implants, tools, drugs and disposables. Even if I worked for free, the kinds of surgeries that had even the remotest chance of saving Mabel's left front leg still cost thousands.

All vets, myself included, are faced with situations where it may be possible to save a leg, but where amputation is performed for economic reasons. The truth is that most dogs will manage fine on three legs unless they have disease affecting the other legs, are overweight or are a giant breed, and even then, some giant breeds manage OK. Also, the truth is that most vets are genuinely offering what they believe to be the best option for a dog by recommending amputation. I, for one, will hold up my hand and say that in the past I have amputated limbs for economic reasons when I worked in general practice or in someone else's companion animal practice in the '90s, which I knew were likely saveable at the time and would almost certainly be saveable nowadays. Even today, across the world I see many limbs amputated for imminently fixable trauma, purely due to lack of funding, implants or expertise to repair them. Poor Mabel carried the scars of her previous incarceration as a breeding machine; she had osteoarthritis affecting both elbows and both hips and she remained pot-bellied. So, due to her body weight, arthritis and her other broken leg, amputation would not be the best option for her.

Mabel might cope on three legs but she was getting on in years and Mark was struggling to get around too. In the days that followed, Mark and I talked about the ethics of trying to save the left front leg and the ethics of a skeleton-anchored limb amputation prosthesis. I had the technology and I could indeed give her this option if the money could be found. Mark himself could also have a skeleton-anchored limb amputation bionic leg prosthesis to improve his own quality of life if money and technology could be found.

Mark and I had an instant and easy rapport, and in the several conversations that followed, he told me his remarkable story. I told him how I wanted to gift the intellectual property that I had developed with limb amputation prostheses for dogs to a human implant company. Twice I have come close to making this happen, but it never has. Sheep were sacrificed to discover how the bone grows into the metal and yet, in spite of more than fifteen years of getting skin to grow onto metal mesh in dogs, human implant companies have not welcomed what I know even if I give it to them for free, because, as I've explained, human medicine is set up in such a way that generally only a sacrificed research animal can act as a subject for testing an implant designed for use in human patients. To put it bluntly, because I feel very strongly about it, we sometimes kill animals to know what is already known from clinical veterinary practice, and because that's the status quo and how companies own technologies and make profit, that's how business continues.

The vast body of knowledge veterinary surgeons like myself have developed over the years through surgery on the spines, joints or bones of dogs in clinical veterinary practice is not utilised to help humans because there is no legal or ethical infrastructure for transmitting this hard-won knowledge into human medicine. As I have said before, the flip side of this coin is that medicines and implants tested on sacrificed research dogs are then not available to help dogs who are family members because it often doesn't make financial sense for the drug companies to license them for animals affected by those same diseases. But I believe that together we could find a way for companies to make the same profits if veterinary and human medicine worked side by side through One Medicine in a more compassionate world for both animals and humans.

So, it turned out that Mark's friend had left the door ajar when he had gone out and our conversation was audible in the waiting room. I cursed myself for not checking the door was properly closed because I insist on client confidentiality.

But I shouldn't have – I should have welcomed the mishap, because a man in my waiting room walked up to me as Mark left the room to think, and before I could go back to the preparation room to look at Mabel again, he told me that he would pay Mark's bills for his dog (he didn't know her name) and he didn't want Mark to know who he was. I was gobsmacked. I had met this man shortly before with his dog, who I had fixed. He had come back for a check-up and was clearly very grateful. As it turned out, he was also quite wealthy and an ardent supporter of the principles of the army. I shook his hand and assured him that I would tell him the truth at all times. He said, 'I know you will.' I rechecked his own dog, who was doing great, and before he left, he paid a deposit for Mabel's care and left his phone number for me to call in due course.

I went back to Mabel filled with the light of this miracle and also the miracle that, even after a tour of duty and being away for more than a year, the women at the shelter believed that Mark would return and adopt Mabel. They believed this with all of their hearts. And Mark believed with all of his heart that I would do my best. And the guardian angel who had just appeared also believed that truth and love would prevail. The only problem was that I had absolutely no idea if I could save Mabel's left front leg. I never perform an operation unless I really do believe I'm going to win. That's the starting point. But there's always a chance I may fail, and, in Mabel's case, a significant chance.

I assessed the injury of the left front leg. It would indeed be very challenging. But if the blood and nerve supply held up, there was a possibility. Following a couple of long chats with Mark, who was also stunned by the generosity of his guardian angel, he asked me to try my best to save both of Mabel's front legs. To begin with, I cleaned the tarmac and grit out of the bone and surrounding tissue of the left front foot. There's a term I use, MD, and it doesn't stand for managing director; it stands for 'maximum death'. This is what I need to wait for in limb-crush injuries like Mabel's. Not all of the tissue that is going to die is visibly dead at the time of initial presentation, and I needed to dress her limb with appropriate bandaging and support for a few days before I could cut away all of the tissue that had actually died. Then, once MD had occurred, I could set about reconstructing what was left. In the meantime, I performed a straightforward repair of the fractures of her right forearm with plates and screws. A few days later, it was apparent that, fortunately, the blood supply to the digits and pads of her left front foot had held up against the odds.

As I alluded to regarding a previous patient called Shadow, I had invented a type of external scaffolding based on a comic book hero who had helped inspire my entire journey to be an orthopaedic veterinary surgeon in the first place. His name is Wolverine and he has an adamantium endoskeleton and can regenerate his own tissue. I had on many occasions used stainless steel pins which looked like Wolverine claws to repair fractures of the palm (metacarpal) bones of the front foot and the arch (metatarsal) bones of the hind foot. One could thread the splintered bones like tubes along pins emulating Wolverine's claws, leaving the pins sticking out and bent upwards at the knuckle joints (metacarpo- and metatarso-phalangeal joints). Then one could put further pins crossways through the wrist (carpus) or ankle (hock) bones and bend them upwards too, joining them all on the top of the paw using a kind of plumber's putty called epoxy resin. This I called a SPIDER, which stood for Secured Pin Intramedullary Dorsal Epoxy Resin frame (and because it looked like a spider).

Some years later, I elaborated on this frame so that it could bridge broken palms and arches of feet and could also support securing toes back in place and facilitating healing of a foot. Instead of linking the pins with resin, I attached them to aluminium arches and rings, which spanned from the lower forearm (radius and ulna) or shin bone (tibia) to the toes of a foot. This provided security for the broken bones and also a metal scaffold within which I could address the wounds and soft tissue loss. I built another bit on the frame with arches subtended below the foot, meaning they were held on pedestals below the foot like horseshoes. I called the frame a PAWS construct – Pedal Arch Wire Scaffold.

I constructed a PAWS frame for Mabel's left front foot, reattaching her dislocated toes and realigning all of her splintered palm bones along four long Wolverine-like pins. I drilled out the remaining cartilage from her wrist and grafted all of the deficits where bone had been sheared away with bone marrow graft harvested from the wings of her pelvis (ilium bones), to fuse her wrist solid. The Wolverine pins and various other wires and pins placed at angles through the toes, wrist and forearm were attached to rings and arches on the external frame. I then built the lower-down pedestal bit of the frame like a shoe for her to walk on. I used special gel and collagen to grow pink tissue known as granulation tissue over the transplanted pelvis bone, all supported inside the PAWS frame. Then I constructed yet another bit of the frame attached to nylon fishing line so that I could gradually pull the remaining skin back over the wounds day by day. And finally, I grafted skin from her belly to fill any gaps. That belly was good for something after all.

I placed wrapping around the frame so Mabel could walk on it and, needless to say, Mabel and Mark made many trips to the practice throughout her healing, which took about twelve weeks. Mabel was super-patient and remarkably compliant. It took me a while to overcome her initial anxiousness and growling, because I am, after all, just a man. But gradually, with more than a little patient coaxing, I too gained her trust. I also had several conversations with Mark's guardian angel. It turned out his father had been killed on active duty for his country and he told me that he was honoured and privileged to have been in the right place at the right time and with the wherewithal to help a soldier who was down and bleeding his heart out. I remarked that I was privileged to only ever have to soldier in the battlefields of biology.

The day the frame came off and Mabel could walk with her fused wrist joint and functional foot, Mark was over-joyed. He clasped me in a giant bear-hug. Tears welled up in his eyes and he told me how grateful he was for all that my team and I had done and how extraordinarily grateful he was for the anonymous angel paying for her treatment. And then he said something I shall never forget. We had got to know each other very well, which itself was a blessing.

He held my shoulder, looked me in the eye and said, 'Thank you. I have seen the worst things people can do to each other, unspeakable things, but now – that man who paid and you, saving my little girl – I've seen the best things too.'

He cried a little and shuffled out of the room with Mabel bounding by his side, evidently eager to bark loudly about the things she had seen and done.

12

I don't trust anyone who doesn't like dogs

Prince the Labrador and Craig

In my veterinary referral practice I am fortunate to meet dogs and their humans who both have truly remarkable vocations in life. I have met humans who dedicate their lives to helping others, some of whom put their lives on the line for others daily. I am lucky enough to hear stories of bravery and sacrifice that remind me every day of the incredible things that humanity is capable of. I see the best that humanity has to offer by way of the animals they love; from the perspective of my consulting room, behind every good human is a truly great animal friend. And it's the trust between a dog and their human that makes this particular partnership so extraordinary.

Prince was a sleek black Labrador. His mum, Teresa, brought him in one unremarkable winter day and we quickly worked out that he was suffering from osteoarthritis affecting both of his elbows and both hips. I have had the privilege of meeting several thousand Labrador Retrievers in my career. I can say this with confidence because I have spent the past three years reviewing my caseload to publish three book chapters on developmental elbow disease, which is a central endeavour of my professional career, and the most common orthopaedic disease Labradors are affected by. It used to be called elbow dysplasia, before I gave it this more appropriate name. I've written a couple of dozen scientific papers on this subject and on hip dysplasia too, which was the cause of Prince's painful hip joints. Arthritis is the inevitable consequence of both of these genetically predisposed joint pathologies and there are a variety of treatments available, some of which I have invented. The most appropriate intervention is guided by many factors, including the stage of the disease, age and lifestyle of the patient, experience of the clinician and attitude of the dog's human. Sometimes it's just medicine; sometimes injections of anti-inflammatory stem cells into the joints which are cultured from the patient's own fat; sometimes arthroscopic (keyhole) surgery; sometimes it's placing special plates on cuts in bones (an osteotomy) to shift weight to good parts of the joints; sometimes partial or full joint replacements, to name a few options.

I'd been treating Prince for a few months with medication and injections into all four joints (elbows and hips) of anti-inflammatory stem cells derived from his own fat, platelets from his blood and a viscoelastic lubricant, as I have referred to earlier, and things were all pretty standard. He was clearly very intelligent and extremely poised but I didn't think much about it if I'm honest. There are always a thousand plates spinning at the practice – always a new emergency, never enough hours in the day. My solution is to spend as few of them as possible sleeping, but even that has its limits. So, when a standard case comes along, you feel grateful, then sprint over to the next spinning plate threatening to fall to the floor.

But for the next visit for his injections, which were usually repeated about twice a year, Prince was accompanied by his dad, Craig. Craig was a big guy with tattoos on his arm and the sort of handshake that always screams military man to me.

I brought him up to speed on how Prince's treatment had progressed to date and we chatted a bit about what was going on in his life because he was back for treatment sooner than I had expected him. I asked him if there was anything that Prince might have been doing recently to exacerbate his underlying condition.

'Ah, he's retired now, but he must have jarred his elbow on top of the chronic effects of his job,' he replied.

'Which is?'

It was then that I found out Prince had been a dog who jumped out of planes. At first, I thought I'd misheard. But it turned out Craig was his handler in the Parachute Regiment. The two of them would jump out of a plane strapped together; Prince would be wearing ear speakers and a camera and would be involved in both search and attack missions on the ground. He was an essential part of the ground troops and had been involved in more than twenty missions. As I watched Prince smiling his chops off as his dad scratched his head, I was impressed, as I often am, by how much joint pain Labradors will put up with without complaining, but I was also struck by just how much a dog has to trust you to let themselves be strapped to you and jump out of a plane.

There is a long history of dogs and war. It's not for nothing that Shakespeare famously refers to 'the dogs of war' in *Julius Caesar*. He's drawing on a tradition that stretches back to the Egyptians, Greeks and Romans. Attila the Hun used huge war dogs in his campaigns. During the First World War, dogs were a key part of the trenches. They would pull machine guns or supplies. They would carry messages through gunfire, where their amazing reflexes would allow them to dodge bullets humans could not. They would go out into no-man's land and find the wounded. Sometimes they would even have first-aid packs strapped to them, so they were literally the first responders of the war. They would stand guard, listening through the darkness for sounds no human could hear. They would venture out, looking for explosives and tracking missing soldiers. They were also essential in dealing with the rats and other pests in the trenches. During the First World War alone, it is estimated that there were as many as 20,000 dogs trained for front-line duties.

One group of American soldiers became so attached to Stubby, the Bull-Boston Terrier who wandered over to watch them training, that they smuggled him with them to the Western Front. There he followed them into the trenches, was involved in seventeen battles and was injured in the leg by a grenade and endured multiple gas attacks.

Stubby had his own uniform. Afterwards, he was taken back to the US, where he took part in parades and would meet three presidents.

Dogs' involvement in warfare continued in the Second World War. When cities in Britain were regularly bombed, it was dogs who found the survivors, running through the rubble and barking until every last person was found. Just as important as any other role, they were also on the battle-field building morale and offering comfort to soldiers so far from home.

Craig told me about Brian the Alsatian, who had joined the Parachute Regiment in 1943, and by June 1944 was parachuting into Normandy. In 1947 he received the PDSA Dicking Medal, which is the animal equivalent of the Victoria Cross for humans, the highest possible decoration for bravery.

Hero dogs have won similar awards in every major conflict for the last hundred years. Whenever the horror of war is there, dogs are there, alongside us, trusting us to do the right thing, as we trust them in return, sometimes with our actual lives.

But it was one thing knowing all this, and quite another sitting in my consulting room actually looking at a hero. Craig told me that Prince was a very special dog. He really enjoyed the jumps. He swore that sometimes, when the parachute fired and they were up there with the canopy above, he could feel Prince's tail wagging furiously.

Once on the ground, they were utterly synchronised. Prince was his eyes and ears, responding instantly to commands given via his ear speaker and trained to let him know if he heard or smelled anything. Craig and his regiment could see the terrain ahead, and even behind walls and doors in buildings, because Prince ran in first with his headcam on. Craig said that Prince had saved lives more times than he could count and now his job was to make Prince's life as comfortable as it could be. The aim wasn't to get him jumping out of a plane any time soon, but rather to make sure that he could fully enjoy his extremely well-deserved retirement. We had frozen cells from his own fat and could thaw them out in our regenerative medicine facility, multiplying them into tens of millions of anti-inflammatory stem cells for injection into his joints whenever the pain flared.

Craig told me that we had to get Prince better because his brother Charlie missed going for long walks with him. 'Does Charlie jump out of planes too?' I asked, half in jest.

'Ah no,' said Craig. 'His job's much more exciting.' I caught his eye to check if he was joking. He wasn't. 'Charlie is a hydrocarbon dog,' said Craig. My blank look clearly showed I had no idea what that meant.

'Charlie goes into fires,' said Craig.

Over the next ten minutes, he told me the remarkable story of what Charlie's vocation was. He had been trained to sniff out hydrocarbons, which are flammable liquids that fuel the origin of fires. But through our conversation, it became apparent that he was an expert at finding survivors in fires too. Equipped with a high-visibility harness and special boots to protect his feet, he would be sent in once the blaze was out to find survivors. In fact, he had been sent into the aftermath of the Grenfell Tower fire in London. Both of us stopped talking for a moment at the thought of what the humans had been through in that tragedy.

Craig also told me how more and more dogs were being used to gather evidence after a fire because their sense of smell was more precise than any equipment. They would be able to tell if any sort of accelerant had been used, which might suggest the fire was started deliberately. They could then search an arson suspect's house and find evidence of that same substance.

Craig said that the funniest thing was that because of Charlie's intense training to find survivors, he responded really well to people who were full of life in everyday situations as well. In Charlie's head he had found a 'survivor' and would be waiting for his customary reward. But sometimes, Charlie would meet someone who didn't give him 'alive vibes' and he would utterly ignore them. Craig joked that this should be a lucrative sideline for Charlie. If he didn't think you were alive, you clearly needed to make some changes in your life. I always trust a dog's instinct in these matters of life or death!

I said goodbye to Prince and Craig until the next check-up. Later that night as I sat in my office, writing the medical reports required for every patient I see, I thought about the remarkable acts of bravery and trust between dogs and their humans that I have been lucky enough to encounter throughout my life.

I have operated on innumerable service dogs like Prince and Charlie over the years. There was Wayne, the airport sniffer dog who came to see me after a cruciate ligament repair of his stifle (a dog's knee) had gone badly wrong. He could no longer climb over boxes and crates of luggage sniffing out drugs. We used an implant I developed called a FROG plate – Fitz Rotation Osteotomy Guide – to repair the failed surgery and within three months he was bouncing around like a frog. He later broke a record for the most cocaine found at his airport. At any one time there are thousands of dogs sniffing out danger and we place our trust in them to keep us all safe.

Then there was Maximillian the police dog, Max for short, who took a bullet for his dad during a botched burglary. He jumped in front of his dad as the gun discharged, saving his human's life and risking his own. Thankfully, after retrieval of the bullet from his abdomen, stitching up his punctured intestines and several nights with his life in the balance, Max survived.

I once had the honour of treating Poncho, a Newfoundland affected by bad arthritis of both hip joints due to dysplasia, like Prince. He was a trained sea-rescue dog, who kept people afloat with his vice-like jaws clamped on their clothing in choppy seas and who was capable of pulling a boat full of people to safety with his massive limbs, paws and physical strength. I was thrilled that after I had performed double total hip replacements, he pulled eleven people in a boat to safety. With his lifeboat crew he had attended to a yacht foundering in a ferocious gale. Eleven people had entered the water in lifejackets but were in a position that meant the boat couldn't get to them safely.

Into the water went Poncho, swimming over to them, dragging them all individually towards his trainer in the rescue dinghy, who hauled them aboard. But even then, his work wasn't done. He pulled the rescue dinghy with all twelve people in it away from the foundering yacht. Poncho was one of the hairiest dogs I have ever encountered. For him to be pulling the weight of all that water-soaked hair on top of the humans was an astonishing feat of strength, bravery and trust.

I have also performed double hip replacements on a Border Collie called Prudence, who went on to achieve the top grade, seven, in agility championships. To see her rocket up the A–frame, bullet through the tunnel and gyrate through the weave poles with even greater alacrity after her surgery than before was truly awe-inspiring. To put this in human context, here was an Olympic competitor winning double gold medals in sprinting and gymnastics with two metal and plastic hip joints. I had been most honoured that her mum had trusted me to perform the procedures and that their mutual trust thereafter propelled them to the highest level of achievement.

Dogs have such a deep desire to help and to please us. To find things like missing people, to chase things like would-be attackers, and for us to tell them what we need, whether it's something life-saving or the enjoyment that both dog and handler get from an agility course. For them to make us happy is often their greatest joy and for us to make them happy is the least we can do in return. What we need can be all different kinds of things, and sometimes we don't even know what we need until a dog gives it to us and saves us anyway.

I remember Nigel the German Shepherd who dragged his dad from a rain-swollen river, where he had fallen when fishing. He was a retired rock star, weakened by Alzheimer's, and Nigel stayed with him all night as he lay freezing on the bank of the river. At dawn Nigel ran and got help. He saved his human's life. In the ambulance, Nigel wouldn't let him out of his sight. This might sound like an episode of *Lassie* or *The Famous Five* that I used to watch on our old TV when I was a kid, but it happens every day. The bravery of our canine friends is born of loyalty and unshakable trust. If we always do the right thing for them, they do this and more for us too.

It isn't just in dramatic ways that our trust in dogs can save our lives. I once mended two broken legs of Flower, a Border Collie who was a doggie-dancing champion with her human. She had been badly injured by running full pelt after a training toy and falling off a steep ledge. Flower and her mum, Abigail, both wore tutus when performing and were in tune with each other pretty much every moment of the day and night. They went everywhere together, always dressed in the brightest colours possible, usually with matching sparkly jewellery and collar accessories. They socialised together, ate together, slept together and danced together, inseparable in the waltz of life. I was particularly chuffed that dancing and tutu-wearing were still firmly on the agenda after Flower's career was almost cut short by the accident, and that they continued to win competitions.

In dancing, agility and obedience training, I have seen an intelligent, respectful, kind and grateful symphony of dog and human that is nigh-on impossible to explain if you haven't experienced it. This indelible trust between dog and human lifts each to be the best versions of themselves, both physically and emotionally. These dogs all have a vocation that lifts them up with joy. Before she adopted Flower and, on the advice of a friend, took up dance classes to use up some of Flower's energy, Abigail had been unable to get out of bed, crushed by a depression so heavy she thought she would never get out from under it. She told me that Flower had saved her life, as sure as if she'd taken a bullet for her. Some heroes wear tutus.

If we were to add up how many people dogs have saved through the simplest acts of trust, by giving humans hope, giving them someone to look after, giving them a routine, getting them out of the house, it would be an enormous number. They are our everyday heroes and we should be incredibly thankful for them.

The reason I don't trust anyone who doesn't like dogs is that I have seen this love bring about extraordinary trans-formations for both dogs and their humans, time and again throughout my life. For me, if someone doesn't like dogs wilfully, it means their capacity to follow the evidence of their own eyes is lacking. Not liking dogs, to me, is like someone saying they don't trust doctors, nurses, the police, the coastguard, mountain rescue and their family, all rolled into one. If you're that bad a judge of character, I'm afraid we're never going to see eye to eye.

I was thrilled to see Prince at his next check-up. Through the window of my reception area, I saw him jump out of the back of Craig's car into the yard with a spring in his step and I knew instantly that the treatment had worked and he was doing well. And then I watched as two dogs followed him out of the car and Craig led all three of them in to greet me.

One was Charlie, who had come to thank me for giving him his pal back in the doggie playground of life, but I was greeted as well by another dear friend of theirs who was also a most deserving member of the club of dogs that I would trust more than any human. She was a gorgeous yellow Labrador called Petal. Catching on quick, this time I asked what amazing job Petal did.

'She's a breathing specialist!' Craig answered delightedly.

'Er, what's that exactly?' I asked, expecting that she must have some way of breathing that calms anxious people or some such. But no. It turned out that Craig had trained her to detect Transient Ischaemic Attacks (TIAs). Also known as mini strokes, they are caused by a brief blockage of blood flow to the brain, usually by a temporarily trapped blood clot or fatty plaque. The symptoms only last for a short period and it's important that they are detected in time because people can lose control of a limb, have slurred speech or blurred vision or dizziness and can fall over and badly hurt themselves. Plus, TIAs are often precursors to full-blown strokes.

But what was really interesting about the bond of trust that Petal needed to have with her dad was that he himself was the actual patient. He had suffered three TIAs over as many years, and on each occasion, Petal detected these by the change in his breathing, because she was an expert in such things. On one occasion he fell over and on the other two he lay down. Each time, Petal pushed her muzzle under his head to roll it over so there was no chance of him choking and she barked loudly until someone came.

'I trusted Prince with my life in the army,' said Craig, 'and I trust Petal with my life every day I'm lucky enough to share my life with her.'

And then he added, 'But there's only one problem!'

'What's that?' I innocently asked.

'Well, Teresa can't do yoga in the house any more because if she lies on the mat and even begins to change her breathing pattern, Petal is immediately snouting her face and barking like a maniac.'

Craig and I laughed loudly together and all three dogs looked up at us and barked their laughter too. Craig is the best that humanity has to offer. I would trust him with my life, just as he has trusted Prince and Petal with his own. But I will never trust anyone who doesn't like dogs.

13

We are all the same

Guy the Beagle and Meghan

Guy is an extraordinary dog. And luckily, he found an extraordinary family. But it could have been very different. He was rescued from a kill shelter in Kentucky. This kind of animal shelter is the norm in most cities across America and it has to exist because there has to be a place where people can take stray and abandoned animals. For this reason, often there are no restrictions, health standards, age limitations or behavioural requirements and such shelters are often forced to euthanise animals even if they are healthy, not because they want to, but just because nobody has adopted them and they have to make room for other animals. As a result, it can be disheartening to work there, and these shelters not only need people to adopt more dogs and cats, but are often also constantly in search of more volunteers and resources.

Guy had been found in some woods where he was abandoned. He was taken into the shelter and given ten days before he would be put to sleep. His eventual mum,

Meghan, saw him online and found that a Canadian rescue organisation was bringing him and a few other dogs to a rescue centre in a town near Toronto where she lived. He seemed to call out to her from her computer screen with his deeply kind molten brown eyes. His nails were curled into his paws, he was very frail and ten pounds under weight, he was scared and he had never been in a house before. She fell instantly in love and adopted him because of this rather than in spite of this.

Guy is a Beagle, and not only did Meghan fall headlong into the deep pools of his eyes, when she first met him they immediately bonded for life. The long white smiling whiskers on his muzzle and big fawn-coloured floppy ears. His flowing beard of wispy white rivulets of the softest fur radiated his soft gentle nature out into the world. A lightning strike of white blazed across his snout, between his eyes and over his muzzle like a magical scarf from which his soft snuggly black nose welcomed one and all with a big 'sniff, sniff, sniff' so he could get the measure of you straight away.

His name, Guy, came because . . . he didn't have a name. At the shelter he was so weak, they simply referred to him as 'the little guy', so that's what Meghan named him. She said that with one look into his eyes, you could immediately know what he was thinking, and in that moment, he was your 'sweet guy', your 'cheeky guy', your 'clever guy', but forever and always 'her Guy' . . . and she was most certainly his human.

He'd had a very rough ride until he met Meghan, but I

have a huge soft spot for Beagles for another reason too. As I've mentioned, the central goal of my life is to give animals a fair deal in medicine, which means refining and replacing the use of animals in medical experiments, learning from naturally occurring diseases in animals and humans side by side and making new drugs available for animals at the same time as they become available for humans. After all, diseases such as many types of cancer and arthritis are nigh-on identical in animals and humans. This is the philosophy of One Medicine. Because Beagles are small and gentle, they're the breed of dog that gets used most often as the subject of experiments. Official figures reveal that in 2022, 4,014 legal regulated experiments were carried out on Beagles in Britain. The US Department of Agriculture estimates that between fifty and sixty thousand Beagles are bred in the United States for use in research testing and experimentation each year. All humans want safe drugs and implants of course, but I have always believed that the need for experiments carried out on dogs and other animals to benefit humans alone can be refined, reduced and indeed replaced if we invest in the study of naturally occurring diseases and in the new era of alternatives such as cell-based assays, organ chips, computer models and other technologies.

I met Meghan on a FaceTime call. So many people had told her that Guy wouldn't be able to walk again and she would have to put him to sleep, that she was shaking with fear and almost immediately near tears. She was utterly terrified and, by the end of the conversation, she was crying from fear mixed with some relief, I think, because as far as I could see, though his injuries were really bad, they were likely fixable. I find it genuinely extraordinary when I hear such things, which I often do, because for me, where there's a blood and a nerve supply, there is nearly always hope. Without wishing to sound either self-indulgent or egotistical, since I am only too aware that biology will always humble me, and I have long since grown distant from my surgical ego, I genuinely thought that it was probably relatively straightforward to fix him.

I had already seen Guy's X-ray pictures and instantly knew that his injuries were way more serious than had initially been suspected. In the recent days before our call, this had become abundantly apparent. I also sensed that the profound anxiety and apprehension that Meghan felt about Guy was heaped on top of all of the changes and challenges she faced in her personal life too. She welled up as I explained that, in my opinion, he likely had a 'jump-down' injury. I've seen this more than a hundred times in my career and often there are very limited signs on standard X-ray pictures. In Guy's case there was just some swelling and a chipped bone. But he couldn't stand on his front legs at all, so it was super-clear that the radiographs weren't revealing the full picture.

Meghan was an actress, and since she'd rescued Guy, he'd been her constant companion, his love an immutable anchor amid the choppy seas of endless hours on set filming, early mornings and late evenings. Every night the two of them cuddled next to each other, each an oasis of comfort and peace for the other. But one day, while she was working, Guy was spooked by something and escaped from his mortified walker. An immediate search was launched through the streets, alleys and parks of Toronto. Meghan stayed up all night looking for him, through a severe thunderstorm, as did several of her friends. They spread out from where he was last seen, and after many tears shed and many miles trodden, finally Meghan found him, huddled, freezing and terrified, at the edge of a lakeshore, unable to run any further.

She picked him up and took him straight to the emergency vet. Guy was in deep shock, very weak, and was put on a drip immediately. Painkillers were given too since it was clear that he had damaged both front legs badly, but how badly wasn't immediately apparent. Meghan was crying her eyes out. Her local vet reached out to me as Meghan had been due to fly to the UK imminently. And so, I found myself on a call to her. Of course, I knew who she was. The press had been immediately obsessed and you couldn't help but know who her boyfriend was. But none of that actually mattered amid the crisis we would need to manage.

I generally see this injury when a dog is running full pelt and doesn't notice a sharp drop of some kind coming up. It may be a wall or sharp edge hidden in a jungle of concrete, or a cliff edge obscured by vegetation, or a retaining wall covered in sand on a long beach. This all seemed to make sense when Meghan explained the circumstances in which she found poor Guy, miles from where he had been lost, across a highway, through busy city streets of construction and scaffolding. I explained that I thought it was likely that he had jumped down from a height, landing with huge force on his front legs, which had likely exploded the ligaments holding his wrists (carpi) together. It's called a hyper-extension injury.

Her primary care vet had done their very best and had placed Guy's forearms and wrists in splints. Soon Guy was on a flight to London and was quickly transported to my practice. Some people think there is some sort of VIP service at my practice. There isn't. Every dog is a VIP in my practice and my colleagues and I treat every one as if they were a member of our own families. Every shared heartbeat is precious, whoever you are. Every animal crisis matters an equal amount because in that moment, for everyone I see, it's the only thing that matters.

I feel that Guy and I formed an instant bond of mutual respect. He would recognise my voice a mile away forever more. Some dogs are initially scared and I do my very best to let them have their space, let them discover me before I impose myself on them, touch them in safe places rather than appearing domineering, and do everything in my power to build some trust. I think Guy also recognised my scent, as he tucked his nose tightly in my armpit. And then of course I have to go and ruin it all by giving injections, performing horrendous procedures and putting a plastic lampshade on their poor heads. It's not easy being me!

But Guy understood I meant well from the get-go, and so did his mum and dad. We all sat on the floor and held the poor little fella. Meghan cried, Harry comforted her and I held paws and hands. That's how it always goes, because we're all the same.

It isn't until one takes what are known as 'stressed' radio-graphs that one can really see what's happening with hyper-extension injuries. I sedated Guy, pushed his front paws into full extension and took X-ray pictures. As I suspected, the swelling and small bone fragments were the tip of the iceberg. Guy had indeed ruptured many of the ligaments of his wrists, was in significant pain, and would never walk again without very invasive surgery.

Most of the time, one cannot simply reconstruct ligaments and what is known as palmar fibrocartilage, which keeps a dog's wrists very pliable and resilient. They can take huge load when withstanding the full force of jumping impact for the front legs, but they can't take the force of plummeting down a cliff-face or accidentally running off the side of a building, and I would need to intervene as soon as possible. The solution would involve fusing all of the bones of both wrist joints solid: two pancarpal arthrodeses. I would grind away all of the cartilage from the articular surfaces of the bottom of the radius and ulna bones, the seven carpal bones and the bases of all the metacarpal bones, graft them with marrow bone and apply plates and screws to bridge the entirety, as I explained earlier when telling Lucia's story. That means that I would take the joint surfaces off the forearm, wrist and palm bones and fuse them solid with plates. I would perform this procedure first on one limb and then the other a couple of weeks later.

As Meghan and Harry gave Guy a hug and gave me a hug and left, I felt their heart-rending pain quite deeply. Here was a man and a woman who fell in love like any other man or woman, but Guy, who was very much an integral part of their relationship, was now in life-threatening danger. I had a deep inner sense that as their love for each other grew, they had entrusted me with the fulcrum of this love. The love of a dog brings people together like no other. When a dog's life is in danger, that profound love screams inside the heads of those who hear it: 'This is your life right now. Wake up and smell the coffee because it isn't gonna last forever and this is all you've got. Love and be loved, be kind and encourage understanding always, pull together rather than pull apart, because this could all be over tomorrow . . . or even today.'

I have learned from the animals I treat to avoid precon-ceptions and also to take people as I find them rather than what anyone else says or thinks. A dog sees it as it really is rather than how human minds may warp perceptions.

In my consulting room, it doesn't matter who you are; we'll try to help your best friend, whatever it takes, as long as it's the right thing to do, and you're fully informed and on board for the journey. I do not take that responsibility lightly. I carry that burden of caring desperately into the operating theatre, knowing how high the stakes are. But then, to do my job, while I don't switch off the caring, I have found a place inside me where I can compartmentalise these thoughts. I visualise a swirling orb in my chest, where I park all unhelpful emotions. Inside the orb, all of my fears and the fears and pain of the patient's family are stored, in the hope that they will radiate into the world as light once my job is done. If you spent your whole time as a pilot only thinking about the fact you had 500 people's lives in your hands, you wouldn't be able to actually fly the plane. I have to land my plane with my passenger in better shape than they were when they took off.

Within hours, Guy was anaesthetised and on his back with me drilling a hole into the top of his humerus bone just beneath the shoulder joint, into which I repeatedly plunged a sharp-edged metal spoon, called a curette, gouging against the inside cortex of the bone as if scooping an egg from its shell. Soon I had enough bone marrow graft to fill a small bowl. Then we flipped him over into what we lovingly call the 'Superman' position, in which he was sat on his chest, the arm to be operated outstretched, and the other one by his side, his head held up on a sand-filled sterile bag.

I burred the joint cartilage away, packed graft into all the gaps, bridged all of it from forearm to toes with two plates and screws, bandaged the leg and, bish-bash-bosh, he was soon awake being cuddled by a ward nurse. I called Meghan and Harry and they were profoundly grateful.

But, of course, there was a long journey of rest, physiotherapy, hydrotherapy and rehabilitation ahead. And after a couple of weeks, all of us had to go through the exact same surgery on Guy's other front leg – especially poor Guy himself. There are risks intrinsic to every surgical procedure I perform and only biology itself is my master. Infection, poor healing, swelling, blood vessel and nerve impairment, skin damage, fracture and implant failure are all risks of the procedures I performed on Guy – and in fact most procedures that I perform on limbs. I hold in my hands the scales of risk versus benefit every day of my life alongside blade, scissors, forceps, drill and hammer. And it is on the balance of this judgement that life or limb is lost or saved.

Thankfully my judgement was sound and Guy made slow and steady improvement. He was incredibly brave and good-natured throughout his journey of surgery and recovery. He made the job of looking after him less of a job and more of a joy. I sat with him often and he appeared to love the smell of my armpit throughout, nuzzling tightly against his human Irish cushion. We fell in love, as Meghan and Harry did. He delighted in my night-time visits, wagged his tail furiously at the sound of my voice and rejoiced in licking my face, no matter how sweaty I was after a long day in the operating theatre – in fact, the sweatier the better.

Guy stayed at my practice for almost three months during his recovery. Because Meghan and Harry had announced their engagement during this time, the press scrutiny was intense and they could only come to visit him under cover of darkness. Luckily, I often sleep in my office, and usually I do what I do until after midnight anyway, so this was no problem. We had a wonderful system in place. It was an hour's drive each way for Meghan and Harry. I'd get a text, a car would arrive, I'd open the back door, my two friends would come in, we'd make tea and then we'd sit on the floor in my consulting room snuggling Guy on a rug and having our 'fireside chats'.

I'd like to think that these evenings of trust, openness

and integrity, all revolving around the beacon of hope that was 'Professor Guy' (as I called him), enriched all of our lives as I was trying to enrich his. I got to know two deeply committed dog parents, whose love for Guy and for each other had no bounds. I take people as I find them, and so does the dog they are lucky enough to share that love with. I learned much about human nature and the difference between dogs and humans through our friendship, which has stood the test of time.

Sometimes Harry was busy, but Meghan came religiously as often as she could to hold Guy and 'will' him to wellness again. In fact, on 13 December I celebrated my birthday with Meghan and Guy and let him eat cake. That was a glorious day of rejoicing in his recovery.

Over the years, I've seen what the press say about Guy's humans. But here's a life rule that I live by: pay less attention to what people say about people and more to what their dog says about them.

Dogs are without exception great judges of character, I believe. They don't care about the small stuff. They know who you are inside. They like you or they don't and they don't care what you think about that. It doesn't matter what your status is, dogs treat us all the same. They care not if we are a prince or a pauper, what colour or creed or gender identity we are. They care about the big stuff. Kindness, care, nurture and generosity. They don't judge you. They don't want to change you. Sometimes we refer to this love as unconditional. Admittedly, they do expect you to feed them and pick up their poo, but that's a fair deal. I can honestly say that I have had abundantly more love back from all of the dogs that I have had the honour of treating than the love I willingly gave to them.

Dogs know who you really are. If you treat a dog with selfishness or cruelty, or if you are unkind, it will be incredibly difficult to regain their trust. But if they do trust you, they will do so forever unless you badly mess it up. There's a reason why the word loyalty so often comes up in relation to the dogs in our lives. They don't listen to what other people say about you. And perhaps that's one of the greatest things we can learn from them. Humans have evolved to care about other people's opinions; of course, it made sense when we lived in small communities. Some people even think speech came from the urge to tell others stories about other people and experiences. Perhaps we should be called *Homo gossipiens*? It's human nature to judge each other. There's likely nobody you or I know that we don't have an 'opinion' about, including ourselves. But the problem is that this bit of our brain is set off by the media. What was once a useful evolutionary urge is in danger of becoming a toxic element of society. They may try to recreate the sorts of stories that scratch that itch within us – clickbait – because it makes money. And if they can't find real stories, they might just take a tiny kernel of something that did actually happen and make up the rest, or make it all up entirely.

It's human nature – but not a dog's nature. To a dog, we are all the same, except of course they might give some of us special treatment – especially when it comes to the senses most important to them. Guy didn't care who I was, other than the fact that I sometimes smelled of antiseptic, sometimes of sweat and always of love. Guy has fondly remembered both my voice and my smell despite his arduous journey. Thereafter he always greeted me with a joyous wag of his tail and an eager lick of my face as I bent down to say hello. Dogs have no idea what your social status is, but one thing they mostly seem to remember is my accent. I've heard from numerous past clients that whenever my show comes on the television, tails start to wag and they go looking for me behind the sofa or just watch the screen intently. I am very grateful that folks generally don't report dogs running and hiding away from the man with the syringe and the scalpel.

I remember vividly a microcosm of the ridiculous world we live in when I visited Meghan and Harry at their house in the countryside several months later. Two helicopters with paparazzi buzzed overhead like unwelcome lascivious locusts, while we sat on the grass admiring a brass sculpture of Guy that a wonderful artist called Beth Cullen-Kerridge had made. It was a gift I gave them for their wedding. I had brought identical plates to those bridging Guy's wrists to Beth's workshop and we embedded them inside the sculpture, which had an uncanny likeness to Guy. As we revelled in the joy of life and love we embraced in the garden that sunny afternoon, and as Guy ran around pain-free with his friend, a Labrador called Pula, the nonsense judgement and fabrication of the outside world sought to intrude on what was real and impose what was made up.

Meghan thanked me again for saving Guy and giving him a great quality of life. She had her Guy, now her 'bionic guy' thanks to the metal plates I put in his legs, and he forever had his Meghan. A dog is a sanctuary of calm in any storm, a comfort blanket to wrap around you and a refuge for your tears. A dog doesn't just bring joy when one comes home; a dog actually makes a home, where one can be oneself without judgement and with unconditional love.

To Guy and to me, Meghan and Harry are two people who love each other, their dogs and their children very much and would do whatever it took to protect them. Since then they have adopted another rescue Beagle called Mia, who came from a drug-testing facility. And so, it comes full circle. In a dog's mind – 'You put out love, you get back love.' So, why can't it be that way for us humans too? If only dogs could teach their old humans new tricks!

Meghan has since explained to me, 'You were the only one who gave me hope and gave him life. Which in many ways gave me life. Guy has been my anchor in my life before, during and after all of it. All of everything.' That's because he was and is the epicentre of everything that matters – love, hope, joy, truth and integrity. She said very touchingly, 'You healed my dog. You healed my heart.' It was a privilege, as it is for every family that I am lucky enough to serve.

I am blessed to witness three constants in my life. First, dogs always tell the truth and they never lie. Well, even if they do lie because they've stolen a sausage from the bin, they pretty much tell you with their eyes straight away. Second, as I've mentioned, dogs never have an opinion about you if they've never met you. In my experience, they generally make up their own minds about you within a minute or so of your first meeting and it's difficult to change their perspective thereafter. However, they do allow an old human to learn new tricks if you work hard to change and earn their respect. Forgiveness is an admirable trait. And third, as I've also explained, dogs don't care who you are or where you come from. We are all the same. To the dog who loves you, you are always Number One. Guy was a reminder of that I will never forget.

Next time you read an article encouraging you to dislike or to judge someone you've never met, stop for a moment and think about why that might be. Be more like Guy!

14

He knows me better than I know me

Bobby the Springer Spaniel and Finley

Finley's little knuckles were white as he clutched hold of Bobby's brown and white fur.

'Finley, love, you need to let go.' His mum's voice was soft. He shook his head fiercely, blinking back tears. His sobs began to turn to trembling, then tremors and then a low rumbling grew within him like far-away thunder. Finley and Bobby were lying on the floor of my consulting room on the blood-stained blanket with which they'd carried Bobby from the car. He was the most adorable three-year-old liver roan Springer Spaniel you could ever imagine. Luxurious brown floppy ears that sprung from the side of his head with rivulets of russet fur cascading down the sides of his face. He had the most extraordinary lion's mane under his chin, fluffed out proudly and tailing off in bearded tufts towards his elbows and forearms.

Finley's mum, Steph, told me through the journey which was to follow that they'd first noticed differences in him at nursery. Tiny differences. He didn't play with the other kids, but played his own games next to them. He would get upset if another child touched him. He didn't like any change to his routine and was extremely sensitive to noise and the textures of his clothing. At first, they'd dismissed it. Kids learn at different speeds after all. Some people are shy. But when he started school, his parents were encouraged to have Finley assessed and he received a diagnosis of Autistic Spectrum Disorder. Growing up as I did in rural Ireland in the '70s, there wasn't much understanding of this sort of thing. But I recognised so much of what she described. I had always found it hard to talk to the other children. I wasn't interested in the stuff they were interested in but I was *really* interested in the things I was. I had hated any clothes with labels and rough seams and I found loud noises physically oppressive, so I wore some old blue plastic ear defenders that a tractor driver on our farm had allowed me to have.

As I looked down at Finley then, I didn't know any of that. I just saw an eleven-year-old boy and the love of his life. Finley's mum popped ear defenders on him and stroked his hand gently, shushing him. 'Bobby will be OK, darling . . . he'll be OK . . . the vet will take good care of him . . . and he will be home soon.' Gradually he began to unclench his fists.

Finley and Bobby had been in the garden playing fetch, which was their favourite thing to do in the whole wide world. He would throw the old tennis ball with all his might and Bobby would race after it, a blur of joy and a lightning strike of hair. Both of them especially liked it when he had to rough and tumble with a bush or a hedge to retrieve the ball. It all just added to the adventure and the excitement. They were both enthralled and consumed by the endless repetition. The tennis ball was worse for wear with a million teeth-marks. But this time, Finley had thrown the ball a little too far and too fast and under the hedge it went. Bobby sprinted to the edge of the fence, nuzzling his nose as deep into it as possible, but no ball to be had. He pawed the ground with his massive hairy bear-paws, but still no ball to be had. Finley bent down and peered through the under-growth and the mesh wire fence that his dad, Darby, had put around the garden to protect them both. There it was. Out on the street. The mesh didn't quite go to ground level.

Without thinking and ignoring all of his dad's warnings to the contrary, Finley flicked open the side gate in the hedge. The ball was no more than a few feet away, but Bobby couldn't resist, and before Finley could react, Bobby was through the gate, desperate to get his ball. Out he flew, skidding onto the ball with ferocious speed and sliding off the path and into the road. Just as a car came. Finley's mum heard the scream and came running to find Finley with his face buried in Bobby's blood-spattered fur. Normally that was his safe place, where he went to calm down when he was in 'the zone'.

Now, as Steph unfurled Finley's arms from around Bobby's neck and, with Darby, almost had to lift him from my consulting room into the reception area, he began to kick and punch the air and from deep within him came a guttural wail that I shall never forget. I could imagine the mixture of guilt and sadness and anger he was going through.

It was one of the most deeply traumatic preludes to 'what-happens-after-the-consulting-room' that I have ever witnessed. It was all I could do to hold myself together, as I held Bobby's head and as Darby came back into the room.

'I'm so sorry,' he began.

'Don't worry about it. It's OK. Is there anything I can do for Finley?' I proffered.

'No, but thanks,' said Darby. 'Can you save Bobby?'

'I don't know,' I said.

I had seen the X-ray pictures that their local vet had taken, but I knew that was just the tip of the iceberg. The vet had told me that one hind foot was ripped off completely and the other hind foot was 'at a funny angle' with bones sticking out through the skin. I also knew that it wouldn't be right for Bobby to stay alive with no hind legs, even though I'm well aware that some such dogs do stay alive on trollies. He was only three years old and Steph and Darby had made it quite clear that if I couldn't save both hind legs I should put him to sleep, no matter how traumatic that might be for Finley. I gave Darby a hug, and told him I'd do my very best and that I'd call them later.

But I kept thinking of Finley and the look in his eyes. Of what Bobby clearly meant to him. I have seen time and time again how important dogs are to non-neurotypical children. The soothing act of stroking a dog can bring them back from meltdowns. The magic powers of a dog's comforting weight, of feeling the texture of their fur and receiving their licks of love. They offer a sense of consistency in a world that can often feel chaotic and difficult to understand. Dogs love routine.

They want to eat and walk at the same time. They want to play the same familiar games. And they give back love consistently. Focusing on a canine friend can mean that children who find it hard to go outside can leave the house, get exercise and release all the chemicals that help with regulating their mood. Children can talk to the dogs in their life in a way they often can't to the humans in their life. Dogs can be a bridge to an interest in the world. They can also help develop a sense of empathy. They make the world feel like a less scary, lonely place.

But Bobby was in a bad way. The family had already been to both their primary care vet and a specialist referral centre, but alas, the potential solution didn't exist elsewhere . . . yet. I sincerely hope the solution will exist in many places in the future. Because it is into this very pursuit that I have channelled my own obsession, in getting knowledge and adding to knowledge with innovation and scientific papers and lectures, so that dogs and cats are in a better world than they were when I began my journey to save as many of their lives as possible. I have always been happiest when I immerse myself in something. It began in childhood, when I sought refuge from the darkness and pain that came from humans and became obsessed with helping animals. So many of the things that were difficult when I was a child – obsessively checking ten times if a door is closed and locked, for example – are a benefit in my professional life. There's a kind of superpower that I have been gifted, as I obsessively review every detail of an MRI or CT scan or can automatically feel the length or positioning of a screw in a bone as if I have X-ray vision. I knew I would need every morsel of my experience to help Bobby, as I called a nurse and an intern and we gently lifted him onto a table and wheeled him into the preparation room. In the hours that followed, as I elucidated the full extent of Bobby's injuries, I was deeply troubled by his plight.

As I get scrubbed, gowned and gloved, I experience a range of emotions, but one of them is relief. In my operating theatre, surrounded by the comforting glint of surgical instruments, the routine of an operation, the knowledge that with anatomy I know where most things are most of the time, I embrace the rules that often elude me in other parts of my life. As I take the scalpel in my hand, there is a calm that comes over me. *This. This I can do.*

Throughout my life, my tendency to deeply internalise pain and churn it in the washer that can never clean anything in my head has found refuge in the company of the animals I have been blessed to take care of. My patients have saved me from deep-seated feelings of inadequacy, worthlessness, anxiety and frustration. There is a quiet promise that I have made to every animal I operate on. That I will do for you what I would do for any of the animals who have saved my life. This is a reassuring and profound comfort for me.

And now my job was to save Bobby's life.

When first assessing a severe RTA, as we call it – a Road Traffic Accident – one has to look for everything and miss nothing. This could be the difference between life and death for our patient. A full clinical examination revealed brutal truths. Bobby's left hind foot below his ankle (the hock) was hanging off by sinews – a couple of tendons and a bit of skin. The blood and nerve supply were pulverised, the toes were all ripped off, the arch of the foot (the metatarsus) was crushed in more than twenty pieces. Grit from the road, full of bacteria, was ground into the macerated tissue and it looked absolutely awful. And so, when I took off the bandage that the local vet had put on there, it was no wonder that all opinions offered so far were grim.

I took the bandage off the opposite hind limb and it was clear that there was both a shearing and degloving injury. Bobby's right ankle had been dragged along the road by the tyre of the car screeching to a halt, which ripped off all skin, ligaments and tendons, and the bottom part of the shin bone and the ankle bones, the tibia and tarsal bones, were sheared off as if a cheese-grater had been repeatedly rubbed against them. And then it was also obvious that there was a dislocated left hip joint and maybe a fractured left pelvis as well since even just gentle movement under sedation revealed the crepitus, the grating sensation that one perceives when one feels such an injury. It was a truly nightmarish collection of injuries.

The only good news was that there did not seem to be any fractures of the spine. Bobby could still feel his hind limbs – well, at least down as far as his left ankle. Also, there didn't seem to be any trauma to his head, which was good on any level, not least that his head and Finley's head were usually entwined. One funny little thing in the midst of all of the tragedy was that Steph had said to me before she left that I must get the ward teams to comb Bobby's ears regularly. Apparently, this was one sure way to get Bobby to fall in love with you, but also he was prone to ear infections if his glorious ear hair became matted.

But we had big problems. In taking the clinical history, which as I've said is called a signalment in medical speak, Darby had mentioned in passing that they had noticed that Bobby had been limping on one of his front legs for a few weeks before the awful accident. Sure enough, when I performed a CT scan of his front legs, I could see he had a genetically mediated problem affecting both elbows, which is very common in his breed and which I suspected based on his history. He was affected on both elbows by humeral intercondylar fissure (HIF). There have been numerous attempts to explain this disease over the years. The bottom part of the humerus looks for all the world like a human bottom sitting in a saddle formed by the ulna and the radius beneath. When I graduated from vet school a long time ago, HIF was viewed as a genetically predisposed failure of fusion of the two 'butt-cheeks' of the bottom part of the humerus, which is called the condyle.

My own personal theory, which I proposed many years ago and which has been alluded to in publications by some of the people I have mentored, is that the butt and part of the saddle (the condyle and the ulna) don't fit together properly, and so the 'butt-crack' actually cracks. In flexing, extending and twisting repeatedly a zillion times when walking and running, the ulna effectively chops into the bottom part of the humerus like an axe in a block of wood, gradually splitting it.

In order to save Bobby's life, I would need to perform

multiple staged surgeries. All of my clinical suspicions had been confirmed on CT scan and radiography. First, I'd need to fix his dislocated left hip joint and fractured pelvis if the family wanted to consider keeping his left hind leg, rather than chopping it off with full limb amputation. It was indeed advisable to keep it because surgery was warranted on all three other legs, but I'd need to remove what remained of his hanging-off left hind paw. Later, if they wanted, I could attach a special bionic limb implant to the bottom part of his left shin bone so that it was possible to keep a functional left hind leg. I'd also have to fuse his right ankle solid. And even after all of that, the HIF affecting both elbows meant that they were quite literally on an axe-edge of fracture and, if left untreated, especially when taking all the weight from the hind limb incapacitation, they would almost inevitably sustain catastrophic and explosive fracture, akin to a strike of lightning through the bones.

People have put dogs to sleep for way less than this combination of problems. It was very much an imperfect biological storm. I removed his hanging-off left hind foot with Darby and Steph's permission and stopped the bleeding. Then, looking at Bobby's X-ray pictures and CT scans as guides, I replaced his dislocated left femoral head in its socket with two anchors attached to a special synthetic fibre through a bone tunnel in the femoral neck, stitching the joint capsule and muscles around it to keep the hip joint in place. I repaired the pelvic fractures with a couple of plates and screws and made Bobby comfortable on a continuous-rate infusion of 'happy drugs'. I called to tell Steph and Darby that this first surgery had gone according to plan and that Bobby was peacefully sleeping. They told me that poor Finley was most certainly not. His normal insomnia had been replaced by a perpetual pacing around his room, they told me on the phone. They had just called the medical counsellor he had been seeing for a while because he refused to put on his pyjama top, and just paced up and down, wrapped in a sheet, repeating 'Bobby' over and over and screaming if anyone so much as tried to enter his bedroom. It was a truly awful situation.

Over the coming weeks and months, I learned a lot about Finley. And I reflected on what it had felt like to be his age. How familiar so much of what his parents described was. I thought of the time in a supermarket not that long ago where, with the sounds of people talking, tills bleeping, packets rustling, I had been so overwhelmed by two women calling out 'Supervet!' at the same time that I'd left my trolley and run out into the car park. How I couldn't be around people munching loudly on crisps, or the slapping, slurping noise of feet in flip-flops.

Finley and I also fixated on some seemingly normal things – in his case, types or colours of cars; in my case, the shape and glint under light of surgical implants. And we love routine and hate change on the one hand and on the other we embrace change readily if introduced to it in a way we understand. Finley had a certain way to go through the day: the same morning routine, the same types of clothes and trainers, the same route to school, a very well-defined school day and the same routine every evening and at weekends, a lunchtime trip to the same park and the same food places.

Routine is king and change is hard. I am a bit like that too, but I have found that when people try to get me to change my mind about something they have to tap into either my love of animals or music to give me a window 'in'. Sometimes playing heavy rock music will not only calm me down, but allow me an aperture of perception in which I can see things a different way. This is very strange, since other types of loud noise unsettle me. Likewise, I don't like change in my life, but it's amazing how my love of animals has allowed me to question everything we do in surgery and, when I'm unhappy, I change it automatically − because the animals told me to do it, or at least that's how it seems to me. Whereas a person can tell me to do something a hundred times and I may not even listen if I fundamentally disagree. It's all about finding the right way into my mind without judging me. Dogs don't care where you are on any spectrum. They don't judge or label you. They just love you.

Finley disliked wet textured food. So, there was no gravy for him. Also, he had very regular mealtimes and the various types of food, of which there were no more than half a dozen that he would touch, needed to be in separate sections on a special plate. Bobby had helped him with this. Bobby also had regular mealtimes, and initially he didn't like his dry and wet food mixed, but Bobby loved gravy and so gradually their mealtimes and their mutual permissiveness of tiny changes helped Finley to cope with change, little by little. Finley wouldn't role-play. He refused to dress up as anything or anyone other than himself, but gradually he took delight in Steph and Darby dressing Bobby for various events such as Christmas, Easter and Halloween and then all the made-up events such as Tuesday Tyrannosaurus club or Sunday Clown parties. Bit by bit, all of the little things with which Finley struggled were in some small way alleviated by Bobby's comforting, reliable and loyal presence.

Finley and I tend to just blurt out exactly what we feel without filter and take everything anyone says as literal and completely to heart. I have learned to control this when I'm lecturing or performing or on live TV or radio. I've found the switch the same way I always do – animals or music. At that particular moment I think of Keira, or my feline friends Excalibur and Ricochet, or a song that I love. Also, for Finley and me, there are no grey areas. Everything is black and white. Luckily for me, X-ray pictures and CT scans of the skeleton are exactly that!

Based on Bobby's CT scans, my colleagues and I manufactured a special plate for his sheared-off right ankle joint called a FitzPTA (Pan-Tarsal Arthrodesis plate), which had a keel like that beneath a sailboat embedded in the bone such that the metal took up as little space as possible under the skin, since I knew it would be challenging to close the surrounding tissues in this area where the skin is almost vacuum-wrapped around the ankle bones. I drilled out all the joint cartilage in all ten bones of the tibio-tarsal joints and packed the gaps with bone graft I'd harvested from the pelvis on the same side. As I have mentioned, the front bit of the pelvis which forms the tip of the wing of the ilium can easily be removed in a dog and donated to another area of the body that needs it.

Once the left hip joint repair was secure and as the right ankle fusion was healing, I set about salvaging the bottom part of the left hind leg. I would have liked to save the main moving part of the ankle joint of the left hind foot even though the foot itself was mangled beyond repair, but I didn't have enough skin to cover the implant that would be necessary to create a bionic foot, plus the foot I had chopped off had been infected with bacteria in grit from the road, which could spread to an implant from any residual infected skin. So, I chopped even more of the limb off at the bottom end of the shin bone, the tibia. Then I designed and manufactured a bionic limb implant system alongside my engineering colleagues. This consisted of a highly specialised endoprosthesis, which comprised a peg inside the tibia and two specially coated titanium plates, one on either side of the outside of the tibia, attached with screws. Below this was an abutment region on which the tibia sat, and below that a doughnut-shaped mesh of trabecular titanium that would hopefully act like Velcro for the skin to attach to. As I've said, it's called the dermal integration module, and if the skin is prepared properly, it should form a permanent seal around a strut of metal called a spigot that protrudes to the outside. Onto this spigot I would attach a clamp that fixed an exoprosthesis or external foot to the endoprosthesis implant inside the body. The exoprosthesis would be an aluminium blade attached to a bearing surface, which we sometimes build from the same kind of rubber used on the tyres of Formula 1 racing cars, or sometimes a skateboard wheel, depending on the position needed and the predicted wear pattern. If the foot gets caught in something, the aluminium should break before the titanium, and one can simply unscrew the clamp and pop on a new foot.

Three weeks after fusing his right ankle solid, Bobby was hopping reasonably comfortably on this leg and I then operated using the bionic implant system to create a new left hind foot the same day the implants came out of the factory. The implant is called a PerFiTS, which stands for Percutaneous Fixation To Skeleton. Exactly the same kind of implant should work for a human too, and as I had explained to Her Majesty the Queen, it would be great if human and veterinary surgeons worked together on implants like this and learned together for the betterment of both species. Certainly, Finley didn't see Bobby as anything other than his brother in their family.

Throughout the journey I had the opportunity to talk to Finley several times and get to know him a little so that I was no longer the strange vet man. Visits to the hospital to see Bobby became part of his routine over the several weeks of surgery and rehabilitation, and he and I grew close since we were surely companions in terms of how we perceived the world. It was particularly scary for Finley on the day I was to implant the PerFiTS, but with my hand and Bobby's paw, he found a window to understanding and coping with change. Fortunately, it all worked out for the best and the skin and the bone grew well onto Bobby's bionic implant. Both he and Finley were irrevocably changed by their journey together and they both learned a way to not just cope with their world, but in fact to rejoice in every step of the journey (quite literally), side by side.

Finally, I scheduled Bobby for surgery to fix the cracks in his elbow joints for fear of sudden fracture as soon as he was allowed to exercise a bit more. I would use screws which I had invented called HIFFS – Humeral Intercondylar Fissure Fitz Screws. I explained to Finley and his parents that this would be a kind of bolt that would be placed through a large drill hole to bridge the crack in each elbow, and that I could inject a special substance called bone morphogenetic protein through the bolt mechanism to help healing. The cracks would then have resilience both mechanically and biologically to prevent catastrophic fracture in both elbows.

I left them in the room to visit for a while with Bobby. About ten minutes later I popped back in. It turned out that Steph had gone to the toilet and Darby was in the car park taking an important call from work. I walked in to find Finley lying on the floor with Bobby, arms tightly wrapped around his neck. I went to leave as I didn't want to burst the beautiful bubble of serenity. But Finley raised his head. So, I stayed.

He looked up at me, peering between Bobby's beautiful ears, his chin resting on his forehead. He said, 'Thank you for saving Bobby, Uncle Noel.'

Darby and Steph had called me 'Uncle Noel' throughout all of the phone calls and visits. I sat down on the chair nearby and I left Finley and Bobby in an embrace on the rug. I wasn't too worried about the final operation because it was relatively straightforward and Bobby was already walking on all four legs. There was some risk, but not much by comparison with what he'd already been through, so I relaxed as I enjoyed this scene of peace and absolute understanding I was privileged to witness.

'I was just like you when I was your age, Finley,' I said. 'My friend was a dog called Pirate.' I thought about the times that Pirate had been my only comfort. 'He was my best friend.'

Finley looked at me and thought about it. Then he nodded.

Bobby's final operation on both elbows went very well and within twelve weeks he was running around the garden again chasing the same old tennis ball that had got them into trouble in the first place. Bobby was constantly smiling, his long tresses of hair like a Greek god. Those magical ears. His white top coat and brown undercoat made him look dappled. His tail was a giant magical broom handle of voluminous crimped brown and white hair, upon which he flew onward to every new adventure. Finley had his best friend back.

Some weeks later, on the final day of our collective adventure, it was time for us to hug each other goodbye and for Bobby to return home after his final CT scan check-up. I'll never forget what Finley said to me from his new state of contented happiness curled up with his soulmate on the floor of my consulting room, both of them healed in so many ways. Because it's true for all dogs and their humans everywhere.

He looked down at his best friend, raised his head and then looked straight at me with his piercing blue-eyed stare and simply said, 'He helps me with things I don't understand. He knows me better than *I* know me.'

15

What is death?

Sparkle the Bouvier des Flandres and Nicola

'What is death, Mummy?' asked Nicola from the back of the car. Amy didn't know what to say. She looked in the rear-view mirror at the innocent face of her just-turned-eight-year-old daughter.

'Well, it's when someone isn't around any more, darling,' said Amy, hoping that another question wouldn't follow. Inevitably it did.

'Is Barney dead, Mummy?' asked Nicola.

'Yes, darling, you know he is. We buried him, didn't we,' said Amy. Barney had been Nicola's best friend and she had spent many hours with her face buried in his fur. Amy wondered if she should pull over since she doubted that she could concentrate on the road at the same time as having the 'inevitable transience of life' conversation with her inquisitive and very perceptive daughter.

'But his spirit lives on, darling, and we remember him as if he was here with us every day. Remember we talked about the rainbow bridge?' she said hopefully.

There was a long silence, three roundabouts and a set of traffic lights. Amy kept glancing in the mirror to see if the storm had passed. She knew it was unlikely.

'Barney is panting, Mummy,' said Nicola.

That was too much. It was all Amy could do to stay on the road. 'Barney? Panting, darling?' she asked.

'Yes. I think he's hot, or maybe getting sick from all the roundabouts. I feel a bit sick too,' said Nicola.

'Do you, darling? Oh, I'm sorry. I'll pull over,' said Amy, now bewildered and more than a little concerned.

'No. It's all right, Mummy. He's OK now. He's fine now. He's resting,' said Nicola.

And then not another word the whole way home, which was another five minutes or so.

'Bye bye, Barney,' said Nicola as she jumped out of the car and skipped towards the front door of their house.

This wasn't the first time I had heard about a child talking to a much-cherished and sadly deceased dog. I don't know what it is or what to call it, but it is a 'thing'. Perhaps children are more attuned to this sort of thing.

The only reason I knew about Barney was because of Sparkle. Sparkle was a Bouvier des Flandres crossed with some unknown breed, according to Amy. I'd not seen another dog quite like her before. Her beautiful long shaggy flowing hair rippled through the air like a field of magical molten barley. She didn't walk through life, but rather floated on her hovercraft of hair between bounces.

Sparkle came bouncing into my consulting room, a joyous effervescent pogo-dog. No amount of fun was too much for this russet-tinged, black-bearded, spiky-haired puppy. As far as Sparkle was concerned, everything was 'hers'. And she was right! Everyone and everything was hers for the taking, including any toy she could grab and fling about in wild abandon, often ripping it to shreds. There was no amount of face licks, cuddles, jousting play or tearing through the fields that could satiate her irrepressible love for life. From opening her eyes in the morning to very reluctantly closing them at night, she bounced about, in her house, through her village, through her park and through the practice where her human mum, Amy, worked as a vet, like a ball in a pinball machine.

And the only possible reaction to her bouncing off you was to smile. Just to see her revelling in every moment of joy that the day might offer brought immeasurable delight to everyone who met her, including me. Her name was very apt because she brought a sparkle wherever she went and the world was so much better off for having her in it.

However, the leap in my heart as she bounded in through my door was tempered by the obvious reason that Amy had brought her to see me. She was very lame on one front leg because she had been born with an elbow joint that didn't fit together properly. As I described earlier, there are three bones in the elbow joint – the humerus, radius and ulna. The radius hadn't fitted in the joint from birth. It's called congenital radial head subluxation. As Sparkle threw her front legs up on my knee, wanting to lick my face, I could see that her right elbow was swollen. And as she jumped down and walked across the room, she was noticeably lame, her head bobbing in concert with her poorly elbow.

When Sparkle was first diagnosed, Nicola asked, 'Mummy, is Sparkle going to die?'

'Of course not,' said Amy. 'We're going to fix her.'

They had only just had the Father Christmas conversation, after Nicola had interrogated them about the logistics of delivering all those presents in one night.

It's tough for any family contemplating serious surgery on the love of their life. And Sparkle was only three and a half months old and already an integral member of Amy's family; by far the bounciest member. Many of my clients have explained to me how the passing of their dog has been more painful for them on a deeply indescribable level maybe even than the passing of their spouse or another close human family member, and this is especially true for very young or very old people. I have held paws and hands countless times in the gateway to the other side.

I have also pondered my own mortality more acutely as a result. Like most people, I am afraid of disease, but, truth be told, I am not afraid of death. I just want to share as much of this ineffable, incredible love that I am blessed to be allowed to take care of with as many beings as I can in my lifetime.

And so it was too for Amy and Sparkle. Unlike in human medicine, euthanasia is always an option for our patients. Sometimes Amy and I, in our respective practices, are asked to perform euthanasia and we entirely agree with our clients that it's for the best from an ethical perspective. Sometimes we do not agree, and that's a tough one. We can decline to put a dog to sleep, sometimes giving rise to arguments and ill-feeling with clients, or we can recommend rehoming or other possible routes. And then there are cases that could go either way – a huge grey area. As she had made clear to Nicola, Amy wasn't considering euthanasia and neither was I, but we both knew how 'close to home' these decisions were in our hands.

Amy was understandably very upset since she knew that, left untreated, Sparkle would endure inevitable pain, osteoarthritis, lameness and poor quality of life. She would grow up to be a very large dog, possibly weighing 40–50 kilograms. Nicola had been told by Amy that Sparkle would one day be enormous and possibly even bigger than her, but she didn't yet grasp the enormity of the situation. We both considered full limb amputation, which would have been an acceptable option, except that Amy had found out belatedly that there was a family history of developmental elbow disease in Sparkle's breed line, and if this occurred in her other front leg, inevitable arthritis and pain would mean she would have great difficulty getting around on one front leg. As I've explained, I coined this term some years ago as a better descriptor than elbow dysplasia, which is what it was called when I graduated and still is by many today.

One can visualise developmental elbow disease as a poor fit of the elbow bones. I have already described the bottom part of the humerus (the condyle) as being shaped like a human bottom with two butt-cheeks sitting in a saddle formed by the radius and ulna bones of the forearm. In this disease, the butt does not sit evenly in the saddle, giving rise to excess pressure between the surfaces of the humerus and ulna, with cartilage abrasion and fragmentation of the lower part of the ulnar surface and abrasion of the humerus surface against it, like a human getting 'saddle sore'.

Sadly, I had also detected another problem affecting one of her hind legs because I'd noticed a swelling of her ankle (hock) joint. We acquired CT scans of all four limbs for thorough interrogation of Sparkle's predicament and this had shown that she was affected by a genetic problem called osteochondrosis, where the cartilage and bone hadn't developed properly on the main moving bone of her ankle joint, the talus. The disease was so badly affecting an atypical area of this talus bone and supporting tissues of the joint that I wouldn't be able to fix it at some point in the future with a resurfacing partial or complete joint replacement implant system. Amy and I knew that the cartilage and bone in this area were already progressively fracturing off, which is called osteochondritis dissecans, and worse, in Sparkle's first year of life, the tissues around the joint would gradually degrade too. We would likely end up fusing her ankle joint solid to get rid of inexorable pain.

So, we faced a dilemma about what to do for the best. It would be great if we had a crystal ball like some kind of medical soothsayer and could see into the future of whatever intervention we may or may not perform, but neither life nor medicine can conjure a crystal ball. Many of my clients ask me for the percentage chance of success with an operation. I used to give percentages based on my experience, but I have long since learned that people hold on to numbers as cast-iron facts. Now, I just explain what will most likely happen with or without surgery and also that there is no surgery in the world that comes with a guarantee or that always works.

Both Amy and I knew this most acutely. In this sense I bonded with Amy straight away and felt as if I was her brother on the decision-making journey since both of us were very aware that others would judge us no matter what decision we made. I suspect many people would have just put Sparkle to sleep, snuffing her life out before it had really begun . . . and in fact, such a decision would have been entirely legitimate in the circumstances.

I do worry sometimes that because simple operations can often make more profit than complex operations, regardless of the total cost, there may be a misconception regarding the options available in situations like this. Operations such as those I carry out, which require complex engineering planning, implant manufacture and implemen-tation, may not produce profits equivalent to more standard 'off-the-shelf' procedures that require less equipment and aftercare, and more of which can be performed in the same time frame it takes to plan and carry out a single challenging procedure. But I vehemently believe that the guardians of animals deserve to be offered all of the possible options for the dog or cat they love, and Amy believed the same. Otherwise, how can they choose the best option?

I knew there were good options for Sparkle and I do not accept the inherent limitations of techniques already published as the only 'best option'. I have published techniques that were performed by me for the first time that have since become commonplace. As I've alluded to, our perception of the 'best option' in medicine inevitably changes over time because otherwise nothing gets better at all.

A second, related challenge currently facing the profession I love is that the public often don't know who owns their local vet practice and whether this could affect the choices they are offered. I think that the public has a right to know whether primary care vets, which most people think of as their local neighbourhood vet, are in fact owned by a large corporate group or not, and whether they ask clients where they would like to be referred for non-routine surgeries or merely refer patients to specialist practices owned by *the same corporate group*. This makes sound financial sense for shareholders, and if those companies can also only use implants where a cost-effective deal has been done with a like-minded company or one that they also own, that obviously makes sense too. I have no problem with business models and, as I've already said, the vast majority of vets of all qualification levels are trying to do their best at all times, in my opinion. But I believe that the paying public should be made aware of any such financial associations between companies, otherwise it doesn't feel quite right to me. Families can't choose options they aren't told about.

A third challenge, which I alluded to earlier, is that there are currently no specific regulations regarding the safety or efficacy of implants sold in the veterinary marketplace in the UK, and many suppliers are owned by the same parent companies. Implants can be launched for sale to any vet with any level of training for operations in dogs and cats in the UK without the same stringent standards applied for human patients, and there is no formal requirement for follow-up or outcomes analysis.

There are also no specific requirements outside of the expected 'standard of care' regulating the qualification or skill level of individuals deploying implants. I have no problem with anyone choosing any vet to operate on their dog or cat. Every vet, including me, has to start somewhere and they are undoubtedly doing their best in their circumstances, as I have said. But I advocate for transparency at all times. In my view, a vet who is about to operate should inform the family whether their training has been a one-day course, an online course or an intensive practical mentorship such as that offered by a one-year internship or a three-year residency. When I was starting out, I always told clients exactly where I was in my training curve for any proposed procedure, and then it was their decision entirely who they chose as the 'best option' for their animal friend. After all, most members of the public have absolutely no idea what the letters after a vet's name actually mean. Recently, the Royal College of Veterinary Surgeons, my governing body, has revised the code of conduct for all vets to include explaining to clients their freedom of choice and the difference between levels of expertise.

Discussing these challenges in my profession can, of course, be perceived as my ego and arrogance talking, because, after all, I am a surgeon, I own a clinical practice and an implant company and I need to pay wages. But I know that one day I will no longer be here, so I need to write my experiences down, since, as I have mentioned, my caseload of surgeries that have failed elsewhere has grown exponentially, while the caseload of routine surgeries referred to my practice has diminished. Routine surgeries are now often operated before they get to my door, and it should be emphasised again that all of these surgeons, regardless of training, mean well. But skill levels vary considerably, and when these surgeries fail, the family may ask for, or need to demand, a referral to see someone like me. Sadly, I have factual evidence of hundreds of cases of this nature. Families don't know they have a choice of surgeon amid the initial crisis facing their best friend, and one trusts one's vet, because as a profession we are still lucky enough to enjoy the trust of the public.

Amy very much knew that, while she had chosen me as Sparkle's surgeon, I too could fail, regardless of best intentions. When my best friend Keira was hit by a van and nearly died, there was no way I would have attempted some of her soft-tissue reconstruction surgeries, because I wasn't the best man for the job, but for the orthopaedic procedures she needed, I truly felt that I was and so I performed them. I would want my best friend to have all options offered with full transparency around the training and skill level of the clinicians, the providence of the implants to be used and any potential conflict of interest, such as a company's ownership of both the primary care and referral facilities. Then people can choose whatever they think is right for the animal they love, and that's fair.

Every surgeon has an ego; otherwise, we'd never pick up a scalpel blade. Ego wins marathons, builds successful businesses, sends people to the moon and it writes this book. Without ego, nothing gets done no matter how altruistic the goal. I wish love and light to all my detractors, but I'm too busy changing the world for the better to listen to narrow-mindedness. If anyone can show me a valid, ethically well-founded and non-biased argument against any technique or implant I've ever pioneered, I shall listen, but otherwise I'm going to spend what limited time I have left saving life and limb and spreading love in the world.

Amy was a veterinarian who trusted that I would only do the right thing for her best friend. Together we decided that the best option was to try to get Sparkle out of pain and keep her elbow moving. I invented and published a technique years ago using an external frame attached to the radius and ulna bones of the forearm with wires affixed to scaffolding rings like a suspension bridge outside the body (a circular external skeletal fixator). Other wires with anchors on them were attached to a moving bit of the frame to pull the radial head back into position in the elbow. But nowadays, I plan relocation of the radius into the joint using CT scans and computer modelling software and then use a special 3D-printed cutting guide and plate system plus a new synthetic elbow ligament to address the problem. As I've said, it's essential that we responsibly embrace new technologies for the benefit of our patients.

I did exactly this for Sparkle and she was doing very well for a while. But then it became apparent that the operated front limb was not growing at the same rate as the other because she had a genetic problem affecting the cartilage plates from which bones grow, the so-called 'growth plates'. We didn't know this when we performed the first surgery. No medical crystal ball unfortunately. So, I cut the forearm in the middle and suspended the radius and ulna bones from the wires inside the scaffolding rings I've described. This time, though, special turnbuckles between the rings, called linear motors, were twisted to grow the limb by 1.5 millimetres per day for a few weeks.

This too was going well . . . then tragedy: the ulna bone dislocated from the humerus because the ligaments holding the elbow together were too weak. Again, Amy and I were faced with a full limb amputation, which we still didn't want to perform for the same reasons as before. So, we manufactured a special implant and I operated to remove the cartilage from the joint and pack in bone graft harvested from her pelvis, fusing the elbow solid as this would at least give her a leg to walk on, albeit stiffly.

Unfortunately, tragedy unfolded again for poor Sparkle. Infection is the single biggest reason for failure in the career of any orthopaedic surgeon, including mine, and very sadly, the elbow became infected with a bug that stuck to the metalwork with a recalcitrant biofilm. Antibiotics can't get rid of such an infection unless the metal is taken out, which we couldn't do without the limb falling apart. Our only options were: to take the metal out and put an external frame on until the infection cleared and then put in more metal; to amputate the limb; or to put Sparkle to sleep. We decided it was in Sparkle's best interests to amputate the limb, even knowing the risks for the remaining limbs.

Nicola asked Amy why she and I hadn't done this in the first place and saved Sparkle from going through so much. Notwithstanding the cost implications, Amy and I felt exactly the same of course, except we couldn't predict the future. Amy explained to her insightful eight-year-old that life is full of 'what-ifs'. What if I hadn't dated that person? What if I hadn't got married? What if I hadn't driven that day of my car accident? What if I hadn't gone out that night I got robbed? What if I hadn't taken the job that ended in heartache? By the time they returned for Sparkle's inevitable ankle fusion surgery, Nicola was fully on board with the unpredictability of life. I looked straight into the tearful but infinitely wiser eyes of an eight-year-old as she raised her head from Sparkle's big fluffy ears and kissed her before I brought her through to surgery.

Nicola's perceptions of life itself had changed forever. But there was yet more unpredictability to come. Initially Sparkle had coped well on three legs. But she gradually struggled, which Amy thought was due to her ankle pain worsening. In the back of her mind, though, she well knew that the remaining front leg could be developing the elbow problem we had feared from the outset, and as soon as she saw my face, she knew it was true. Now Sparkle was struggling to get around, with significant pain affecting two of her remaining three legs. This was sadly confirmed on CT scan and via arthroscopy, where video images of the inside of the joint are obtained by a needle attached to a camera and light source. The talus bone had an unrepairable chunk fractured off and the inside part of the elbow joint was badly wearing away, both due to genetically predisposed problems.

Amy and I discussed possible euthanasia or performing surgery on Sparkle's remaining elbow and one of her hind legs at the same time. This would be really hard for Sparkle and her family to go through – especially Nicola. Amy told me how, many times on the journey so far, she had been judged by others who didn't understand their love for Sparkle. Couldn't she just get another dog? Why spend so much money? Wouldn't death be kinder? I get judged like this all the time, but though she was also a vet, this was a first for Amy, one of the kindest and most compassionate human beings I have ever met.

It's a tough one. Is death kinder when a dog is suffering, but there is reasonable hope of a resolution with further surgery? Does the fact that the dog has already been through multiple surgeries change that balance of decision-making? What about when the dog is a puppy with her whole life ahead of her? There are many vets and many people who aren't vets who would absolutely feel that euthanasia was the best decision in such circumstances. But this wasn't cancer. And I could treat both problems effectively and potentially give Sparkle more than a dozen years of good quality of life. She was in a loving family who knew the risks and didn't want to send her over the rainbow bridge if they didn't have to. And yet there are those who might judge us for deciding not to euthanise Sparkle.

Debate still rages in the UK whether to legalise euthanasia

of humans as a law-enforced right of choice to end one's own life. In countries where this is legal, initially assisted suicide was sanctioned only for untreatable permanent suffering, but this line became gradually blurred so that people who feel they have irretrievable mental illness or even lack the financial means to treat their unremitting pain can be sanctioned for assisted death. There are hugely divergent opinions on what should or should not be allowed. And there are those who will judge anyone for deciding for or against death.

Amy had gone out of my consulting room to fetch something and I was alone with Nicola. She sat on the chair, with her hands under her legs, posture hunched, and as tears welled up inside her she said, 'My biggest fear is that I will lose her.'

Nicola now knew what death was. She knew that, in spite of feeling Barney's presence in her car, that he wasn't coming back. She loved Sparkle beyond words, like I had loved Keira when I chose for her to have serious surgery after her vehicle trauma, in spite of being thirteen years old. Many people would have put Keira to sleep and many would have put Sparkle to sleep, but do we have the right to judge the choice for life any more than we do to judge another's choice for death – canine or human?

I performed a procedure to unload the painful 'butt-cheek' of the elbow with a special customised plate I'd developed called a FitzSHO (Sliding Humeral Osteotomy). Then I fused the painful ankle solid with a custom-made implant, which was different from the one I used for Bobby's ankle fusion in that earlier chapter, because of Sparkle's particular disease pattern. Most of the metal stabilising the joints was buried inside the bones as it would have been even more challenging than it had been in Bobby's case to find enough skin to cover bulky metal implants. As with other joint fusions I have described, I transplanted bone graft from Sparkle's pelvic bones to the ankle to fill the gaps between the ankle bones and facilitate healing together in fusion. We carried her to the garden and back for a couple of weeks until all swelling had subsided and she'd healed enough to bear weight on three legs confidently. And then Sparkle went home.

As I write this, Sparkle is in the early stages of her recovery. I won't know how she is faring by the time this book goes to print. On television and in books, there's social pressure to tell the stories with the right ending, which in my case would be a happy ending. Through ten years and nineteen series of my TV show I have insisted on always telling the truth no matter what happens. I have taken considerable flack for showing failure and death, not from the clients involved, who are all fully on board with spreading the message of love, truth and integrity, but from vets who feel that I shouldn't have performed the procedures in the first place. And yet when I see failure of routine procedures almost every week of the year, those same vets may well feel that's entirely acceptable. I see no difference. We are all doing our best in our own circumstances, with the experience and equipment we have, and we all fail some of the time. What seems extreme surgery to some vets is routine to me. For any vet performing any surgery, for much of the time, we do not know for sure what will happen. We simply do our best for the patient with our best judgement at the time. One can never know if one made the right decision until after the decision is made. Here are three possible endings for Sparkle's story.

Ending 1

I didn't see Sparkle or Nicola until the six-month check-up. Sparkle was running around on three legs, without pain, happy as the day was long, exhilarating in every moment and sparkling her stardust on everyone and everything she could.

Nicola had just turned nine and it seemed to me that she was already an old soul. Sparkle had taught her that there is no crystal ball in life and that every decision made has consequences. She ran into my consulting room hot on the heels of Sparkle and gave me a big hug. She thanked me for 'doing the right thing' for Sparkle and she said that she understood how difficult it must have been for Mummy and me.

I took X-ray pictures of Sparkle and confirmed all was well with the implants in her remaining front leg and in the ankle of one of her hind legs. Off she went to live the rest of her life. Amy gave me a hug as I signed Sparkle off. She thanked me for taking the time to explain things properly to Nicola, for including her in every part of the journey and for treating her with kindness and respecting that she had a point of view, even if she had been only eight years old. Amy also thanked me for making her feel like she was the only client I had, which is the biggest compliment that anyone can ever pay a vet. Coming from a fellow vet, this meant the world to me. I think Amy and I also gained some sense of our own mortality through our journey with Sparkle. We will all die someday, but not all of us have the blessing of being able to choose life, even in the most extreme circumstances.

We chose life for Sparkle and, as she ran off towards the car park, dragging Nicola behind her, I knew with all my heart that Nicola would never need to wonder 'what is death?' again. Sparkle had come very close to death and her human knew what it felt like. They would make the most of every moment of every day for the rest of their lives.

Ending 2

About a week after returning home, Amy was on the phone in great distress. Sparkle's operated hind limb had blown up with swelling overnight and she was in great pain. Unfortunately, the resistant bug that had resulted in amputation of her right front limb had come back in the metalwork of her left hind limb. Amy was in bits, as was all of her family; Nicola was inconsolable.

Everybody knew that Sparkle was suffering beyond reasonable hope of recovery and that sadly biology had made the decision for us. We collectively felt that the kindest thing to do would be to let her slip peacefully away rather than go through the whole process of implant removal, building an external support frame, infection treatment and re-implantation again. The family held each other and held poor Sparkle as I administered the final injection into her vein. Amy couldn't bring herself to do it alone. It was utterly devastating and we all cried.

This moment would change all of our lives forever. Nicola would never need to wonder 'what is death?' again, because she had felt the searing pain of loss in spite of our best efforts, even at such a young age. The weight of these difficult decisions would linger in her soul forever, but so too would the light of Sparkle's stardust. Amy and I knew that, though this pain was indescribable for Nicola, the compassion and empathy it would instil inside her would also last forever.

'Sparkle has made me a better vet, I think,' said Amy as she cried on my shoulder. 'Until now I never knew what it really felt like. I thought I knew . . . but I didn't. It's a love like no other, a love that makes you tremble with fear and uncertainty; makes you question everything you have ever learned at vet school . . . a love that really makes you wonder when it's the right time to say goodbye . . . a love that forces you not just to think about what death is, what it means, but to confront death head-on and welcome it as the kindest choice.'

Ending 3

About a week after returning home, Amy was on the phone in great distress. Sparkle's operated hind limb had blown up with swelling overnight and she was in great pain. Unfortunately, the resistant bug that had resulted in amputation of her right front limb had come back in the metalwork of her left hind limb. Amy was in bits, as was all of her family; Nicola was inconsolable.

Having discussed the situation with her husband and then with me, Amy made the very difficult decision for me to take the metalwork out of the ankle fusion site and suspend the leg in an external skeletal fixator frame, in the hope that the infection might resolve without the metal acting as an anchor within which the bacteria could hide in biofilm. A subsequent operation would need to be performed to put more metalwork in if we could clear the infection, and I cautioned that this was the absolute last-chance saloon. If Sparkle was suffering beyond reasonable hope of recovery, then euthanasia would be the kindest and only right thing to do.

Fortunately, the bacteria did clear with appropriate anti-biotics, and when much of the transplanted bone graft had already been incorporated, supported by the external frame, I again stabilised the hock joint with the best off-the-shelf plates and screws available for that location.

Unfortunately, as I had feared when making the original custom implant, I could not get enough skin to cover the bulk of metal I'd put in for stability, no matter how hard I tried. But the bone was healing well and infection had ostensibly subsided, so we engineered and manufactured a world-first fusion implant system based on CT scans, which was slimline and used exactly the same holes for anchorage as had already been drilled for all of the specific angles of the previous screws. After a few weeks in conjunction with appropriate antibiotic therapy, the skin healed over and thankfully all was well. Sparkle was walking well and soon running well on three legs, sprinkling her magical dust of joy wherever she went.

Neither Amy nor Nicola would ever need to wonder 'what is death?' again because Sparkle had come close and had taught all of us everything we ever needed to know about the value of living every moment to the max. Everything is transient and it is biology and not ourselves that determines when time has run out, unless we feel with all our heart that we must welcome the end.

I know which ending I'd prefer. But I also know that so much of what happens is entirely out of my hands. I can make the same decisions, informed by the same knowledge and experience, but biology is in control, not me. For the hundreds of happy endings, there's a handful that end in tears. I need you to understand that the scalpel blade of any surgeon, human or animal, is not a magic wand. At each fork in the road for Sparkle, we made a decision that we felt was the best thing to do. Usually there is laughter and success. But we must all never forget that there can be tears and failure too.

'What is death to me?' Something that I spend all of my career pushing back from the gateway to the other realm with all of my might. Something that all of my study and endless days and nights of experience seeks to quench even as its darkness swirls. But sometimes, just sometimes, it is something I embrace as the kindest and most compassionate act of love I can ever bestow for my patient and their humans.

16

He smells like peace

Captain the Labrador and Mary

'I'm so sorry, Mary,' I said, 'but I think it's unlikely that Captain will live longer than six months.'

Captain was a ten-year-old black Labrador who had been coping with severe elbow and hip osteoarthritis for many years. I'd first seen him when he was two years old. As we know, this is sadly all too common in the Labrador breed due to hip dysplasia and developmental elbow disease, which occur for genetic reasons. Mary had wanted to avoid surgery if possible, which was understandable. So, we had successfully maintained a quality of life for him with a combination of tablets and injections into his elbows with anti-inflammatory stem cells propagated from his own fat combined with platelets from his blood and a special visco-elastic lubricant, as detailed earlier.

But he'd been limping on one of his front legs for a couple of weeks. Mary thought he had some sort of strain or sprain or that his arthritis was just flaring again. She stroked his head as I examined him. He was clearly incredibly sweet-natured and had half sauntered, half limped over to my chair, tail wagging, his huge liquid hazel eyes looking up at me as he plonked his chin on my knee. Even though he was clearly in pain as I examined his poorly leg, he waited patiently, every now and then checking to see if Mary was OK.

I had known Mary for almost twenty years. She had brought her previous canine friend, Fred, to see me when I worked in the very small practice, which was a converted house beside a kebab shop. The parking was shared with the neighbouring pub. It hadn't been a great place to have a practice. A popular gag with the locals was to mutter, 'Don't go to see that Irish fella, cause the dog might go in fine and come out in a kebab.'

Mary and I had laughed and chatted all those years ago, but this time it was very different.

An X-ray picture had shown a suspicious lesion in the bottom part of the radius bone of Captain's forearm and a CT scan had confirmed the worst. He had a very serious bone cancer and it was likely a tumour called an osteosarcoma. This is the same kind of tumour that Bob, Dave's friend, had in an earlier chapter, but in a different location. We performed a full-body CT scan to see if it had already spread to the rest of his body. As I mentioned earlier, osteosarcomas have almost certainly spread at a cellular level to the lungs or elsewhere in the body by the time they present to any specialist like myself, so early diagnosis is really important. With high-powered CT scans, we cannot pick up spread at a cellular level but we can detect if tumour cells have spread and grown into small nodules, known as metastases, within or around the smaller blood vessels of the lungs, which is the usual site of first spread from the primary tumour. This is a process we call 'staging the tumour'. Unfortunately, it was clear that the cancer had already spread to Captain's lungs.

Tears streamed down Mary's gaunt white cheeks when I told her. 'Oh no,' she said. 'I just can't believe it. Not my little boy.' I held her hand as her shoulders heaved and strangled sobs came out of her. I was heartbroken for her, but I was frustrated too, because she'd told me that her primary care vet had recommended that she did not come to see me, but rather go to another centre because 'Fitzpatrick's are too expensive' and 'he only sees celebrity dogs'. Mary knew better and remembered the care I'd given Fred with great fondness, so she demanded to be referred to see me with Captain.

I've kept a spreadsheet with more than a hundred fabricated and even delusional reasons why the families of dogs or cats are dissuaded from coming to my practice. Others include that I'll experiment on their dog or invent the need for a complicated procedure. I've stopped being surprised by it but sometimes it still stings. As I explained earlier, vets are good people trying to do a good job, and I am keen to support them, but most people who come in to see me have absolutely no idea that their local vet practice is owned by the same company as the referral practice which they are then commonly sent to for business reasons. They may assume they're an independent vet because the name hasn't changed for years, but more than half of the primary care practices in the UK have been purchased by a handful of large companies, as have the vast majority of referral practices.

Our professional guidelines state that clients need their primary care vet to refer them to a specialist facility for continuity of care and patient safety, and in my opinion the specialist vets at referral centres across the UK are generally truly excellent, highly skilled and deeply conscientious veterinarians. However, as I have mentioned, I am concerned that there could be an undisclosed conflict of interest. I can understand why a vet practice may hire peripatetic surgeons to operate on patients and why business groups often refer in-house. These may be good choices for clients, but I believe that all options should be given to all families at all times. I have seen paperwork used in some corporate groups where dogs and cats are referred to as RGUs. This stands for Revenue Generating Units. A consultation or treatment is a monetary transaction, but I think it's really important that the stakeholders and shareholders who hold the purse strings in my profession, who are *often not veterinarians*, do not confuse the 'kindest' or 'best' option with the option where the easiest profit is consistently to be made. In my experience, many vets at the front line of practice feel a discordance between the values they signed up to and the need to increase fees for the businesses they work in. In some cases this can sadly be a cause of significant mental health issues. I feel very bad for vets who take the brunt of cost criticism from the public when it's often not their fault.

And I know for some people there's a whiff of 'thou dost protest too much, Fitzpatrick'. The television show focuses on the most extreme cases. The bionic limbs and world-firsts and only-times-ever. Of course it does, because out of all the cases filmed, those are the ones broadcasters prefer since they're of most interest to potential viewers. But I promise you the vast majority of what we do is far less dramatic. It's the slow, careful, painstaking business of getting as many more shared heartbeats between people and their animal friends as we can.

My practice remains independent and is reliant on the goodwill of vets and families to allow me and my colleagues to see patients because they deem us good enough, and hopefully the work we do reflects well on the trust they place in us. It's a care partnership — a referral practice sees a patient for a short time and primary care practices see them for a lifetime. But if people think we only try to fix the extreme cases, if we don't get referred any routine cases, or are actively stopped from seeing clients because of bias or ignorance, we will cease to exist. Then many of the unique advanced procedures that I have described in this book would not be performed at all, since they require a compromise of some kind on costs versus profit, which is just not within the power or remit of the vast majority of veterinarians.

As I was writing this chapter, an important report by the Competition and Markets Authority was set up to look into the massive rise in vet fees. The objectives are ostensibly to assess whether the veterinary industry is working in the best interests of companion animals and their families, and to ensure that recent massive corporatisation of my profession doesn't result in a lack of trust from the public. Vets want to help animals and families and be respected for the wonderful job they do. Hopefully this report will help clear up misconceptions and improve communication so that families have total transparency regarding all costs and all treatment options available for the animals they love.

Of course, some media outlets chose to take the angle that 'TV shows like *The Supervet* drive up vet fees'. I'm an easy target because I'm in the public eye, but the reality is that a few dozen advanced procedures performed annually by any specialist surgeon do not drive up vet bills generally. The root cause resides in tens of thousands of cases elsewhere. As I mentioned earlier, there is potentially more profit in performing multiple shorter surgeries using off-the-shelf implants than there is in complex procedures requiring days of engineering planning, weeks of implant manufacture, many hours of surgery and many weeks of aftercare.

I welcomed the report, as I believe anything that contributes to transparency in veterinary care is important. All I've ever wanted is for a dog's family to know their options and be free to make the best decision for themselves. The simple fact is that, unlike most families, Mary was able to fight to see her specialist of choice because she knew she could. But every family should know they have the right to ask to be referred to any advanced care or specialist vet, no matter which company owns their primary care vet.

I hugged Mary. All she needed to know was that I cared desperately and that we'd do our very best for her boy.

She once told me her husband Liam had been a great hugger. He'd come and wrap his arms around her while she was making a cup of tea. He hugged her with all of his strength until he himself got cancer and was too weak from the chemo and the disease and then he was gone. She found herself standing in the kitchen and suddenly realised that he would never be there to wrap his arms around her again. When that happened, she'd go and find Captain and give him a squish until the tears subsided. He had lived up to his name, she said. He had been her solace, her confidante and her guide, she told me. When it felt like she might crash on the rocks, he'd kept her going, found a route through the storm. They looked after each other.

His elbows and his hips had hurt for a very long time, so Mary had built a 'bed ramp' for him. The ritual was the same every night. She had trained him to go up the stairs slowly, one foot at a time, alternating front and back, step by step in spite of his painful hip and elbow joints. Mary would recite: 'One step, two step, three step, four,' and then: 'All right, my boy, up the ramp, the ramp, the rickety ramp,' whereupon Captain would get halfway up to the mattress on the ramp, and Mary would lend a helping hand with the final words: 'Yay, bedtime, my boy.'

Captain would paw the duvet to get it exactly how he liked it, which wasn't really any different from before the pawing, but it made him satisfied enough to curl up into a ball. Mary would negotiate a position and squeeze in beneath the duvet. She told me that in her desolate sorrow following the passing of Liam, sometimes she cried. She said, 'Captain always knows. It's as if he can taste my tears in the air even with his eyes closed. He lifts his head, and paws my hand, as if to say, "It'll be all right, Mam."'

During the years I had known Captain, Mary had told me just how special his senses were. He had a highly developed sense of smell and Mary explained to me that he was a 'super-sniffer'. He didn't have any formal training as a medical detection dog, and we all know how much dogs sniff other dogs' bottoms, but Captain had actually saved a man's life by bottom-sniffing. He was a friend of Mary and Liam's who often came to visit. One day, Captain would not leave him alone, and on several occasions, he was sniffing this poor man's bottom. Mary said to him that it was 'a sign' and he should go to the doctor. Remarkably, it was subsequently discovered that the man had colorectal cancer. He had surgery and chemotherapy and survived.

As we've seen, a dog's nose is a magnificent 'bio-sensor'. I've already told the stories of dogs who can sniff for explosives or drugs, but dogs can also be specially trained to detect a whole range of diseases very effectively. In fact, they can detect around one part per trillion of the 'smell particles' or molecules that are sometimes called volatile organic compounds, which are specific to diseases such as some types of cancer, some neurological diseases like Parkinson's, some infections like pseudomonas and some parasites like malaria. This is the equivalent of one teaspoon of sugar in two Olympic-sized swimming pools, which is truly extraordinary.

Now Mary cried and Captain knew how upset she was, but she couldn't tell him that it'd be all right, because it wouldn't be, for him, and neither could he tell her it would be all right for her, because it turned out that it wouldn't be either. I was well aware that they had done everything together since he had been a puppy and they had never spent a night apart in his entire life. Even when he was neutered at the local vets, Mary picked him up that same evening lest he be lonely or afraid.

But now, Mary was very afraid indeed – and not just because her best friend had just been diagnosed with a severely life-limiting cancer. It turned out that Captain had been behaving very peculiarly around her for a few months – sniffing her tummy when she had been lying on her bed with him. She initially dismissed it as a simple case of empathy because she had been having gut upsets and stomach cramps for a while. But, remembering what had happened with her friend some years previously, she too went to the doctor. Profoundly sadly, it turned out that she too had cancer . . . of the worst kind . . . involving the pancreas. It was stage four and was terminal. Just two days before I offered a six-month outlook for Captain, her own medical consultant had also given her six months to live.

'We have done everything together,' she said, 'the poor fellow has given all of himself to every day of my life and now I suppose he is doing the same in death too.' And then, through her tears, she asked, 'Can you help him?'

I could of course help him. I can help every dog with bone cancer, but what that 'help' might look like varies wildly. To help may be to hold a paw and a hand in saying goodbye as compassionately as possible; it may be to just give painkilling drugs or chemotherapy drugs; it may be to put a plate across the tumour to try to prevent fracture of the bone, to zap a tumour with radiation, to replace the tumour with an implant called an endoprosthesis while retaining the bottom part of the limb, to chop a part of the leg off and apply an endoprosthesis inside the skin and a new bionic external foot called an exoprosthesis, or to remove an entire limb by amputation.

The decision on what to do is far more nuanced than anything that can be represented by an algorithm or found in a textbook. First and foremost, every patient–guardian dynamic is different, and then there's the age of the patient, the stage of the disease, the classification of the tumour in terms of aggressiveness, other co-morbidities and a plethora of other factors. But two similarities are shared by all guardians – everyone is terrified of the big C and everyone asks the same question: 'What would you do if he/she were your dog?'

But then you have to factor in all sorts of other things, not least what the family can afford. I would never want to emotionally coerce anyone. All I can do is explain the implications of all options and let them make their own minds up. I can make recommendations, but everyone is different and every patient is different, so the question about 'what would you do if he/she were your dog?' is laden with potential pitfalls. For my own part, I try to encourage all guardians to do what I truly believe is the right thing to do based on my experience, on my gut feeling about prognosis and on their unique circumstances. I know in my heart that's what I would do if he or she was indeed my own dog.

'All I want is for whatever time he has left to be comfortable,' said Mary. 'I won't keep him alive or suffering for my sake, and I couldn't bear to remove his leg because he won't cope with the arthritis of the other legs.' She was right.

'You know, he kept Liam company every day when he was dying. He would lie with him on the bed, put his head on his chest,' she added. 'It brought Liam great comfort, he said, the smell of our dear boy.'

'I understand,' I said. 'When Keira lay on my chest, just the smell of her soft fur brought me great comfort too.'

'When I am feeling at my lowest after my chemo, he pushes his nose up against my nose, and when my chin is resting on his snout, he has pulled off the most remarkable feat . . . because he has made me a super-sniffer too!'

I asked her what she meant and she simply said, 'When I am in pieces, he smells of peace!'

'We're a right pair, aren't we?' she continued. 'I have his pills in containers at one end of the utility room and mine at the other. I sometimes borrow his omeprazole when I run out. He doesn't mind.' They were both on the same drug that reduced stomach acid to protect their guts because they were on so many painkillers for arthritis and cancer.

Mary had taken to sleeping on a mattress on the floor beside Captain, enduring some discomfort so that he could have some comfort by her side, since he was now having great difficulty getting up the ramp into her bed and she was too frail to lift him. She showed me a photograph of Captain and herself, each on flimsy foam mattresses on the floor. I asked her why she didn't choose a thicker, more comfortable mattress. She explained that it had to be thin because she didn't have the strength to pull around a thicker mattress, and she allowed him to decide whether they slept in the living room, the dining room or the kitchen near the back door, as was his preference on a particular night.

Once she had fallen over and badly hurt her pelvis, unable to move. Captain had run out of the back door, which fortunately was nearly always open, and had barked incessantly until a neighbour came to rescue Mary. They truly were comfort blankets for each other.

I didn't really want to broach with Mary the subject of her own imminent passing, but she just trotted out the elephant in the room anyway without a thought for herself, but rather only with concern for her best friend.

'What happens to him is more important than what happens to me,' she said. 'I don't want him to have to cope with big changes or loneliness if I go first . . . but you must tell me when I should let him go, even if I'm too out of my mind to hear it. We are all going to die, but he and I have had great lives. It's quality rather than quantity of life all the way. You understand?' I nodded.

Unfortunately, Captain didn't have much 'rest of his life'. We administered chemotherapy multiple times with the best drug we have for this cancer, which is already more than three decades old. It's called carboplatin. As I talked about earlier, I can't get hold of a better drug even though research dogs and other animals have given their lives to give better drugs to humans. I will say again that this is an utter travesty in my view. We controlled pain in the bone being 'eaten away' by the tumour with an intravenous drug from a medication group called bisphophonates, which was another pharmaceutical that Captain and his mum Mary had in common, since it is often prescribed for women to reduce the risk of bone fracture due to osteoporosis associated with menopause.

And then one day I got 'the call'. I had given Mary my direct mobile number, knowing that she would only use it on that one occasion and I wanted her to have the safety net of knowing that I would do the right thing when the time came. I really didn't ever want to have to tell her when the time had come, and I didn't know whether she or Captain would die first. At one visit for chemotherapy, she told me that if she lived in a country where assisted suicide was legal, she would ask me and a doctor to allow them both to pass hand-in-paw. Such decisions are made by two doctors independently for humans in such countries, and the rate of duo-euthanasia has risen in countries like the Netherlands, where doctors agree that a human couple can die together as they have lived together. I don't know if there's ever been a discussion between a human doctor and a vet about euthanasia of a human and a dog side by side.

In the end Captain blessed us both by clearly making the decision for himself and for us. He had finally given up wanting to saunter out through the open back door into the garden, he had begun heaving his chest and abdomen to suck air into his clogging lungs and he had stopped eating for a few days. It was time. Mary asked if I could come to her house to allow Captain to pass peacefully away.

In referral practice I don't commonly visit homes for any reason, but Mary and I were friends of long standing and I requested the go-ahead from her primary care vets, who were lovely and totally supportive. When I was in general practice years ago I performed home euthanasia frequently. Holding a paw as a soul passes over the rainbow bridge remains emotionally traumatic for me, though I have done it hundreds of times over the past thirty-plus years. In fact, I think it gets more difficult the closer I come to my own mortality. For Mary it was intensely painful but also absolutely necessary and my role was twofold – to allow the most peaceful passing possible for Captain and to give Mary peace of mind that she was absolutely doing the right thing for her very best friend.

When I arrived at her home, her daughter greeted me, inviting me into the living room, where Mary sat, Captain's head resting on her lap. I hadn't seen either of them for a few weeks since the chemo visits had finished and it was very sadly clear to me, and to her daughter, that Mary didn't have long either. She was skeletally thin as she raised a hand to greet me and yet her inimitable warm smile crept feebly across her sunken and ashen-white cheeks.

I sat by her side for a while on a faded old sofa, strewn with hairy pillows, which had clearly been their earthly resting place for the past few weeks, as they both brought peace to the other.

'Together to the end,' said Mary.

I nodded, gently stroked Captain's head, and held Mary's fragile hand. I explained what would happen, which she knew already anyway. Often, I will give a sedative drug to a dog before I place an intravenous cannula for the final injection, since I think it's kinder. But one has to time it exactly right, because the sedative, which is injected under the skin, can result in a drop in blood pressure and within a couple of minutes it may be very difficult indeed to get a cannula into a vein in the front limb.

I don't often put cannulas in dogs' limbs on my own. Captain didn't need a sedative; he was already sedated by the progression of his disease, which had worn him down. I beckoned to Mary's daughter, who obliged as I placed her thumb over the vein in Captain's leg and she squeezed gently so that I could see it fill with blood. Mary held his head, tears gently streaking down her pale cheekbones. He didn't even feel the needle going in, or if he did, he didn't whimper. I pulled the inner needle out, leaving the plastic cannula inside, securing it with some tape. It was indeed time.

Mary's daughter held one of her mum's hands, as the other stroked Captain's head, still on her lap. She was too frail to bend down and kiss his head, so I gently held up his paw for her so she could kiss her dearest friend one last goodbye. I asked her if she needed more time; she shook her head.

There have only been a few times in my life when I have cried openly in front of a client. I know I've already mentioned one such moment in this book. Normally, I need to be strong for everyone else too. But as I drew up the pink phenobarbital solution into the syringe, I felt tears prick my eyes. As the syringe fills up, I am always powerfully aware of the tenuous hold we all have on life, how close to the edge of the precipice we dwell.

What I knew for absolute sure, though, as we all cried, as I injected, as Captain's heart slowed and stopped and as he breathed his last, was that there is a whole realm beyond that of anatomy and physiology which our feeble minds seek to rationalise as life. 'Life' is much more than what and who we 'are'. Life is love itself if we live it well and are kind in its passage and its passing. In kind passing there is peace and in peace there is a passing on of eternal love. This is a oneness that transcends our earthly form – a connectedness to eternal love that those of us who have loved a dog are blessed to share. This I know with all of my being.

I picked up my stethoscope and applied it for one last time to the side of Captain's chest. Death was officially declared by my nod, as is required by my moral responsibility. And as Captain's spirit drifted among us, I held Mary's hand on his head for a few moments. I waited for her nod, and as her daughter held her shoulders, I quietly lifted him off her knees and off the sofa and laid him curled up on his foam mattress on the floor nearby, right next to hers.

I gave Mary a huge hug, both of us sitting on the sofa. She hadn't moved and wasn't able to, it seemed. Then I stood up and hugged her daughter, making to leave. But just as I did so, Mary reached out her hand towards mine. She held my hand tightly, belying her frailty. I kneeled by her side for a moment. I didn't know what to say. I squeezed her hand gently.

'Thank you,' she said. 'Thank you for giving him peace. He smells like peace. Thank you.'

Mary's daughter told me later that Mary had laid on her mattress beside Captain's for a few hours after I left, just cradling him in her arms, their heads resting on the same hairy pillow.

Mary died the following day. Captain held on for her, and she held on for him. They did everything together to the end. Their earthly remains were buried side by side. They held each other and kept on holding forever.

17

Everything is impossible
until it happens

Irena the Airedale Terrier and Sarah

Sarah had blamed herself for a long time. Maybe it was how she dressed. Had she given off the wrong signals? Brought it on herself? She must have wanted it. That's what he said anyway. All she knew was that she felt shame, a shame so deep it felt like it was all there was left of her. And he used that. Told her that she was worthless, that nobody would love her. That he was the only one willing to put up with her. A normal person would be grateful. Grateful that someone like him was able to bear being with someone like her. Even afterwards, when it had stopped, she couldn't tell anyone. Not the girls at school. Not her mum. She stopped leaving the house because she was sure people would be able to see it. That they'd be talking about her to each other. She was scared in busy places, so she stayed in her room. She had nightmares that she woke from screaming at some huge dark shape chewing at her, grinding her down to nothing. She stopped hanging out with her friends.

She was sixteen and they kept wanting to talk about boy-friends and it made her feel like she was going to faint. The teachers all noticed the change and asked her mother what was happening. Her mother asked her but she couldn't tell her. Her dad had left years ago. Then she stopped going to school. She stopped eating, she stopped getting out of bed. When her mum asked her where the scar on her leg had come from, she said she'd done it by accident. But she hadn't.

Her mum, Kate, didn't know what to do. But then one day she'd brought home Irena. She hadn't thought it through. She'd been visiting her friend's new litter of Airedale Terrier puppies, just because she'd been invited and it'd be rude not to visit. And then of course, as is often the case, her friend said innocently, 'There's one little girl who still doesn't have a home, you know, maybe you could bring her to meet Sarah – might bring her out of herself – just for a few hours – just see how it goes – maybe?' She was called Irena because Kate's friend loved exotic names. Irena comes from Greek and means peace, tran-quillity or harmony. All that Kate really wanted for Sarah.

She would lie awake at night wondering if Sarah was all right, listening at her door to check on her. She had no clue whether it was the right thing or the wrong thing to bring Irena home – but what was the worst that could happen, she thought to herself; she could always take her back to her friend.

Inevitably, when Kate got home that first day, Sarah kept the door of her room firmly shut and wouldn't let her mum introduce her to Irena, telling her she wasn't feeling well.

286

Afternoon turned into evening turned into night and in spite of small yipping noises of an excited puppy playing with toys and exploring every nook and cranny of the house, Sarah's mind wasn't for changing. Kate, meanwhile, was instantly smitten. Who could blame her? Airedale Terrier puppies are more like little hairy nuggets of gold than actual dogs. Irena's dense wiry coat was tan-coloured with black markings and she shoved her long snout into literally everything as she explored.

At one point her head ended up in a large bowl of cake mixture which was on a low table, a little too close to a small chair, which she had somehow clambered up onto. She had already developed a noticeable cute little beard and moustache, which is typical for the breed. And now these spiky tufts were doused in cake mixture, and flinging gloopy drips all over everything as she vigorously and exuberantly shook her head like a flailing mop. Kate laughed so loud that she didn't even hear Sarah's door open down the corridor in their bungalow. However, the neatly folded ears of an inquisitive ebullient Airedale Terrier can pick up such a sound quicker than a flick of her whiskers, and before Kate or Sarah even knew what was happening, she was down the corridor like a bullet and straight into Sarah's room. Sarah chased her but she was under the bed, snuffling around. She came out backwards dragging a trainer. Then sneezed from the dust. As Sarah tried to get her trainer back, Irena growled fiercely, refusing to let go of the laces and, as she jumped into the air, the trainer waggling in her mouth, Sarah couldn't help but smile.

'Muuum . . . come and take this mad thing away please.'

But this little shining star of peace and harmony had different ideas. *Very* different ideas. She let go of the shoe and darted around the room so fast that neither Sarah nor Kate could grab her as she jumped on and off and under and over Sarah's small bed, each time stopping for just a split second out of reach, as if daring them to try to catch her. Out the door again, up the corridor, both of them chasing her, until all three of them ended up on the carpet in the living room tumbling, giggling and yipping loudly.

It took forever to get Irena to go to sleep, and the next morning she was bouncing off the walls once more. Kate called her friend, as she had already done three times the day before, half tempted to give the puppy back, but all the while knowing in her heart that this change was probably for the better. Kate's friend had seen it all before, and brought round a training pen, instructing them they were to be strict with Irena and get her into a routine of play time and rest time. 'Mum, I don't think we can keep her, can we?' asked Sarah. 'I mean, I don't have the energy and you don't have the time. It's just too much.' And yet neither of them could bring themselves to take her back to the breeder, and within a couple of days, the deal was sealed.

On day two, Sarah had left her bedroom door open and, as soon as the pen was opened, Irena came sprinting in. It was as if she sensed something in Sarah that needed her. She jumped on the bed and battled a pillow, growling, but as soon as Sarah reached out and touched her tummy, she lay on her back, all of a sudden sinking into some kind of reverie, and remarkably drawing Sarah into this dreamworld with her. Something deep inside Sarah relaxed for the first time in years.

But then a few minutes later, Irena was up and about again, wanting to chew everything and anything. Electrical cables, slippers, dressing gown cords. Airedales are hunters and athletes, and for Irena, everything that even slightly moved was to be hunted down and leaped on. Irena didn't feel useful unless she had something in her mouth, and slowly but surely this became more than useful, and rather an essential part of Sarah's day. Sarah would lie for hours dangling something for Irena to grab hold of. Sometimes she'd get tired and fall asleep lying against Sarah. Sarah couldn't quite believe that Irena trusted her enough to just fall asleep on her like that. She'd watch her little chest rising and falling as she growled in her sleep, chasing dream creatures.

Then one night Sarah crept down the corridor, past Kate's room and did the unthinkable – she let Irena out of her training pen, making small shushing and giggling noises as she carried her back to her room, where she let Irena sleep on her bed. Kate could hear very well what was going on, but she lay there more contented and less worried than she had been for a very long time. For the first time also in a very long time, Sarah didn't have a single nightmare. And so, from then on, that's where Irena slept. She woke Sarah up by chewing her toes as they poked out the bottom of the duvet.

Initially, Kate had done all of the walking training for Irena, because for a very long time Sarah had been afraid to leave the safety of the house. But one morning, Sarah asked her mum if she could take Irena for her morning walk. Not far, just out to the field around the corner of their road. She watched Irena meeting everything animate and inanimate with unbridled enthusiasm and joy. She wondered how many of the things Irena was seeing for the first time . . . flowers, lampposts, letterboxes, a boisterous hairy white dog being held back on a lead, and even some humans who smiled at them as they walked by. And for that half an hour, it was as if she too was seeing all of these things for the very first time . . . and somehow, she forgot to be scared.

But just as she got home, it was as if the world suddenly remembered everything and she felt her heart thumping and a tight band around her chest. She thrust Irena's lead into Kate's hand, ran to her room, closed the door and pulled the duvet over her head. She heard Irena scratching at the door, but buried herself even further under the duvet. All the shame had come rushing back. She couldn't be allowed to be around anyone, not even Irena. She was poison. A few hours later, Sarah went to get a glass of water and found Irena lying across the doorway. She knew immediately that this was Irena protecting her, stopping anyone getting in. Airedales are fantastic protectors of their family, and Sarah was now definitely Irena's family.

Sarah scooped Irena up and kissed her, apologising for shutting her out. They would look after each other. From that time on, Irena and Sarah were inseparable. They went for longer and longer walks. Irena began to get bigger, to adopt a comical loping running gait. Her tail was thick, like an otter's. The thing she loved best was splashing into a pond or stream, huffing about in the water before shaking herself dry as Sarah laughed. On some of their walks, Sarah still felt scared when she saw the shape of another person, especially if that person was a man in darker clothing. And she'd never be out when it was anywhere near getting dark. But over days, weeks and months, with Irena by her side, she began to feel safer and that they could go anywhere together. And because she was exercising, she started to get her appetite back.

She felt she had to take care of herself because Irena got so upset if she was upset. If she was huddled under her duvet, crying, Irena would come and snuffle her way in, wriggle her way up to her face and lean her head against her shoulder. She still couldn't deal too well with people. If she was out walking with Irena and saw another dog and their human, she'd walk the other way. She couldn't bear talking to them, worrying that she wasn't being normal. That they'd be able to tell. But when she realised that everyone was totally beguiled by Irena and that she just happened to be her human, she began not to care so much what they might think of her because Irena became her shield against such intrusive or self-abusive thoughts.

First Kate and then Sarah herself told me this, over the weeks after they'd brought Irena in to see me. She was six years old when I saw her limping into my consulting room on both front legs, clearly in significant pain. She had been getting worse and worse for nearly two years. What they had initially thought was some kind of sprain or strain injury turned out to be much more serious, in fact as bad as it gets. I examined her and quite quickly realised this was one of the most extreme cases of inflammatory joint disease that I'd ever seen. The digits of her front feet were literally falling off. Her toes had become detached from her knuckles (metacarpo-phalangeal joints). They had been told it was untreatable and that perhaps the kindest thing would be to put Irena to sleep. I didn't know any of what had happened to Sarah then, just that she was nervous, glancing around the room, and she flinched when I moved to examine Irena. She was a young woman by then, but had a hunted look that I recognised. And I could tell they shared a special bond. As I examined Irena, if it hurt, she would look up at Sarah as if to ask her to make it stop. Every time she did, I could tell it hurt Sarah like it was her own hand.

I recognised that feeling, and I kind of intuited what was going on for Sarah before I really knew, because of my experiences as a child back home on the farm in Ireland where I had grown up. Back then my best friend was Pirate, the sheepdog who my father brought home from a cattle market one day. He was supposed to be a working dog and, when not running around herding sheep, he was chained up in an old cowshed out the back of our house. To my father he was a functional animal, but to me he was my best friend, confidante and therapist. For there was no human being in '70s Ireland who could remotely fill those roles for me. I would go and sit with him, burying my face in his soft fur, whispering my secrets to him.

Whenever I felt too lonely having to keep my secrets, whenever I was crying and there was nowhere to turn, feeling that the world would reject me, Pirate allowed me to feel like there was at least one being in the universe that understood me, didn't judge me and cared enough to hold me.

As an adult it was the love of my life, Keira the Border Terrier, with whom I felt that bond of innate understanding and mutual support. But when she was hit by a delivery van, I had to switch immediately to professional mode and prioritise her needs above my own. Though I was falling apart inside, I had to try to put that aside and give her the best care I could. She had been with me for thirteen years. For every single animal that comes through the doors of my practice, I would ask myself the same question: 'What would I do if this was Keira?' But suddenly that wasn't a sense check any more, it was real. I always have hope. But that hope was tested. She was so little and had been hit so hard – 5 tonnes of van vs 6 kilograms of dog. She had a ruptured abdominal lining and urinary bladder, a crushed sacrum and pelvis and a dislocated hip. She was bleeding internally and was going to die.

I genuinely didn't know if there was anything that could be done, but I knew I had to try. It took two blood transfusions and hours of emergency surgery just to stabilise her. And then we had to wait before knowing if we could successfully get her walking again. Whether she'd even make it through the initial surgery. Then when I operated on her pelvis, I created an entirely new set of custom implants to optimise my chances of success.

There were so many times I thought we were losing her. But she was a fighter. She came out of the operation too weak to move but trying to lick my face, to check that I was OK. This was her nature – always looking out for me. Over the weeks and months we began the process of getting her well again. But a year later, she was in the hydrotherapy pool at my practice when she collapsed. They called me immediately and by the time I got downstairs she was on a table in the prep area. I felt for her heartbeat. Nothing. I had to cut open her chest to compress her heart manually. I felt her life slip away beneath the tips of my fingers.

That afternoon I sat on the floor of my bedroom crying and there was no Keira to jump up and lick away my tears. When times were hard, it was always her who had helped me get through them. It was always her who made me smile by doing something silly or naughty, by pulling a 'not-me' face when I came back to my office to a torn-open binbag and the biggest display of ham-acting innocence you have ever seen in your life. She kept me focused on the unique love that only exists between a dog and their human. The night before she died, Keira was snuffling for things to play with in some packaging on the floor of my office and nudged something towards my feet to show me – a scented candle in a small glass votive. The next day I lit that candle and then buried it with her in a little grave outside the window of my office at my practice. She had chosen the light to take with her, but I have since realised she left a far greater light behind.

When Kate told me it was a matter of life and death and we had to try whatever it took to get Irena back, I knew with every fibre of my being what that meant.

As I said, I had never seen such a severe case of immune-mediated polyarthritis of the digits in my life and certainly not in an Airedale Terrier. This is a disease in which the immune system attacks the joints of dogs or indeed humans and sometimes they fall apart, as it was for Irena's toes falling off the knuckles of both front feet. As I mentioned regarding Crystal earlier in this book, the cause can be infectious or can prove elusive, but the immune system goes haywire and attacks the body itself, which it is supposed to protect. It is a case of being eaten from within. Sarah was eaten from within too, by all the ghouls of her past from which Irena had protected her so well. But now Sarah was terrified for her best friend, who truly was the immune system of her soul.

Irena had been in constant pain for a long time and was getting repeated infections in her front feet because the skin between her toe pads was taking her weight as the dislocated metacarpal or palm bones pressed down into the ground. She kept trying to walk and even to jump, yearning and limping to be near Sarah, but it was agonising to watch. She was clearly a tenacious dog but she had reached her limit. Airedales are very often physical and energetic. They like bounding around, chasing after sticks or balls, especially if they need to jump into water to get them. They are friendly too and love to run down at the first sound of visitors, both to warn them that they'd better not harm their family but also to say hello. To see Irena so subdued by terrible pain was heartbreaking.

This is a moment I often reach in my consulting room: the existing treatment paradigm may be that nothing can be done, and indeed the kindest thing may be to euthanise the patient. More than that, a desire to challenge the finite list of treatments is sometimes frowned upon by some very well-meaning members of my profession, who are good and kind people. They may see efforts in such extreme cases as needlessly prolonging the suffering of an animal, as I have mentioned previously. So, and I say this without vested interest in my own ego, sadly the two alternatives in any other vet's consulting room in the country and possibly the world might be drugs to try to control uncontrollable pain or simply death. But in my consulting room there was another option. It wouldn't be easy, but it was an option that meant that Sarah and Irena might have the chance to share cuddles and walks for a long time to come, for them to run side by side in the park again. It could mean that Sarah may continue to have the one being in the universe next to her who made her feel that she deserved happiness. That life wasn't over at twenty-two, but stretched out in front of her.

Because it turns out it wasn't impossible to treat this condition. It was just very difficult. Those are two extremely different things. As I explained regarding the treatment of both Shadow and Mabel earlier in this book, I have been inspired by comic books my entire life and one of my great heroes is Wolverine. Again, it doesn't take a genius to work out what I found so compelling about the man with an indestructible body and adamantium endoskeleton who could heal whatever wounds were inflicted upon him. In one of my favourite storylines by Chris Miller, he realises that life is not about winning or losing but about 'making the attempt'. That matters. The alternative is stagnation, 'a safer, more terrible form of death, not of the body, but of the spirit'. So that has always been my attitude.

There is a very long list of impossible things just there waiting until someone starts to make it shorter. Everything is impossible until it happens.

Irena didn't want to leave Sarah and Sarah didn't want to leave Irena. Echoing my hero, I whispered, 'Whether we win or lose, we have to make the attempt, don't we?' Sarah nodded. I said that I would do all in my power to have them back together soon.

With Irena, the simplest route of putting plates and screws on all her knuckle joints to fuse them solid wasn't possible since there wasn't enough room for the plates, and the sites were infected, which meant that the bacteria would almost certainly seed on the plates, resulting in ultimate failure. I burred off the cartilage that was left on the bottom of each metacarpal bone and the top of each phalanx, which is the equivalent of our knuckle, between the palm bones and the fingers. Then I skewered the joints in place at the appropriate standing angle using long rigid wires just like Wolverine's claws. I packed marrow bone graft around them, which I had harvested from the humerus bones near her shoulders. Then I bent the wires and attached them to a series of arches and rings made out of aluminium, which formed a scaffolding around her front paws, wrists and forearms that she could stand on. This was a PAWS frame – Pedal Arch Wire Scaffold – as explained in the chapter about Mabel. Then I taped worn-out rubber croc shoes to the soles of these scaffolds, so that Irena could walk around without difficulty.

The procedure was long and arduous for me and my surgical team operating on both front limbs simultaneously, but it seemed even longer for Sarah and Kate. I assured them that Irena would have a peaceful night on an appropriate intravenous infusion of painkillers and calming drugs, but they were well aware that she would stay with us for several days to get used to walking on her 'high-fashion' new shoes. It was a joyful reunion when Sarah and Kate came to pick her up, crying with both relief and fear of the impending weeks of recovery. There were many things that could go wrong, including lack of healing of the knuckles in their fused positions, before I would inevitably have to remove Wolverine's claws and their support frames, or the infection could scupper our chances of success, in spite of antibiotic treatment.

When Irena returned home, the training pen of her puppyhood re-emerged out of the garage and they built an extension on it. Poor Irena rested her beard and moustache on her plastic collar, looking glum, but the 'cone of courage' had to stay in place or she would chew her frames. She could only be walked for a maximum of ten minutes six times a day for nearly three months. Sarah and Kate had to be constantly vigilant that Irena didn't run too fast, jump or bash into something, in case she did real damage to her feet. But Sarah was there for her. She would lift her up onto her bed at night and down again in the morning. Every single night, she whispered to Irena that everything would be OK, that they would soon be back jumping into streams.

During Irena's many visits for check-ups and radiographs to monitor healing and to adjust her frames, Sarah and I had many chats. We spoke about our love of dogs and how their companionship had been our mutual salvation. We spoke about how hard it was to open up with people most of the time. I told her that I sometimes felt unable to deal with people and retreated like a tortoise into my shell. She told me that she was scared sometimes that she was broken and would always be broken. That people would know this and that she would attract people who are drawn to broken people. I told her she was stronger than she knew. I hoped that I was too.

Ten weeks later, radiography and a CT scan of her front limbs revealed that Irena's knuckles were fused. I removed her external skeletal fixator frames. Sarah and Kate hugged me with relief and delight and when Irena walked into the room without pain for the first time in years, she flung her Wolverine-fused paws around Sarah's neck and they danced in delight. These are the days that I live for, the days I dreamed about looking at my hero in a comic book when I was ten years old, the days that make the long days and the even longer nights worthwhile. These are the days when love triumphs and when 'making the attempt' elevates the spirit like Wolverine always promised it would.

One day some months later, my phone vibrated and it was a message from Sarah with a video of her and Irena running and dancing in a field. The sun was shining and I could hear Sarah laughing and Irena yapping joyously, a streak of golden joy in the green of the field.

Keira lived nearly a year more. A wonderful year. A blessing stolen from the ravages of time.

Before we are alive there is darkness. Once we are gone there is darkness. But here's the thing − it's the bit in the middle that counts, the bit you're living today, right now. If the light of right now is robbed of its brightness by fear of darkness of the past or the future, you're missing out. And let me tell you, from one who has lived through that darkness and seen it almost destroy lives − dogs live in the now, and we can make a choice to live there too, by their side. A dog is a glorious beacon of light in any darkness.

The love of a dog is an anchor in the choppy seas of life; a love that tells you every day how precious each moment of being alive really is, that all you ever need to achieve is *you*, and that every dream you have ever had is only as far away as you choose to travel. Ego, money and power can be forces for good or bad, but none of them will lick your face when you are crying. And as I have seen time and again, the light of unconditional love lives on long after our crossing of the rainbow bridge. We must always appreciate this light. Dogs can turn the darkness of fear into the light of hope. Sometimes living can feel impossible. But in reality, it's just difficult.

Everything's impossible until it happens.

Snatched moments

I wrote this book in a succession of moments snatched from my working days. At night, once consultations, surgery, clinical reports, implant design and academic work had finished. In the minutes between operations as my next case was prepped for surgery or in stolen moments between phone calls to worried clients, emails to worried vets and visits to worried dogs in the wards of my hospital.

I have lived through each and every one of these words, and in the journey of my thirty-plus years of being a vet, I have been truly blessed to serve the most luminous dogs and their humans. This book gave me a reason to reflect on time itself and how valuable every minute with those we love actually is. To every human who has ever loved a dog, you'll know exactly what I mean.

I was surprised at how viscerally I was transported back into the past to the incredible journeys I have shared with dogs and their humans. Sometimes I cried, sometimes I laughed. From time to time, my fearless feline companions

Ricochet and Excalibur, two Maine Coon cats who follow me everywhere, would jump onto my desk to see what strange thing their dada was up to when we'd normally be tucked up in bed. It's probably a good thing that they couldn't read that it was a book about dogs, though they would have loved the parts about their beloved friend Keira.

I wrote much of this book in my office at my practice, from which I can see Keira's grave through the window. But, of course, that's not where she is really. She's alive in the light of every moment I think of her. Every face she would pull. Every look she would give me. Every time that she made me feel that my return to her was a miracle. Every time she ventured out, determined to grasp every sunbeam of the day or shadow of the night with her paws. Every time she taught me that what really mattered was love, joy, truth, integrity and loyalty. With every one of the heartbeats we shared, she made me an infinitely better person.

That's where all the dogs that have allowed us to be part of their lives are — in our hearts, making us better people. Teaching us how to be the best version of ourselves if we are willing to listen. Keira's unconditional love still shines bright in every single journey of every dog and their human I try to help, willing me on to do for them as I would do for her. Whatever it takes. If it's the right thing to do.

I often wonder how the dogs we love or have loved might see this world we have created; how they might see politicians, power brokers, war or even how we treat the people we meet each and every day of our lives.

I spend my days trying to deliver the best treatment in the world for my patients, with a team around me who work as a family for every family we are blessed to serve. That's all I want. To treat my patients well. Because we know what they mean. I do this for them. And their humans.

As I write this, I have just been in the wards of my hospital with a critical care doggie who is a member of someone's family. The dogs I meet remind me every day that we need to look after each other, that we only get one chance at life, that the more love you put out into the world, the more you get back.

I hope this book reminds all of us how lucky we are to share our lives with dogs. They tell us daily that we are *enough* just as we are. They tell us that we are *not* our past, to be completely in the present and to look to the future. Every story that I have shared in this book tells us that we cannot change what *has* happened, but we can change what *will* happen next. Dogs even teach us the secret to eternal life, if we choose to listen: because love is the most important thing in life and love transcends death, if we never stop loving, then those we love will never die.

I hold life and death in my hands most days, and please believe me when I tell you that I have felt something transcending our physical form in moments when my patient is close to death and all that stands between the darkness and the light is me. I feel it too in moments when I sit on the floor with a dog and their human; when all of our earthly trappings are stripped away; when we are our vulnerable, raw, kind, beautiful selves – all we ever need to be.

For amid the vast darkness of our not being, those moments we spend with dogs allow us to be the brightest we can ever be.

All Love,
Noel xx